CHOOSING TO LEAD

CHOOSING TO LEAD

Understanding Congressional Foreign Policy Entrepreneurs

Ralph G. Carter & James M. Scott

Duke University Press · *Durham & London* · 2009

© 2009 Duke University Press
All rights reserved.
Printed in the United States of America on acid-free paper ∞
Typeset in Miller by Tseng Information Systems, Inc.
Library of Congress Cataloging-in-Publication Data
appear on the last printed page of this book.

CONTENTS

PREFACE

Before you get to be president you think you can do anything.
You think you're the most powerful leader since God.
But when you get in that tall chair, as you're gonna find out,
Mr. President, you can't count on people.
You'll find your hands tied and people cussin' you.
The office is kinda like the little country boy found the hoochie-koochie
show at the carnival, once he'd paid his dime and got inside the tent:
"It ain't exactly as it was advertised."
—Lyndon B. Johnson, quoted in Cronin (1979, 381)

In many ways, Congress is the poor relation in the American foreign policy–making arena. Scholars describe "presidential preeminence" and "congressional grandstanding," presidents claim foreign policy prerogatives and decry the perils of "535 secretaries of state," the courts declare the "plenary power of the president over foreign affairs," and some members of Congress themselves note their support of congressional deference. The institution and its members are the Rodney Dangerfield of the foreign policy game: they get no respect.

While most observers prefer to characterize foreign policy as the product of an administration and its appointees in the executive branch, there is another view, less often heard but just as inaccurate. As a congressional staff aide colorfully described the situation to us in 2001, "If Congress speaks with one voice the game is over. Congress has the money. And the president can't flush the toilet at the end of the day without approval from Congress. . . . And if there's the will in Congress, the president will . . . see the writing on the wall and he'll take action" (Munson 2001). Critics sharing this view have railed against the "imperial Congress" and the illegitimate and harmful intrusion into presidential territory that they believe it represents.

In our view, neither of the perspectives outlined above suffices, and both significantly distort the reality of American foreign policy making. Clearly, presidents are central to foreign policy making and have a wide range of formal and informal powers and tools with which to exert policy leadership. No account of foreign policy is complete without the president, and the White House is a good starting point for most foreign policy analyses. However, there are far too many entries in the historical foreign policy record showing Congress and its members as important players to relegate their participation to the margins as a general practice. At the same time, neither is there much evidence to support the "imperial Congress" thesis, or to place Congress at the center of foreign policy making as a general rule. Congress and its members may be central to foreign policy, but they are not "the center" either.

On balance, the field is severely tilted toward the presidential preeminence perspective, which we believe is problematic for attempts to understand both the foreign policies of the United States and the processes through which foreign policy choices are made. Addressing this shortcoming has informed much of our scholarship, both individually and cooperatively, as we have both attempted to bring Congress into the foreign policy analysis picture, without either exaggerating or understating its role and influence. In fact, it was a panel on Congress and foreign policy at the Midwest conference of the International Studies Association in 1993 that first brought us together and began the friendship and collaboration that led to this project.

We seek a balanced, accurate accounting of United States foreign policy making. As we discuss in chapter 1, we believe that one reason why the field is tilted toward the presidential preeminence perspective is that there is a tendency to oversimplify Congress by treating it as a monolithic institution rather than a collection of individuals, and by focusing solely on formal legislation rather than the various other avenues of congressional influence. Correcting these oversimplifications yields a more nuanced view of congressional behavior and influence; achieving this more nuanced view contributes to the more balanced, accurate perspective that we seek.

In the following pages we carefully examine the nature, activity, role, and influence of a select subset of the members of Congress who choose to lead in foreign policy. Our goal is to present and assess the empirical record, which we believe demonstrates that these members of Congress are both influential and regular features of the foreign policy landscape. This demonstration demands more respect for the involvement of Congress in foreign policy generally, as these individuals are key to overall congressional foreign policy behavior. Our emphasis on these members of Congress does not mean that we believe Congress as a whole is more important than the presidency on foreign policy matters. We do not seek to replace a presidential preeminence perspective with an untenable "congressional preeminence" perspective. Instead, we believe that policy influence and leadership are variables, and we seek to understand when and how both arise from the White House or from members of Congress. Unfortunately, given the tilt of the scholarly field toward the White House, doing so requires some focused attention on Congress to balance the scales.

Hence this book explores a particular facet of congressional foreign policy behavior—what we term "congressional foreign policy entrepreneurship." We set the context for this phenomenon and then examine the record since the Second World War to explore the ways these entrepreneurs have shaped foreign policy. To do so, we have blended five types of evidence into our study. First, as we describe in chapter 3, the study rests on an extensive quantitative dataset spanning the period from 1946 to 2000. Second, we have examined a vast record of writings by key entrepreneurs themselves: books, articles, chapters, and contributions to newspapers and magazines. Third, we have reviewed and made extensive use of the public record (congressional hearings, the *Congressional Record*, other government publications, and sources like the *Congressional Quarterly Almanacs* and accounts in key newspapers). Fourth, we have examined memoirs of presidents and administration officials across the period of our study, as well as histories of those administrations, with special attention to evidence of the role and impact of entrepreneurs from the perspective of the White House. Finally, we conducted about two dozen interviews of members of Congress and their staff aides from 2001 to 2003. We are obliged to each of these public servants for the time and insights they provided to us. We are grateful to both those who were willing to talk to us only on condition of anonymity and those prepared to go on the record. These include Representatives Barney Frank (D-Mass.), Jim Leach (R-Iowa), Curt Weldon (R-Pa.), Charles Wilson (D-Texas), former House Speaker Jim Wright (D-Texas), Senator Chuck Hagel (R-Neb.), and the staff members Bill Tate (Leach), Bill Johnstone (Senator Max Cleland, D-Ga.), Ken Meyer (Senator Richard Lugar, R-Ind.), Lester Munson (Senator Jesse Helms, R-N.C.), and Andrew Parasiliti (Hagel).[1]

Completing this project has left us indebted to many. We would like to thank the Dirksen Congressional Center, the Research Services Council at the University of Nebraska, Kearney, the AddRan College of Arts and Sciences at Texas Christian University, and the College of Arts and Sciences at Oklahoma State University for their financial support of this project, which enabled us to work together on this project, collect our data, and travel to Washington to conduct most of the interviews woven into the study. In particular, a grant from the Dirksen Congressional Center funded our first interview trip to Washington. That trip was during the week of September 10, 2001. Like others around the world, we were stunned by the Al Qaeda attacks on the World Trade Center and the Pentagon on September 11, which we watched from our hotel room. Given the crisis facing the nation, we can only say a heartfelt "thank you" to those members of Congress and their staffers who kept their scheduled appointments with us. As one representative put it, "If we let them disrupt our normal business, they've won."

Many scholars provided valuable advice and comments during the development of this book, and we are deeply indebted to them. Marijke Bruening, Polly Diven, Cooper Drury, Jean Garrison, Ryan Hendrickson, Marie Henehan, Heidi Hobbs, Steven Hook, Patrick James, Brian Lai, James Lindsay, James McCormick, Gregory Marfleet, Thomas Preston, Jerel Rosati, David Skidmore, Peter Trumbore, John Vasquez, and others we have probably—and unintentionally—overlooked shared their insights with us as we worked our way through the project. Anonymous reviewers for Duke University Press also provided helpful comments and suggestions which improved the final product substantially.

As we shaped our ideas and worked through our evidence, we also benefited from the many helpful comments provided by the participants and audience members of many panels at academic conferences. Unfortunately we cannot name them all, but we thank everyone who took the time to attend and share questions and comments with us. We also benefited from the assistance of our students over the years, including Emmy Treptow, Melissa Willis, Daniel Money, and Neal Jackson. Special thanks go to those students who not only assisted us with the research but also shared their insights on the ideas and collaborated on conference papers and articles that we developed in the process of producing this book. For their time gathering and entering data, transcribing interviews, brainstorming ideas, writing, editing, and participating in conference presentations, we are tremendously grateful to C. James DeLaet, Charles Rowling, and Carie Steele.

At Duke University Press, Valerie Milholland was our acquisitions editor, assisted by Miriam Angress. Managing editor Fred Kameny also did the copy editing. Charles Ellertson designed the text. We sincerely appreciate all of their efforts on behalf of our project. Margaret Allyson prepared the index with efficiency and thoroughness and we thank her, along with Susan Petty of TCU Press, who recommended Margaret to us.

Finally, we both have debts that we can never repay. For Professor Carter, these include the constant love, support, and encouragement provided by Nita. She did all that a spouse could do to create a setting in which he could work. He also extends his thanks to both family and friends who understood when he could not be with them. For Professor Scott, those debts are owed to his family for their patience, love, and forgiveness, especially during those times when he was huddled over a notebook computer. He is also grateful to his parents and extended family for their encouragement, and to his friends and colleagues for their support. Each of us has had the inestimable pleasure of working with a conscientious and patient colleague and friend, and those debts we have incurred to each other are among the ones that matter most. As usual, our names are listed on this work in alphabetical order, but each of us contributed equally to what was a shared project in every sense of the word.

Of course, in spite of all the help and support we have received from so many quarters, the final product, with its limitations and any errors of fact or interpretation, are entirely ours. We hope the limitations are few and any errors inconsequential.

1

BEYOND THE WHITE HOUSE

BRINGING CONGRESS INTO
THE FOREIGN POLICY PICTURE

President George H. W. Bush once claimed: "I have an obligation as president to conduct the foreign policy of this country the way I see fit" (Devroy 1989, § A, 27). The president's claim reflects a common perspective widely adopted in popular accounts as well as academic models and conceptual images of foreign policy. Yet this characterization of foreign policy is fatally impaired, as it fails to account for consequential policy makers in Congress who play important roles and have significant impacts on American foreign policy. The lens suggested by the former president is simply not wide enough.

Foreign policy "can be said to be the sum of official external relations conducted by an independent actor (usually a state) in international relations" (Hill 1993, 312). For a country like the United States, a wide range of choices typically exists to confront any given issue. Understanding the choices requires attention to the actors, preferences, and processes of policy making. As Peter Trubowitz (1998, 241) argues, "it is the realities of power inside a country, not the distribution of power in the international system, that determines the course of the nation's foreign policy." Along with the actions themselves, the origins of and motivations for the actions are important. Thus, in this book foreign policy is defined as the goals that the federal government's officials "seek to attain abroad, the values that give rise to those objectives, and the means or instruments used to pursue them" (Wittkopf, Kegley, and Scott 2003, 14).

So, from where do the goals of United States foreign policy come, and who selects the instruments for their pursuit? Which policy makers would a wider lens include to better understand foreign policy? These questions defy easy answers. On one hand, most observers stress the role of the president as the preeminent actor in foreign policy making, and most studies of the subject focus on the president and other White House participants in the process (Rudalevige 2005). Bert Rockman (1994, 59) summarizes this view well when he writes that "because of constitutional interpretations of presidential prerogatives in foreign policy and the president's unique ability to act, leadership in foreign policy is normally thought to be the particular responsibility of the president." Put more simply, *the captain of the ship of state is the president*" (Crabb and Holt 1992, 297, emphasis in original).

Although an equal branch of government, Congress is less often mentioned as an important actor in the foreign policy-making process. Although there are exceptions (e.g. Blechman 1990; Hersman 2000; Howell and Pevehouse 2007; Lindsay 1994a; Martin 2000; Ripley and Lindsay 1993), relatively few studies attribute any systematic or significant influence by Congress in foreign policy. Moreover, in the eyes of many observers Congress seems neither prepared nor willing to challenge presidential preferences in foreign policy making (Hinckley 1994). Instead, "Congressional acquiescence in foreign affairs . . . is the product of a powerful set of internal norms and attitudes, customs and institutions, a veritable culture of deference" (Weissman 1995, 3).

Yet inside the Washington Beltway, a different perspective is found. According to Lee Hamilton (R-Ind.), longtime member of the House Foreign Affairs Committee, more recently a leader of the 9/11 Commission and the Iraq Study Group, and currently the director of the Woodrow Wilson International Center for Scholars, "although the president is the chief foreign policy maker, Congress has a responsibility to be both an informed critic and a constructive partner of the president" (Hamilton 2002, 7). Some observers go much further and claim that "it is impossible to understand fully the foreign policy-making in the United States without accounting for Congress" (Ripley and Lindsay 1993, 6). Most presidents would ruefully agree. Virtually every president since World War II has at some point castigated Congress for intruding into the "presidential" realm of foreign policy making. President Ronald Reagan illustrated the typical Oval Office frustration when he pounded his desk and told Republican congressional leaders, "We've got to get to where we can run foreign policy without a committee of 535 telling us what we can do" (Hoffman and Shapiro 1985, § A, 22).

In foreign policy making the president cannot be both preeminent and hamstrung; Congress cannot be both acquiescent and an important actor that must be taken seriously. Thus a puzzle is posed: Which view is correct—the preeminent presidency or the assertive Congress?

A careful examination of all the facts suggests that the balance favors the latter choice—the assertive Congress. Even the most diehard defenders of the preeminent presidency admit that Congress occasionally plays important roles (Weissman 1995). Well-known instances of congressional assertiveness in foreign policy making include:

—ending United States participation in the Vietnam War, passing the War Powers Resolution, and investigating and publicizing covert operations and intelligence community activities in the 1970s;
—prohibiting funding for the Nicaraguan contras, promoting a greater emphasis on human rights in Central America, promoting and encouraging the Central American Peace Plan, legislating a nuclear freeze, and imposing economic sanctions on South Africa in the 1980s;
—codifying the economic embargo on Cuba, funding the dismantling of Soviet nuclear weapons (thereby keeping Soviet nuclear scientists and engineers gainfully employed), and voting down the Comprehensive Test Ban Treaty in the 1990s.

Part of the analytical problem is that "Congress is not truly an 'it' but a 'they,' and the hundreds of members who constitute that plural have their own political needs and substantive agendas" (Rudalevige 2005, 428). As one recent study of Congress characterized it, "Congress does not check presidential power, individuals within it do" (Howell and Pevehouse 2007, 34). So if one studies individual legislators instead of Congress as a singular entity, additional instances of significant foreign policy impact can be found (Mayhew 2005; Mayhew 2000), policy effects that are not always publicly attributed to the members of Congress (MCS) who initiate them. The following examples of congressional foreign policy impact, to be detailed in this book, are rarely appreciated by most observers:

Lesser-Known Examples of Congressional Foreign Policy Impact

From the 1940s
— Framing the debate for the creation of the United Nations and the European Union

From the 1950s
— Originating the ideas for what became the Peace Corps and NASA
— Providing aid to Franco's Spain, thereby helping to end Spain's alienation from the West

From the 1960s
— Framing the debate for détente with the Soviet Union and rapprochement with the People's Republic of China
— Creating rules for high-technology trade with communist states that led to the creation of COCOM
— Raising the issue of the return of the Panama Canal to the Panamanians
— Reforming the procedures of the United Nations
— Calling for an end to the economic embargo against Cuba
— Outlawing political contributions by foreign agents

From the 1970s
— Improving relations with Mexico
— Pressuring American citizens to stop funding the Irish Republican Army
— Banning military assistance to the Pinochet regime in Chile
— Aiding the Afghan mujaheddin
— Providing relief for refugees
— Funding the V-22 Osprey tilt-rotor aircraft

From the 1980s
— Focusing United States foreign policy more squarely on the issue of human rights, particularly as it applied to both communist regimes and right-wing military regimes
— Publicizing Soviet violations of the ABM Treaty

From the 1990s
— Proposing the creation of an International Criminal Court
— Ending the intervention in Somalia by cutting off the funding

—Pressuring the administration to intervene in Haiti

—Originating the idea for the successful bailout of Mexico's peso

—Pressuring the Swiss to return looted Jewish art

—Promoting the idea of HIV and AIDS programs funded by the World Bank

—Promoting debt relief for the poorest countries in the world

—Pushing for the democratization of Chile

—Highlighting Russian-Iranian exchanges in missile technology

—Creating Radio Free Asia after the massacre in Tiananmen Square

—Promoting improved ties with Russia

—Pressuring the administration to intervene to protect Bosnian Muslims

—Promoting democracy in Zimbabwe

—Pressuring the administration to recognize Vietnam

—Exempting humanitarian sales (food and medical supplies) from unilateral American embargoes

—Abolishing the Arms Control and Disarmament Agency (ACDA) and the United States Information Agency (USIA)

—Proposing sanctions on Iran for its pursuit of missile technology

—Framing the debate in support of enlarging NATO

—Reforming the IMF

—Withholding dues from the United Nations in return for reform of its operations and a reduction in United States dues

—Repudiating the International Criminal Court and passing the American Service Members Protection Act

—Contributing to the diplomatic formula to end NATO's bombing campaign against the Milosevic regime in retaliation for its "ethnic cleansing" of Kosovars

—Promoting withdrawal from the ABM Treaty and the creation of a national missile defense system

—Extending the "war on drugs" by promoting United States military intervention in Colombia

—Pushing for the abolition of abortion activities abroad funded with aid from the United States

From the 2000s

—Banning the trade in "conflict diamonds"

—Creating a Russian-American exchange program

—Pressing the administration for a greater commitment toward reconstruction in both Afghanistan and Iraq

The list includes "high politics" illustrations like aiding the creation of the United Nations and the European Union, reaching out to Franco's Spain, promoting détente with the Soviet Union, proposing the return of the Panama Canal, banning military aid to the Pinochet regime in Chile, providing military aid to the Afghan mujaheddin, ending the intervention in Somalia, pushing for a military intervention in Haiti, promoting the recognition of Vietnam, framing the debate for enlarging NATO, forcing reform in the United Nations and the International Monetary Fund, promoting a diplomatic solution to end the NATO bombing campaign against Yugoslavia in 1999, extending the "war on drugs" to include military intervention in Colombia, and promoting the creation of a national missile defense system.

So-called low politics examples are found as well: originating the ideas for the Peace Corps and NASA, regulating high-technology trade with communist states, pushing the ratification of the Genocide Convention, promoting the economic embargo against Cuba and subsequently codifying it into law, exempting humanitarian supplies from unilateral United States embargoes, advancing the peace process in Northern Ireland by hindering the ability of the Irish Republican Army to raise money from Americans, promoting a human rights focus in United States foreign policy, finding a way to bail out the Mexican peso, opposing the creation of the International Criminal Court, promoting HIV and AIDS programs and debt relief for the world's poorest countries, abolishing the ACDA and the USIA, and banning the trade in conflict diamonds.

When one adds congressional oversight activities and Congress's penchant for cutting budget requests (e.g. Carter 1998; Lindsay 1994b; Blechman 1990; Fenno 1966), it is hard to either dismiss the congressional foreign policy role or to characterize Congress as acquiescent. But more is involved here than one set of observers perceiving the congressional glass as half empty and another set perceiving it as half full. The congressional role in foreign policy making is misunderstood by many for a simpler reason—*what scholars choose to examine determines what they think they know*. When attention is focused on the proper evidence, patterns of engagement, avenues of influence, historical and policy context, and policy activity, the importance of Congress and its individual members in shaping United States foreign policy becomes clearer.

Congressional Decisions

A first corrective step is to change the decisions and activities that scholars choose to examine. For many the most straightforward way to study Congress is through roll-call vote analysis (Burden 2007). This approach has an obvious appeal. Roll-call votes provide scorecards that can tell who won on the foreign policy issue and by what margin. Furthermore, such votes yield interval-level data capable of significant quantitative analysis, thus grist for the mills of eager scholars. There is nothing wrong with relying on roll-call vote analysis to study Congress, so long as one recognizes there are "differences in the composition of the roll-call record across chambers and over time" (Roberts 2007, 355). Roll-call votes are also a reactive form of behavior, and thus they say little about the more proactive behavior of MCs (Burden 2007; Van Doren 1990). However, conclusions go seriously astray if scholars assume that roll-call votes are the *only* mechanism by which important foreign policy–making inputs are made by MCs. As Rebecca Hersman (2000, 19) notes, "observers must not only observe caution when weighing the significance of recorded votes, they must also give sufficient weight to the many ways that MCs and their staffs influence policy that cannot easily be measured or recorded." Howell and Pevehouse (2007) concur, and their examination of congressional influence on decisions to use force—typically regarded as the preserve of the president—indicates that Congress and its members matter more and in a broader variety of ways than conventional studies suggest. In his study of congressional foreign policy assertiveness during the Cold War, the historian Johnson (2006) makes a similar point—that missing what is not easily measured leads to underestimating congressional foreign policy influence. At the very least, roll-call vote analyses ignore what happens before the vote as if such matters are inconsequential, but they are not (Burden 2007).

Barbara Hinckley's *Less Than Meets the Eye* (1994) illustrates this tendency. Chiefly examining formal legislation and official votes, she "finds little evidence for an increase in congressional activity across the years" (Hinckley 1994, 171). According to Hinckley, most foreign policy is the product of bureaucratic inertia, moving policy forward in directions set long ago and over which neither presidents nor Congress has much control. She also argues that post-Vietnam congressional reforms, which increased the impact of individual members, diminished the institutional influence of Congress by diffusing power and making it even more difficult for it to act coherently as an institution.

Hinckley's study, and others like it, suffer from the limits imposed by the evidence chosen for examination. For example, Hinckley focuses on what she calls the "congressional working agenda" (Hinckley 1994, 25), thus ignoring activities such as committee hearings or reports which pressure an administration to change its policy requests, the lobbying of administration officials by individual MCs, the actions of chamber leaders to frame public opinion or shape the overall governmental agenda, the degree to which administrations change their positions in anticipation of congressional opposition, and so on. These activities often have demonstrable policy consequences (e.g. Burden 2007; Johnson 2006; Mayhew 2005; Hersman 2000; Howell and Pevehouse 2007; Lindsay 1994a). Further, this "congressional working agenda" even omits many recorded votes such as "appropriations bills making no substantive changes in foreign policy, defense procurement decisions that do not directly impact on foreign nations or organizations (a B-1 bomber or Trident submarine), immigration policy and treatment of foreign nationals within the United States" (Hinckley 1994, 25).

Excluding such votes means that significant policy effects are missed. Appropriations changes in excess of 5% are significant for the agencies or programs involved (Fenno 1966; Korb 1973). For fiscal years 1947–91, Congress exceeded that threshold 44% of the time on defense spending bills alone (Carter 1994, 162). Major defense procurement decisions, including those surrounding the B-1 bomber and Trident submarine that Hinckley cites, altered the defense posture of the former Soviet Union, organizations like NATO, and potentially other countries like China. Furthermore, immigration policy affects other countries, as evidenced by current U.S.-Mexican relations, and the treatment of foreign nationals, which Hinckley excludes, has impacts on other countries. The international outcry over the roundup in the United States of foreign nationals in the hours and days following September 11, 2001 (not to mention the detention of "unlawful combatants" at Guantánamo Bay, Cuba), illustrates these concerns, as does the decision by the World Court in 2004 upholding Mexico's argument that its citizens arrested in the United States must be allowed access to consular officials. In short, much is missing from Hinckley's data. Her dismissal of the congressional role as "less than meets the eye" is based on an examination of only part—and a narrow part at that—of the relevant congressional behavior.

A similar shortcoming characterizes studies choosing to examine just the "major events" in United States foreign policy. These studies assume that presidents make the important decisions—those regarding war and peace, fundamental shifts in major policies, etc.—and that congressional involvement is only significant for implementing executive branch policies, less important structural issues, or marginal political and diplomatic issues. Hersman (2000, 3) offers an excellent critique of this argument: "A focus on these high-profile events tends to produce a formal, institutionalized portrait of Congress that bears little resemblance to the practical, day-to-day reality of most policymakers . . . Trying to evaluate the state of executive-legislative relations according to these headline-grabbing events is like trying to measure an ocean by counting waves. Dramatic clashes over high-profile issues—'waves'—are important, but they do not tell all, or even most, of the story. It is in the 'ocean'—the day-to-day interactions over unexceptional issues—where most foreign policy is shaped, debated, and made."

This policy-making "ocean" matters for three reasons. First, just because many issues lack media or public attention does not mean that they do not have considerable consequences for bilateral relationships or broader elements of foreign policy. Second, how such issues are handled day to day helps to determine whether they evolve into high-profile conflicts. Third, high-profile conflicts do not arise in a vacuum; they develop from a base of routine, informal interactions (Hersman 2000, 4). Thus the congressional role is not necessarily less important than that of the president; it was long-ago recognized as simply being *less visible* (Moe and Teel 1970).

Patterns of Engagement

Another aspect of congressional foreign policy behavior that requires proper focus concerns the nature of the engagement between Congress and the executive branch. Many scholars employ dichotomies (engaged-disengaged, active-deferent, assertive-acquiescent, etc.) to characterize congressional engagement on foreign matters. These simplistic distinctions have much appeal, but they fail to account for more subtle patterns and therefore miss significant congressional foreign policy activity. For example, Hinckley's focus on congressional foreign policy activity weakens her argument, since activity differs from assertiveness—or even success (Anderson, Box-Steffensmeier, and Sinclair-Chapman 2004). Congress can be highly active and still supportive of (and even deferential to) the president's foreign policy preferences. On the other hand, Congress can be less active, but when active it may challenge the president's policy preferences. Thus, separating activity from assertiveness explains part of the puzzle. *Since World War II, congressional foreign policy activity has generally declined over time, but congressional foreign policy assertiveness has increased over time* (Scott and Carter 2002a). Those who argue that Congress is acquiescent may be looking solely at activity levels, rather than the increasing congressional tendency to challenge presidential initiatives. Both dimensions of congressional foreign policy behavior—activity and assertiveness—are important. Combining them turns a one-dimensional characterization into a two-dimensional conceptualization (more or less active *and* more or less assertive). As shown in figure 1, a two-dimensional activity-assertiveness focus posits four models of congressional foreign policy behavior:

—a *Competitive Congress* whose greater levels of both activity and assertiveness lead it to challenge the president for foreign policy influence, a pattern of behavior reflective of the idea of a resurgent Congress;

—a *Disengaged Congress* whose relative inactivity and compliance with presidential preferences reflect the acquiescent Congress more involved in domestic than foreign policy and more likely to defer to and support the president;

—a *Supportive Congress* whose greater activity is combined with less assertive behavior, indicating a Congress cooperating with the president to achieve shared foreign policy goals;

—a *Strategic Congress* whose combination of less activity and greater assertiveness suggests a Congress that selects its battles carefully but is willing to challenge the policy preferences of the president.

These four models reflect the range and complexity of congressional foreign policy behavior and more accurately represent the varying relationship between the legislative and executive branches since World War II

Figure 1: Congressional Foreign Policy Orientations

(Scott and Carter 2002a). Even a less active Congress may have important policy impact if its members are more assertive when they do choose to act. Moreover, there are powers and avenues of influence that range far beyond formal legislation at the disposal of members who seek to shape foreign policy.

Congressional Powers and Avenues of Influence

A third aspect of congressional foreign policy behavior that requires more careful consideration is the powers and avenues of influence available to members of the institution. Interbranch competition over foreign policy derives from the U.S. Constitution, which establishes the principles of separation of powers and checks and balances by which policy making power is divided, distributed, and balanced among the branches. The Constitution forces a sharing of foreign policy responsibilities by assigning various powers to the Congress and others to the executive. An "invitation to struggle" stems from the failure of the Constitution to specify which branch is to lead in foreign policy (Corwin 1957, 171).

The Constitution assigns to the president powerful but limited foreign policy roles (Lindsay 1994a). Article 2, Section 2, provides that the president is the "Commander in Chief of the Army and Navy of the United

States . . . He shall have Power, by and with the Advice and Consent of the Senate, to make Treaties, provided two thirds of the Senators present concur; and he shall nominate, and by and with the Advice and Consent of the Senate, shall appoint Ambassadors, other public Ministers and Consuls." The use of these specific powers, court decisions (e.g. Silverstein 1994; Smith 1989), and the growth of executive institutions under the command of the president—especially after World War II—established important historical precedents for presidential leadership (Melanson 2005).

Nevertheless, the Constitution assigns Congress more numerous and more specific foreign policy powers. Article I, Section 1, gives Congress the general legislative power, and Section 7 adds the power to appropriate funds (the so-called power of the purse). Section 8 includes a wide array of foreign policy powers:

—to collect duties (thereby affecting imports),
—to provide for the common defense,
—to regulate foreign commerce,
—to set uniform rules for naturalization of citizens (thereby affecting immigration),
—to punish piracy and "other Offences against the Law of Nations" (thereby affecting international law),
—to declare war,
—to raise and support armies and navies,
—to regulate land and naval forces,
—to organize, arm, discipline, and call forth the militia, and
—to make all necessary laws to carry out such powers.

Hence the constitutional delegation of foreign policy powers to Congress is both wider in scope and more specific in nature than its delegation of powers to the presidency (Koh 1990).

The relationship between the executive and legislative branches is further complicated by two other factors. First, Congress is the most accessible federal government institution. Citizens communicate with their elected legislators fairly easily, as can organized interests—both domestic and foreign. Many who seek to influence foreign policy therefore choose Congress as their focal point. Since many legislators are motivated by the desire to make "good policy," they welcome informed input from others. They also typically welcome the financial support that organized interests provide to effective legislators for future elections (Box-Steffensmeier and Grant 1999). Thus congressional activity is complicated by the number of actors who rely on Congress as the best forum for shaping foreign policy in the directions they prefer (Lindsay 1994a).

Second, Congress consists of many actors who both shape policy and serve as access points where policy may be shaped. Individual legislators are the most fundamental actors and access points in Congress. Long before matters come to a vote, they highlight issues, help set the governmental agenda, frame debate, introduce bills, and lobby their colleagues and administration officials for support (Mayhew 2005; Carter and Scott 2004; Koger 2003). Then there are the numerous standing committees and subcommittees where most policy is shaped, if not made (Loomis and Schiller 2005; Rohde 2005; Maltzman 1998). Policy is also shaped in formal and informal policy caucuses that are formed around specific policy issues or regions (Trubowitz 1998; Rieselbach 1995; Hammond 1989). Party structures also play an increasingly important role both as access points (Sinclair 2005; Smith 2005; Nokken 2000; Wright 2000) and in developing foreign policy positions (Smith 1994). As Barbara Sinclair (1993, 231) summarizes, "When the majority party leadership speaks for and acts on behalf of a united majority, it will continue to be a potentially formidable competitor to the president." That congressional challenge becomes even more pronounced when the legislative majority party is also the opposition party to the president. Further, each chamber's floor becomes another access point, as members try to legislate through floor amendments. Conference committees also represent a final actor and access point, in which policy can be shaped before going to the president.

Attention to formal legislation and congressional procedures dominates studies of Congress and foreign policy. Yet with many actors and access points, there are many ways for legislators to shape foreign policy. In addition to formal powers and legislative processes, "members of Congress exert influence over foreign policy through many formal and informal inquiries, investigation, floor statements, and various procedural customs and techniques" (Hersman 2000, 20). Rather than try to enumerate every one, two dichotomies simplify the possibilities. One can discriminate between legislative and nonlegislative actions (Burgin 1997) and between direct and indirect ones (Lindsay 1993). Legislative actions pertain to the passage of specific pieces of legislation. Nonlegislative actions do

Table 1: Avenues of Congressional Foreign Policy Influence

	Direct	Indirect
Legislative	Legislation Appropriations Treaties (Senate)	Nonbinding legislation Procedural legislation Appointments (Senate)
Nonlegislative	Letters, phone calls Consultations, advising Hearings Oversight activities Litigation	Agenda setting Framing debate Foreign contacts

Source: Adapted from Scott (1997).

not involve a specific item of legislation. Direct actions are specific to both the issue involved and the case at hand. Indirect actions seek to influence the broader political context or setting. When these two dichotomies are joined, four broad avenues of influence are identified: direct-legislative, indirect-legislative, direct-nonlegislative, and indirect-nonlegislative (Scott 1997). Examples of activities that fall within each category are provided in table 1.

Most observers focus on only one of these four avenues: direct-legislative approaches to foreign policy. These are, after all, most easily measured. Those who recognize the importance of how setting procedures now shapes policy outcomes later appreciate the congressional foreign policy influence obtained through oversight activities and other actions that fall into the legislative-indirect avenue of influence (e.g. Lindsay 1994b). Fewer observers appreciate the impact that Congress can have through nonlegislative avenues, whether direct or indirect. These avenues tend to be a major domain of selected MCs who seek to shape the United States foreign policy agenda and who fly under the radar of most observers.

Historical and Policy Context

If the decisions, patterns of engagement, and avenues of influence open to MCs are more complex and subtle than many observers acknowledge, so too are the shifting patterns of congressional activity. Although studies of Congress and foreign policy during the Cold War tended to downplay the influence of the institution and its members, often characterizing Congress

as inherently acquiescent or deferential, a substantial portion of the literature on the subject agrees that Congress and its members became more
assertive across a wider range of foreign policy issues during the Vietnam
experience of the 1960s.

During the Cold War a policy consensus simplified both problem interpretation and policy prescription by providing "shortcuts" to United
States foreign policy makers (Melanson 2005). This consensus included
basic agreement on the nature of the world (bipolar), the nature of conflict
in the world (zero-sum between the United States and the Soviet Union),
the role of the United States in the world (leadership), and broad United
States foreign policy goals (containment of the Soviet Union and communism, and promotion of an open, multilateral economy). When the consensus was strongest, the policy debate tended to be more about tactics
than broader strategy or purposes, and the basic agreement generated a
tendency toward executive branch leadership in foreign policy making. As
James Robinson (1962, v) characterized this era, "Congress's influence in
foreign policy is primarily and increasingly one of legitimating and amending policies initiated by the executive to deal with problems usually identified by the executive."

Yet approximately two decades into the Cold War, White House leadership began to erode. In particular, the Vietnam experience destroyed much
of the Cold War consensus, and the ensuing policy disagreements largely
ended the so-called bipartisan era (e.g. Melanson 2005; Destler, Gelb,
and Lake 1984; Holsti and Rosenau 1984). Vietnam, Watergate, and other
events combined "to cause the relationship between the two branches in
foreign policy-making to shift away from the clear executive dominance,
characteristic of the postwar era, back to a more typical condominium
or shared enterprise arrangement" (Drischler 1986, 193). White House
leadership came under increasing scrutiny as congressional assertiveness
increased and domestic pressures proliferated. Of course the White House
(and the broader executive branch) retained important leadership roles,
but the breadth and scope of that leadership was increasingly challenged,
opening the door to greater congressional activism and assertiveness.

The end of the Cold War affected congressional behavior similarly (e.g.
Scott and Carter 2002a; Scott ed. 1998; Wittkopf and McCormick 1998).
In some ways congressional engagement in foreign policy increased even
more after the end of the Cold War, as a greater shift toward dissensus

and fragmentation of leadership occurred (e.g. Carter 1998). Moreover, in the post–Cold War period "intermestic" issues and increasing constituency pressures led to greater congressional challenges to presidential leadership (Conley 1999). Also, in the immediate post–Cold War years, the risk of challenging the president diminished, both because of the apparently more benign international environment and because of a decline in public interest in international matters (Lindsay 2000). Lack of consensus on foreign policy, more diffuse international security risks, and an interdependent world economy therefore combine to provide greater incentive and opportunity for MCs to be less deferential and more assertive.

Admittedly, the preeminent presidency was reinvigorated by the threat of terrorism after September 11, 2001. When it came to national security issues, President George W. Bush seems to have got most of what he asked for from Congress during his first term (Kassop 2003). In a time of war, politics both inside and outside the Beltway favor the president, and although a few MCs tried to challenge the president (see Mayhew 2005, 81–82), most members had less incentive to do so as long as he could claim success for his national security initiatives. How far this congressional deference extended beyond national security issues after 9/11 is another matter. Congress was willing to challenge President Bush on other issues like trade policy, and it made restrictions on civil liberties in the USA Patriot Act temporary, not permanent as requested (Lindsay 2003). In many ways, the extent to which congressional deference to the president extended beyond national security after 9/11 is a question yet to be fully answered.

This sort of variation in congressional foreign policy behavior hints at the importance of context. Returning to the four models of congressional activity, one can see that these patterns fit well with two general trends in congressional behavior: collectively, Congress seems to have become gradually less active in foreign policy since World War II, but increasingly assertive (likely to challenge presidential preferences) when it does act (Scott and Carter 2002a). In fact, using the four models to characterize the postwar period reveals a more nuanced conception of the ebb and flow of congressional behavior. Until about 1958 Congress did not assert itself so much as cooperate with the president in developing Cold War policy (Carter 1986), making "Supportive Congress" the appropriate characterization for this period. This label nicely captures the widely shared view of a bipartisan Cold War era.

Between about 1958 and 1967, congressional activity declined while assertiveness grew. This pattern suggests a "Strategic Congress," increasingly pressing the White House on certain foreign matters, while remaining less active on foreign policy overall. This combination nicely captures the idea of an increasingly restive Congress, uncomfortable with the logic of Cold War policy in the context of Vietnam overseas and domestic unrest at home.

From 1968 through the mid-1980s, a more active *and* assertive Congress emerged: a "Competitive Congress," eager to correct a perceived imbalance of power between the two branches and to reorient foreign policy after the Vietnam War. This categorization is consistent with analyses that stress a resurgent Congress.

Finally, since the mid-1980s the figures suggest a less active but still assertive Congress, indicating a return to the "Strategic Congress" model. This pattern is consistent with the post–Cold War conception of a Congress generally less interested in foreign policy, but willing to challenge the president when it chooses to address key issues.

Hence congressional foreign policy behavior varies in a reasonable and rational way that reflects, at least in part, the foreign policy environment and the political context. Consider the following overview. Immediately after World War II, in the relative simplicity of the Cold War context, not only did greater consensus exist (i.e. less assertive behavior), but there was substantial support within Congress for efforts to counter what then seemed to be an obvious and central communist threat. As the international context evolved and the implications of the Cold War logic manifested themselves in the Vietnam intervention, Congress reacted by first becoming more assertive. Then in the 1970s, with political concerns of an "imperial presidency" joining the changing foreign policy context, Congress became more competitive.

Finally, as the impact of congressional competitiveness took hold and the foreign policy climate evolved in the immediate aftermath of the Vietnam War, divided government and congressional reforms joined these other factors to produce a less active but more assertive Congress that faced greater difficulties in collective action, but in which individuals were afforded greater freedom to assert themselves. Committee and subcommittee reforms in the late 1960s and early 1970s increased both the opportunities for individual members and the fragmentation of power in Congress. This dynamic held into the post–Cold War world as well. As Marie Henehan (2001, 9) has argued, "On the one hand, activity should go down because there is no longer a critical issue over which to contend. On the other hand, the potential for contention increases because the constraint of the bipartisan consensus over containment . . . is now irrelevant."

Congressional Foreign Policy Behavior

A final corrective turns on the recognition that congressional foreign policy behavior is a complex phenomenon. As suggested earlier, there are important differences between activity and assertiveness, but there are also differences between general congressional assertiveness and even more forceful efforts by individual members. Congressional foreign policy activity can be conceptualized into three nested types that can be presented as a series of concentric circles (see figure 2).

In the broadest circle of foreign policy actions, *congressional foreign policy activism* includes any effort by Congress and its members to affect policy, whether in support of or in opposition to an administration's position. Thus when President George W. Bush asked for authorization to use force against Saddam Hussein's Iraqi regime, Congress voted to approve the action. Since Congress was not required to act on the president's request, its choice is an illustration of foreign policy activism.

Congressional foreign policy assertiveness, by contrast, encompasses instances of activism in which Congress and its members challenge the policy leadership of the administration (see Scott and Carter 2002b). Assertiveness fundamentally concerns policy innovation or change but may involve both reactive efforts (opposition to proposals or policy from an administration) and more proactive efforts (initiation of policy). Sometimes MCs are supportive of the direction of policy but unwilling to go as far as the president requests. Budgetary requests typically illustrate this dynamic. In other instances MCs are willing to go farther than asked. Examples include congressional actions supporting Israel to the point of recognizing Jerusalem as its capital or measures to fund military reserve units at levels beyond what the president requests. Sometimes, assertiveness means resisting a presidential initiative, such as when Congress refused to grant President Clinton fast-track trade negotiation authority in the 1990s.

The last type, which is the focus of this book, is *congressional foreign*

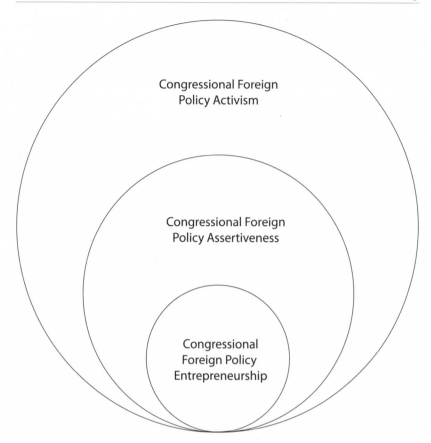

Figure 2: Types of Congressional Foreign Policy Activists

policy entrepreneurship. This activity is a subset of assertiveness, including only those foreign policy efforts by individual MCs that are both assertive and proactive. Because of the time investment required, MCs only become proactive about issues they see as very important (Burden 2007). Entrepreneurship therefore involves congressional policy innovation or change driven by individuals sufficiently dissatisfied with the administration's existing policy (or lack of a policy) to push for their own policy initiatives (Baumgartner and Jones 1993). By definition, innovation means nonincremental policy change. Thus *foreign policy entrepreneurship* entails the initiation of new policy. It may also entail the repudiation of existing policy. One example of policy repudiation was Congress's refusal to continue funding the Vietnam War in 1973. An example of entrepreneurship through new policy creation was the successful effort by Tony Hall (D-Ohio) to ban the importation of "conflict diamonds" from Sierra Leone, Angola, and the Democratic Republic of Congo (U.S. Embassy 2002). The Clean Diamond Trade Act of 2003 (Public Law 108-19) was the result.

Individual Members and Foreign Policy Entrepreneurship

These more subtle and complex characterizations of congressional foreign policy behavior have numerous implications, but none is more significant than the need to focus attention on individual MCs and, especially, on those specific members who aggressively pursue their policy priorities through the various avenues of influence available to them.

In any given situation, "Congress" is really a shorthand term for those individual members who act in its name (Bax 1977). One recent study baldly asserted that "it is nonsensical to treat Congress as a unitary actor" (Howell and Pevehouse 2007, 34). Although Congress is an aggregate body, the few members who choose to act become not only its public face (Mayhew 2005) but also the cue givers who direct the rest of their chambers. According to Frans Bax (1977, 884), "many studies on Congress have shown that the actions of the parent chamber usually constitute a ratification of decisions made at the committee (either standing or conference) level. At this level, action usually follows the lead of those one or two members who have taken a personal interest in a matter and who have developed enough understanding to offer an informed judgment . . . Congressmen have considerable latitude to select for themselves the issue areas in which they will play a part . . . to the extent that the entire Congress supports or ratifies the desires of those members interested in an issue, it can be said that those members embody or act in the name of Congress."

Individuals such as these have considerable power in a largely decentralized body (Hersman 2000; Kelman 1987). "With the member's job goes a license to persuade, connive, hatch ideas, propagandize, assail enemies, vote, build coalitions, shepherd coalitions, and in general cut a figure in public affairs" (Mayhew 2005, 71). As Burdett Loomis (1998, 121) notes, even freshmen in Congress can focus substantial resources on their favorite issues: "From the moment new members take the oath of office, they all control million-dollar-per-year operations of staff, communications, travel, and research capacities that allow them to commit substantial re-sources to reelection efforts, drafting legislation, overseeing the bureau-cracy, or seeking higher office . . . The congressional enterprise helps all lawmakers claim credit for governmental programs, take positions on the issues of the day, and relentlessly advertise their accomplishments. But this is just the minimum enterprise, the stripped-down model that every first-term member gets upon arriving on Capitol Hill." Rebecca Hersman states that "individualized power has come to rival institutional or struc-tural power when it comes to congressional influence over U.S. foreign policy" (2000, 10); thus "congressional influence over foreign policy is a highly personal business" (2000, 29). Those members who choose to serve as "champions and opponents for and against certain issues and policies" are especially important in the foreign and national security arena (Hers-man 2000, 29).

The policy literature has various names for those who use power and opportunity to change policy or force policy innovation. We use the term "policy entrepreneurs" because it is the one most widely used in the litera-ture (e.g. Jeon and Haider-Markel 2001; Kingdon 1995; Baumgartner and Jones 1993; Cobb and Elder 1983), although others use the terms "politi-cal entrepreneurs" (Schneider and Teske 1992), "strategic entrepreneurs" (Riker 1980), "public entrepreneurs" (Polsby 1984; Walker 1981), or even "policy champions" (DeGregorio 1997; Roberts 1992).

As a distinct subset of congressional activism and assertiveness, foreign policy entrepreneurship is an important, but underexamined, phenome-non. According to Mayhew (2005, 2000), these actions by individual MCs matter not only because they become the public face of Congress but also because the actions have important consequences, they were undertaken with a high degree of personal autonomy, and they were done without much notice having been taken by social scientists. Mayhew also estimates that from 1789 to 1988, 23 percent of these individual actions concerned foreign policy.

Thus consistently with the entrepreneurial literature (e.g. Jeon and Haider-Markel 2001; Kingdon 1995; Baumgartner and Jones 1993; Roberts 1992; Polsby 1984; Cobb and Elder 1983; Walker 1981), we define congressional foreign policy entrepreneurs as *members of Congress who seek to initiate action on the foreign policy issues about which they care rather than to await action from the administration.* Furthermore, entrepreneurs take such action continually; they seek to be ongoing "players" in the foreign policy process.

Implicit in this definition is the acknowledgment that congressional foreign policy entrepreneurs engage in these actions for one of two reasons. According to Rep. Jim Leach (R-Iowa), entrepreneurship typically occurs when something is wrong with existing policy, or when something is wrong and there is no policy to address the problem (Leach 2001). In either case—a policy correction or a policy vacuum—congressional foreign policy entrepreneurs seek policy innovation and do not wait for administration initiatives.

While numerous motivations may drive congressional foreign policy entrepreneurs, the most significant seems to be a passion for or commitment to a particular foreign policy issue, a category of issues (e.g. military or security policy), or even foreign policy in general. Policy entrepreneurs want to make "good policy" for the issues they care about (Hersman 2000; Kingdon 1995). As former House Speaker Jim Wright (D-Texas) said, "they have convictions. If they didn't have convictions, there would be little point in their seeking to serve in Congress" (Wright 2001). What else motivates entrepreneurs? Answers vary. To some, it is the matter of getting reelected (Arnold 1990; Mayhew 1974). To others, it may be a genuine effort to represent a constituency for its own sake (Mansbridge 2003; Mansbridge 1999). Or more personal motivations may be at work, such as influence in the chamber or "the simple pleasure in participating" (Kingdon 1995, 204).

Whatever the reason, by taking advantage of the direct and indirect, legislative and nonlegislative avenues of influence, individual members may choose to lead as foreign policy entrepreneurs and thus have substantial opportunities to exert policy influence. Such potentially influential policy makers demand attention. Their characteristics, activities, and impact must be examined.

Given the preceding arguments and evidence, we postulate that congressional foreign policy entrepreneurs seek to: (1) frame policy discussions and mobilize the public and interest groups; (2) direct congressional agendas to require attention to specific foreign policy issues; (3) structure and influence the formulation of foreign policies by the executive branch; (4) revise, refocus, or reformulate foreign policies; (5) fill policy vacuums with their preferred foreign policies. Because many MCs are less interested in foreign than domestic issues, foreign policy entrepreneurs become important generators of congressional activism, making the understanding of these individuals and their behavior a vital element of efforts to comprehend United States foreign policy making.

The remainder of the book explores the characteristics, activities, and impact of congressional foreign policy entrepreneurs since World War II. Chapter 2 develops the entrepreneur concept, elaborating on definitions and the motives, activities, and expectations of the entrepreneurs. Chapter 3 presents a quantitative dataset of congressional foreign policy entrepreneurship for the period 1946–2000. Chapters 4–6 focus on the Cold War Consensus period (1946–67), the Cold War Dissensus period (1968–89), and the post–Cold War period (1990–2000). In each chapter entrepreneurship for the period is discussed, and case studies of entrepreneurs are presented. Chapter 7 presents a synthesis of our findings from 1945 to 2000, the expectations that knowledge generates for the era after September 11, and a preliminary look at data from two randomly sampled years post-9/11 to see if those expectations are met. Chapter 8 concludes by discussing the nature and impact of congressional foreign policy entrepreneurship and trends over time. It also aggregates the lessons of the case studies within and across eras.

2

FROM PROBLEM TO POLICY

A THEORY OF CONGRESSIONAL
FOREIGN POLICY ENTREPRENEURSHIP

There has long been a conventional wisdom about Congress and foreign policy. In large measure because of the seminal work of David Mayhew (1974), members of Congress have often been characterized as "single-minded seekers of reelection." As Lindsay (1994a, 37–38) has character-ized it: "The simple electoral explanation, then, paints a pessimistic por-trait of the role Congress plays in foreign policy making. To keep their seats in Congress, members generally avoid foreign policy. When they do turn to foreign policy, they take positions designed to win favor with voters or attend to narrow parochial concerns. Lost in the pursuit of electoral gain is detailed attention to the substance of foreign policy." A possibly apocry-phal comment attributed to a member of Congress put it more colorfully: a member cannot be bothered with foreign policy because "Afghanistan is not in my district."

And yet, *some* members of Congress clearly do attend to foreign policy matters substantively and persistently. While there may be electoral bene-fit to their doing so, because of increased influence within Congress, the prestige attached to national leadership, and credit for policy successes (e.g. Lindsay 1994a, 41–43), electoral gain simply fails to explain their commitment. The most committed of these members—those we have labeled congressional foreign policy entrepreneurs—choose to devote sig-nificant time and resources to foreign policy issues, choosing to lead and seeking to shape policy. How should those who study U.S. foreign policy making understand the motives, activities, and impact of this select subset of members of Congress?

The Entrepreneurship Concept

When individual members of Congress choose to engage in foreign policy leadership, they are treading a path selected by relatively few of their colleagues. For a variety of reasons, most MCs choose not to invest their scarce time or political resources heavily on foreign policy issues. As former Representative Lee Hamilton, himself an active congressional foreign policy entrepreneur, characterized it, "the preferred stance is to let the president make the decisions and, if it goes well, praise him, and if it doesn't, criticize him" (quoted in Wittkopf, Kegley, and Scott 2003, 403). Some members see foreign policy as the president's responsibility, while others feel hampered by their lack of foreign policy expertise. However the greatest disincentive for MCs to get involved in foreign policy making is the lack of perceived domestic political incentives. As Representative Dave Mc-Curdy (D-Okla.) once observed, "I have no constituency in foreign policy" (quoted in Weissman 1995, 14). Most MCs see no local constituent groups whose support can be obtained by voting a certain way on a foreign policy issue.

However, some members manage to overcome such calculations (Hersman 2000; Kelman 1987). For one, the lack of constituency stakes can often mean more freedom to address policies of interest to the entrepreneur. As a staff member to an active senator told us, "So, part of why there can be more entrepreneurship in the foreign policy field now, in my opinion, is that here it can be done at relatively little cost defined in any way" (Johnstone 2001). Hence, even if most MCs care primarily about getting reelected (Mayhew 1974), Congress is still capable of overcoming narrow calculations to produce collective goods like foreign policy (Cox and McCubbins 2002; Cox and McCubbins 1993; Frohlich and Oppenheimer 1978). Some MCs do become active in the foreign policy arena with reelection in mind, as they can help *create* constituency opinion by their own actions, they can choose the constituency to which they respond, and they know that bold policy innovations may help their chances of reelection. Others want to shape policy for its own sake (Mayhew 2000). Those interested in forcing policy innovation are "policy entrepreneurs" (Jeon and Haider-

Markel 2001; Kingdon 1995; Baumgartner and Jones 1993; Parker 1992; Cobb and Elder 1983).[1]

In this analysis, *congressional foreign policy entrepreneurs are members of Congress who take the initiative on the foreign policy issues about which they care rather than await action from the administration*. These entrepreneurs initiate policy change or innovation, attempting to "seize the initiative to identify policy problems and offer substantive alternatives and solutions" (Conley 2003, 136).[2] In so doing they invest their own time and resources to produce collective goods (Frohlich and Oppenheimer 1978; Salisbury 1969). As discussed later in this chapter, foreign policy entrepreneurs often focus on passing legislation, and work to build support and coalitions for that purpose (e.g. Wawro 2000, 4), but they frequently engage in nonlegislative efforts as well in pursuit of their foreign policy objectives.

Moreover, congressional foreign policy entrepreneurs are both *expert* and *persistent* in advancing their policy interests. Thus to warrant the label of entrepreneur, our conception demands sustained activity, and requires MCs to *engage in more than one instance of foreign policy entrepreneurship*. Like Weissert (1991), we distinguish policy entrepreneurs from policy opportunists. The latter have not invested the time to develop the expertise or demonstrate persistence regarding a policy issue. They simply take advantage of an opportunity to associate themselves with innovative change for their own personal benefit. True foreign policy entrepreneurs, by contrast, represent the apex of congressional foreign policy assertiveness vis-à-vis a presidential administration, and their actions are consequential. In the words of Mayhew (2000, 105, emphasis added), "for any stretch of American history, *no one could write an adequate account of foreign policy without reckoning with MCs who took notable stands*."

Admittedly, Congress as an institution often defers to the presidency or other bureaucratic actors on foreign policy issues, particularly on issues involving the use of force (Hendrickson 2002; Hendrickson 2005). Moreover as suggested in chapter 1, foreign policy entrepreneurship is a distinct subset of congressional foreign policy behavior. Unlike *foreign policy activism*, which means simply taking action on foreign policy, even if it is no more than complying with the administration's requests, and *foreign policy assertiveness*, which involves choosing to shape policy by opposing or changing an administration's request, *foreign policy entrepreneurship* involves developing new policy, either as a correction to existing efforts or to fill a policy vacuum.

Congressional foreign policy entrepreneurship may occur in two situations. First, a *policy vacuum* may trigger entrepreneurship. In this situation the entrepreneur identifies a problem on which there is little effort and no existing administration policy. In such cases, congressional foreign policy entrepreneurs take the initiative to define a problem and generate a policy response without waiting for the administration to do so. Second, a *policy correction* may result from the entrepreneur's recognition that current policy is ineffective or inappropriate. In this situation, the entrepreneur attempts to redefine the issue and goal, highlight the failure or inadequacy of the current approach, and reverse or substantially revise the existing policy.

In either situation, when MCS choose policy entrepreneurship they need not restrict themselves to formal legislative activities. Indeed, they have an impressive number of means by which to press for their policy preferences. Of course, they can draft, introduce, or cosponsor legislation, as well as offer committee or floor amendments, to promote their policy agendas (Loomis 1998). However, they can also engage in policy research (using personal staff, committee or subcommittee staff, and institutional assets like the Congressional Research Service and the Government Accountability Office). They can travel to see the external realities or domestic consequences of policy issues. They can hold hearings to publicize issues, meet with the media to frame issues in preferred ways, and use available public forums to make the case for their policy positions—for example by making speeches on their chamber floor and before public and private organizations, writing magazine articles and letters to newspaper editors, and appearing on local or national television and radio programs. Within Congress they can appeal to other MCS through a variety of means (by means of personal contacts, letters, activities in caucuses, etc.). They can appeal to officials in the administration (up to and including the president) to change policy in their preferred direction. Even if it takes several congressional sessions to be successful (Koger 2003), *they may be able to change the direction of an administration's foreign policy without resorting to formal legislation* (a point missed by typical roll-call vote analyses of Congress).

With active members, flexible policy jurisdictions, and multiple access points, Congress is particularly well suited to the efforts of policy entrepreneurs. Conflicts internal to the institution also help entrepreneurs, as members, committees, and parties compete for control of issues (Baumgartner and Jones 1993). External factors facilitate policy entrepreneurship in Congress as well. Multiple "changes in the political system outside Congress—involving party organization, voter attitudes, and the role of the media—have encouraged members to 'go into business for themselves,' acting as independent entrepreneurs rather than as members of a larger organization" (Kelman 1987, 51). Such individual actions are nothing new. "Since the 1950s, members of Congress have increasingly operated as individual entrepreneurs, independent of political parties" (Sellers 2000, 23).

A Model of Entrepreneurship

We conceptualize congressional foreign policy entrepreneurship as shown in figure 3. As the model indicates, MCs *choose* to engage in entrepreneurship. The most common reason is their recognition of a problem that generates a new personal policy position regarding the issue they think is important or refines an existing position, but for which the administration either has no policy or has a policy that the entrepreneur sees as fundamentally incorrect. This personal policy position (Clausen and Van Horn 1977) is a product of the member's core values, personal experiences, family experiences, and own expertise (Burden 2007). Another factor for MCs who choose to become entrepreneurs is their desire for influence in their chamber (Fenno 1973). They may use the foreign policy issue as a vehicle to gain influence. External factors that may motivate MCs to become entrepreneurs are the influences of policy experts, their constituency, partisanship, the president, the media, and their own staff (Kingdon 1989).

To borrow from the work of John Kingdon (1995), the entrepreneur's choice to engage can take advantage of and shape policy windows. According to Kingdon (1995), policy making occurs in the context of a "problem stream," the recognition by those inside and outside government that a problem exists. For entrepreneurs, the problem stream represents the need to define a problem in such a way as to bring others' attention to it. A "policy stream" implies potential solutions to the problem, generated by experts and advocates. When key institutional, electoral, or societal moods change, the "political stream" changes. When these three streams coincide,

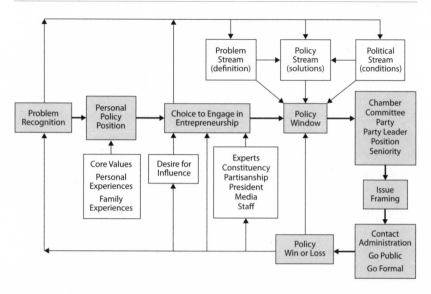

Figure 3: A Theory of Congressional Foreign Policy Entrepreneurship

a policy window opens which allows alert policy entrepreneurs to make rapid and innovative changes in policy.

The choice to become a foreign policy entrepreneur both affects and takes advantage of windows of policy opportunity (Kingdon 1995). Definitions of problems, proposed solutions, and favorable conditions in the political environment combine to open a policy window. Additionally, favorable conditions in the political stream can help generate policy solutions as some solutions become more feasible. However, by their own actions, entrepreneurs can define the events that fill the problem stream—such as through press conferences or committee hearings. Entrepreneurs also can inject important alternatives into the policy stream through their speeches and actions. If they are successful in calling attention to the problems and proposed solutions, they may help create a set of favorable conditions to act—the political stream and their efforts can affect the climate of opinion of which the political stream is partially formed.

Once a policy window opens and the opportunity for meaningful policy impact arises, the chances of entrepreneurial success and the means utilized by entrepreneurs are affected by a series of structural factors. These include the chamber of Congress in which they serve, whether they sit on a policy-appropriate committee, which party they belong to, whether they hold a leadership position within the party structure, and their seniority level.

Two primary action steps follow a decision to engage in foreign policy entrepreneurship. First, the member will try to frame the issue in a way designed to facilitate success (Iyengar 1991; Kahneman and Tversky 1984; Kinder 1983). Second, he or she will typically contact administration officials to seek policy change, go public with the need for the preferred policy, or, where necessary, take the formal step of seeking to pass appropriate legislation. After the general context is noted—which involves the creation of "policy windows"—these theory components are discussed.

The theoretical conceptualization in figure 3 suggests a number of general expectations regarding congressional foreign policy entrepreneurship. Entrepreneurs may be motivated by their core values, personal experiences, or family experiences, leading them to emphasize a particular problem (the problem stream) or to become especially interested in a set of ideas flowing through the policy stream at that time. In response, they may either attempt to generate a policy window or recognize that a policy window is already open, which motivates them to act on the foreign policy issue. Defense-minded entrepreneurs might act to create a national missile defense system to protect against a North Korean attack or to employ out-of-work Russian nuclear technicians so that they do not seek employment elsewhere. Entrepreneurs from immigrant families may want to act on issues affecting the country of their ancestry. Those who previously worked in international trade might seek to end a reliance on unilateral United States economic embargoes. When members in these and similar situations see an opportunity to enhance their legislative effectiveness through foreign policy entrepreneurship, their motivation to act should increase.

When it comes to personal motivations to act, an institution with 535 potential foreign policy entrepreneurs might find any number of idiosyncratic linkages to their behavior; putting these in the form of testable hypotheses rather than more general sets of expectations might be premature. Yet in terms of the rest of the model, a number of hypotheses are readily apparent. They are summarized here:

1. Legislators engage in more entrepreneurial acts when constituency groups important to them apply pressure to do so.

2. Legislators from the nonpresidential party engage in more entrepreneurial acts than members of the president's party.

3. As media attention to a policy issue increases, legislators engage in more entrepreneurial acts regarding that issue.

4. As staff attention to a policy issue increases, legislators engage in more entrepreneurial acts regarding that issue.

5. Members of the Senate are more likely to engage in foreign policy entrepreneurship than members of the House of Representatives.

6.1. Congressional foreign policy entrepreneurs are more likely to be members of foreign-affairs-related and defense-related standing committees.

6.2. Congressional foreign policy entrepreneurs who route issues through the committees on which they serve are more likely to be successful in achieving their aims.

6.3. Congressional foreign policy entrepreneurs who are the chairpersons or ranking minority members of foreign-affairs-related and defense-related standing committees and subcommittees are more likely to be successful in achieving their aims.

7. Legislators from the majority party in the chamber engage in more entrepreneurial acts than minority party members.

8. Congressional foreign policy entrepreneurs who serve as elected party leaders are more likely to be successful in achieving their aims.

9.1. Congressional foreign policy entrepreneurs who are more senior are more likely to be successful in achieving their aims.

9.2. The degree to which seniority aids foreign policy entrepreneurship tends to decrease over time.

10. Since World War II, more members have chosen to become foreign policy entrepreneurs, particularly those from the nonpresidential party.

11. Since World War II, entrepreneurs have used a greater variety of access points over time.

12. Since World War II, entrepreneurs have engaged in a greater variety of activities over time.

13. Overall, entrepreneurship is most common on economic development issues.

14. Issues of political and diplomatic status are more prevalent among Senate entrepreneurs than House entrepreneurs.

15. Entrepreneurs from the House of Representatives focus more on structural foreign policy, while entrepreneurs from the Senate focus more on strategic foreign policy.

Context: Policy Windows

An important contextual prerequisite for successful congressional foreign policy entrepreneurship is the presence of a policy window. As Kingdon (1995) argues, successful policy entrepreneurs take advantage of or generate a policy window. External events may generate policy windows. Thus Chinese espionage activity led to restrictions on the exports of encryption software. Atrocities in West African civil wars led to restrictions on the exports of "conflict diamonds." Policy failures also create policy windows. To many in Congress, the Tet Offensive in 1968 demonstrated that the Vietnam War was unwinnable for the United States, leading to the congressional cutoff of its funding. The inability to protect the American public on September 11 led to the creation of a Department of Homeland Security. But enterprising MCs who are dissatisfied with the status quo can also help create policy windows by contributing to both the problem and policy streams, while using access to the media and the public to influence the political stream. In this fashion, for example, entrepreneurs opened policy windows during the Cold War to try to purge the government of alleged communist influence. More recently, they opened policy windows to recognize Jerusalem as Israel's capital, to commit funds to the overthrow of the religious regime in Iran, to reorganize the State Department, and to reform the United Nations and the International Monetary Fund. Once a policy window is open, an opportunity for entrepreneurial impact arises.

Choices

Building on the observation by Fenno (1973) that members of Congress have three goals—enacting "good public policy," getting reelected, and gaining influence in the institution—we see congressional foreign policy entrepreneurship as the result of an individual choice (Schickler 2001). As noted in figure 3, a primary motivation for an entrepreneur to act is the recognition of a problem that becomes part of his or her own foreign policy agenda, which leads to the entrepreneur's personal stand on the issue. When asked why some members of Congress choose to engage in foreign policy entrepreneurship, former House Speaker Jim Wright (D-Texas) answered: "They have convictions" (Wright 2001). In other words, they have a *personal policy position* as to what constitutes good policy on that issue (Clausen and Van Horn 1977), and they want to mold policy to fit that position (Conley 2003; Froman 1963). "Convictions" is a key word to understanding personal policy positions. While MCs have opinions about many things, personal policy positions go far beyond mere policy opinions. They are intensely held positions on specific policy issues salient to them. These positions provide consistent decision-making guidelines and tend to change slowly, if they change at all. The intensity of these positions is reflected in a statement by Phil Gramm (R-Texas): "You don't have to worry about stepping on people's toes. They get out of the way" (quoted in Ehrenhalt 1991, 28). While it is helpful if such positions make them more popular back home (Schaffner, Schiller, and Sellers 2003), MCs often act on issues that have no apparent electoral benefit because they are committed to them (Parker 1992).

What shapes intensely held personal positions? As noted earlier, the key factors are the individual's core values, personal life experiences, and family experiences (Burden 2007). In terms of *core values*, Senator Jesse Helms (R-N.C.) provides a good example. According to one of his staffers, Helms believed the United States had unique moral values to share with the rest of the world, and that these should be pressed by both direct action and the power of example (Munson 2001). Others may be motivated by particular issues, like human rights issues in the cases of Representative Nancy Pelosi (D-Calif., now House Speaker) and Representative Frank Wolf (R-Va.) (Frank 2001). Clearly core values about foreign policy can also have an ideological component (Mayhew 2000). A good example would be the congressionally led "red scares" of the late 1930s, 1940s, and 1950s. These pitted congressional Democrats and Republicans motivated by anti-communism against congressional Democrats and Republicans concerned about civil liberties.

Personal experiences provide another motivation, as they generate heightened awareness about some issues or provide expertise relevant to particular policy arenas.[3] Military service motivates some foreign policy entrepreneurs—whether in World War II, as with Jim Wright (D-Texas), Bob Dole (R-Kan.), Frank Church (D-Idaho), and George McGovern (D-S.D.); the Korean War, as with Mike Gravel (D-Alaska) and Gerald Solomon (R-N.Y.); or the Vietnam War, as with Chuck Hagel (R-Neb.), John Kerry (D-Mass.), and John McCain (R-Ariz.) (*Congressional Biographical Directory* 2001). Other relevant personal experiences include foreign travel, study abroad, service in the Peace Corps, and prior careers involving international affairs. For example, after becoming the first person to major in Russian Studies at West Chester University, Representative Curt Weldon (R-Pa.) traveled early and often in his career to the Soviet Union and later to the former Soviet republics (Weldon 2002a). According to one of his aides, the entrepreneurship of Senator Richard Lugar (R-Ind.) was influenced by his study abroad as a Rhodes Scholar (Meyer 2001). According to another congressional staff member, the foreign policy agenda of Senator Chris Dodd (D-Conn.) was significantly shaped by his service as a Peace Corps volunteer in the Dominican Republic (Anonymous 2003a; see also Broder 1983). For Representative Jim Leach (R-Iowa), the formative experience was his former career as a foreign service officer (Leach 2001). For Chuck Hagel, part of his formative personal experience was his career in international telecommunications sales (Hagel 1998).

Family experiences also figure among key motivations. For example, the commitment of Representatives Robert Menendez (D-N.J.) and Ileana Ros-Lehtinen (R-Fla.) to anti-Castro initiatives can be traced to their Cuban-American immigrant heritage (Anonymous 2001a). MCs whose families emphasize their immigrant roots may engage in foreign policy entrepreneurship based on their sense of connection with the "old country." The efforts of Senator Edward Kennedy (D-Mass.) and Representative Thomas "Tip" O'Neill (D-Mass.) to nurture peace in Northern Ireland can be seen as examples of this tendency. Simply being a first- or second-generation American might make a member more sensitive to conditions elsewhere. Efforts by Senator Jacob Javits (R-N.Y.) to promote economic development in Africa and Latin America may have been influenced by his background as the son of immigrant parents (Carter, Scott, and Rowling 2004).

Not only are personal policy positions and personal and family experiences important cue givers for MCs, but they are particularly important when considering policy innovation or change. Jane Mansbridge (1999) calls relying on such factors "introspective representation," which she finds to be most important on new issues or issues for which there is no clear party position—in other words, issues for which a policy window may be open.

Another motivator for foreign policy entrepreneurship is the *desire for institutional influence* (Conley 2003). Having a reputation for policy expertise, along with the perception that MCs care more about accomplishing something than about just garnering publicity, can go a long way in helping them to establish a degree of personal influence within the chamber (Hill and Hurley 2002; Wright 2001; Drew 1979). For example, Richard Lugar takes foreign policy very seriously, studies the issues, and as a result often gets both Republicans and Democrats to vote with him (Meyer 2001). Most MCs would like to have that kind of influence, either because it aids their effectiveness in the chamber or because the public perception of their greater influence leads to greater electoral success in the future (Lindsay 1994a). This would be especially true for entrepreneurs, who typically have a high need for achievement (McClelland 1961). Further, those engaging in policy entrepreneurship enhance their ability to move up to more prestigious positions in their committee or party ranks (Wawro 2000).

Another indicator of the strength of entrepreneurial motivations involves "taking credit." For many entrepreneurs, the most important thing is policy success, not who gets credit for it. Former Speaker Wright (2001) stressed this point: "I learned that you mustn't expect credit if you're going to be effective. Satisfy yourself having made some worthwhile contribution." In interviews with the authors, both Representatives Weldon (2002a) and Leach (2001) noted that they were involved in pushing significant foreign policy initiatives for which the administration later took public credit. Getting the new policy "right" was more important to them than getting credit for the idea.

What else influences decisions to engage in entrepreneurship? Six decision-making factors are most important. First, the ideas flowing through the *policy stream* play a central role in persuading a potential entrepreneur to act (Kingdon 1995). Put simply, MCs listen to policy experts (Jacobs and Page 2005). Input from anti-apartheid experts like Bishop Desmond Tutu led Edward Kennedy to visit South Africa and then advocate sanctions against that regime (Carter, Scott, and Rowling 2004). In the late 1950s many leaders in the public and private sectors were talking about creating a civilian form of international public service when Representative Henry Reuss (D-Wis.) began considering a bill to create the Peace Corps (Polsby 1984).

Other factors are suggested by the consensus mode of decision making posited by Kingdon (1989).[4] For some, foreign policy entrepreneurship is *constituency*-driven, as entrepreneurs may be motivated by desires for reelection, the need for campaign contributions, or the propriety of representing the folks back home (Loomis and Schiller 2004; Parker 1992; Arnold 1990; Mayhew 1974). For example, religious groups pressed Representative Leach to push for debt relief for poor countries (Leach 2001). Similarly, Portuguese-Americans in his district persuaded Representative Barney Frank (D-Mass.) to act on the issue of East Timor (Frank 2001). In the view of a foreign policy aide to one senior senator, *most* entrepreneurship is constituency-driven, and the most influential constituency groups are often those that reflect very narrow interests and do not stray far from them. In addition to the pro-Israel lobby, good examples of narrowly focused groups are ethnic lobbies like Armenian-Americans, Greek-Americans, and Cuban-Americans (Anonymous 2001b). Business interests are another important example, as are (to a lesser degree) labor groups (Jacobs and Page 2005). The need to react to strong and well-organized constituency pressures back home is a political reality that affects all MCs to some degree (Lindsay 1994a; Arnold 1990). Since MCs should be more inclined to engage in entrepreneurship where concerned constituencies exist, the first hypothesis stresses that influence.

> *Hypothesis 1: Legislators engage in more entrepreneurial acts when constituency groups important to that legislator apply pressure to do so.*

Another motivation is *partisanship*, which affects entrepreneurship in two ways. First, foreign policy making is a partisan process (Ripley 1998). Widespread bipartisan support of presidential foreign policy initiatives ended sometime in the late 1950s.[5] By the early 1960s MCs of the non-presidential party began to challenge the president's foreign policy agenda (Carter 1998). Since then, party leaders as well as rank-and-file members have shown "increasingly partisan patterns in their support for presidential positions" (Smith 1994, 154–55). Partisanship is a major factor in congressional foreign policy behavior in the post–Cold War period (Howell and Pevehouse 2007; Lindsay 1994b; Wittkopf and McCormick 1998; Carter and Scott 2004). Second, congressional entrepreneurs expect the support of their party leaders. They seek their party's assistance in implementing the policies that they favor, and this applies as much to foreign as to domestic policy (Lindsay 1994a).

The *president*, his policies, and his party identification also motivate foreign policy entrepreneurship. Presidential policies inspire different reactions in Congress (Kingdon 1989). Questions such as "Do I agree with the president's position?" and "Is the president from my party?" are central to congressional decision making (Asher and Weisberg 1978; Howell and Pevehouse 2007). Members of the president's party have a partisan reason to support the president or, if entrepreneurship is called for, to work with or through the administration where possible (Fulbright 1966c).[6] Conversely, members of the opposition party act differently (Burden 2007; Howell and Pevehouse 2007). They are quicker to challenge presidents and to promote their own alternative foreign policy initiatives rather than await administrative action in line with their preferences.

In part because of partisanship, more entrepreneurial activity can be expected from members of the nonpresidential party (Ripley 1998; Carter 1998; Carter and Scott 2004; Wittkopf and McCormick 1998; McCormick and Wittkopf 1990; McCormick, Wittkopf, and Danna 1997; Ripley and Lindsay 1993; Rohde 1994; Sinclair 1993). The literature on divided government suggests this as well (e.g. Foreman 1988; Warburg 1989; Thurber 1991). Challenging the president is "good politics" for nonpresidential party MCs, and partisan or ideological differences generate substantive foreign policy disagreements with a president of the opposite party. By contrast, one would expect fewer electoral incentives or policy disagreements to prompt MCs from the presidential party to challenge the president's foreign policy agenda. Thus the discussion of party and presidential factors leads to the second hypothesis:

Hypothesis 2: Legislators from the nonpresidential party engage in more entrepreneurial acts than members of the president's party.

The news *media* play a motivating role as well. Their decisions about what foreign policy issues to highlight help to open policy windows and thus create the preconditions for getting an issue on the government's agenda (Kingdon 1995). As suggested by the "CNN Effect," dramatic media coverage created pressures on the administration to intervene in places like Somalia, Haiti, and Yugoslavia (over Kosovo) and later to withdraw (Gilboa 2005; Entman 2004). Similar media-created pressures to act can be felt by MCS as well (Baumgartner and Jones 1993; Cobb and Elder 1983).[7]

Even if the "CNN Effect" does not produce an intervention in each instance of graphic news coverage of violence to United States citizens or other noncombatant victims (Strobel 1999), the impact of the media cannot be discounted. In cases like Iraq, Somalia, Haiti, Rwanda, and Bosnia, some entrepreneurs called for the United States to act in behalf of the innocent victims of aggression after widespread media coverage of their plight (Entman 2004; Western 2005). In a different example, media coverage of the landing of a V-22 Osprey on the Capitol grounds helped persuade some members of Congress to support funding of this aircraft (Jones 2002). Thus the third hypothesis focuses on the role of media attention.

Hypothesis 3: As media attention to a particular policy issue increases, legislators engage in more entrepreneurial acts regarding that issue.

Finally, congressional entrepreneurship may be a response to pressures from *staff*. While staff expertise may have been limited before the reforms of the 1970s (Kingdon 1989), thereafter the policy expertise available to MCS increased dramatically (Mann and Ornstein 1993). As a result, staff influence in policy making began to escalate (Fox and Hammond 1977). Staff members now often act as policy advocates and press their principals regarding a particular issue (DeGregorio 1997), as did the Senate staffer Peter Galbraith on the issue of Iraq's genocidal treatment of the Kurds in the late 1980s (Power 2002). According to an aide, Jim Leach began to promote democratization in Taiwan after one of his staffers, whose parents had been missionaries in Taiwan, repeatedly stressed the one-party nature of the Taiwanese regime (Tate 2001). This phenomenon may be more commonplace on the part of elected party leaders responsible for seeing through a legislative product to successful completion (DeGregorio 1997) or committee staffers, who invest their time on a more limited number of issues than personal staffers do (Price 1971). The impact of staff may also be more noticeable in the Senate, as senators have more staff members than House members and, as policy generalists, may be forced to rely on staff members more for information (Kingdon 1989).

Hypothesis 4: As staff attention to a particular policy issue increases, legislators engage in more entrepreneurial acts regarding that issue.

Once members choose to engage in entrepreneurship, certain structural factors may enhance their possibilities of success. Congressional chambers may make a difference. *Senate* membership can enhance one's chances of effectiveness. As many have argued (e.g. Baker 2000; Crabb and Holt 1989), the Senate tends to be more concerned with foreign policy than the House, in part because of its constitutionally mandated foreign policy powers (e.g. ratification of treaties and confirmation of presidential appointments). With fewer members, senators serve on more standing committees than representatives do, thus giving them more access points to affect policy (Ripley 1983). One Senate staffer explained that "under Senate rules, the Senate is a very good body, as opposed to the House, for entrepreneurship because the rules place few limitations on a senator's rights to prospect for gold as it were, on just about any measure that comes along" (Johnstone 2001). As one of just one hundred members, a senator also benefits from the enhanced visibility that his or her advocacy brings to an issue (Schiller 1995; Schiller 2000). Senators may be freer than representatives to pick and choose the issues on which they focus, since they stand for election every six years rather than every two and represent an entire state rather than a district (unlike members of the House, except for those who are elected at-large by an entire state). To the extent that foreign policy represents a more national interest than one driven by a local constituency, senators may be freer to pursue such foreign policy interests than representatives are.

Hypothesis 5: Members of the Senate are more likely to engage in foreign policy entrepreneurship than members of the House of Representatives.

Relevant *committee membership* is a crucial advantage, as both a source of policy expertise and the location of procedural access points from which to affect policy (Deering and Smith 1997; Norton 1999). MCs are expected to develop policy expertise on the subject matter before their standing committees and subcommittees (Groseclose and King 2001; Maltzmann 1997; Krehbiel 1991). Thus those on the foreign affairs and defense-related committees learn the substance of foreign and defense policy, typically becoming the chamber's experts for these issues.

In some cases, entrepreneurs master these policy issues over time simply from being assigned to the committee—as Ron Dellums (D-Calif.) did on the House Armed Services Committee. But mostly they master these issues because they care about them, as reflected by their request to serve on those committees in the first place (such as Chuck Hagel for the Senate Foreign Relations Committee). For instance, Representative Charles Wilson (D-Texas) "had a grander vision. His passion, since boyhood, was foreign affairs, and from the moment he got on Appropriations he set out to position himself on the two subcommittees that dole out all money connected to national security" (Crile 2003, 77).

An extreme example is Stuart Symington (D-Mo.). During the Cold War, Symington dropped all domestic committee assignments and kept only his slots on the Armed Services Committee, Foreign Relations Committee, Joint Committee on Atomic Energy, and the Jackson Subcommittee on National Security and International Operation (of the Government Operations Committee). As one scholar put it "No senator in American history possessed a similar range of committee assignment dealing with American foreign policy and national security issues" (Johnson 2006, 145).

Either way, members' policy expertise enhances their ability to be successful entrepreneurs (Gilligan and Krehbiel 1997). Furthermore, membership on a foreign affairs or defense-related committee or subcommittee provides entrepreneurs with arguably the best structural location from which to influence policy (Baumgartner and Jones 1993; Arnold 1990), whether at the time the policy is initially considered or later in a conference committee (Shepsle and Weingast 1987a; Shepsle and Weingast 1987b). Moreover, according to a congressional staffer it is much easier to bring media attention to bear on an issue if the entrepreneur is a committee or subcommittee chairperson (Anonymous 2003d). These effects are magnified when an entrepreneur is the chairperson or ranking minority member of a committee that is relevant to the issue at hand (Wawro 2000). Since standing committee jurisdictions often overlap (King 1997), congressional foreign policy entrepreneurs can "shop" for the best committee venue from which to influence policy. Not surprisingly, the committees chosen are often those on which entrepreneurs sit (King 1994; Baumgartner and Jones 1993; Weissert 1991). These factors suggest three related hypotheses.

> *Hypothesis 6.1: Congressional foreign policy entrepreneurs are more likely to be members of foreign-affairs-related and defense-related standing committees and subcommittees.*

> *Hypothesis 6.2: Congressional foreign policy entrepreneurs who route issues through the committees on which they serve are more likely to be successful in achieving their aims.*

> *Hypothesis 6.3: Congressional foreign policy entrepreneurs who are the chairpersons or ranking minority members of foreign-affairs-related and defense-related standing committees and subcommittees are more likely to be successful in achieving their aims.*

One's party matters as well. Majority party membership increases the potential for entrepreneurial effectiveness. The structure of Congress makes it easier for the majority party to process legislation than for the minority party to do so. The majority party controls each chamber's leadership, committee and subcommittee leadership (e.g. Mayhew 2000; Deering and Smith 1997), and floor agenda (e.g. Campbell, Cox, and McCubbins 2002; Cox and McCubbins 2002; Jean Smith 1989). Thus majority party members will have more opportunities and presumably greater success in influencing policy. There are more potential allies based on shared party loyalties. For example, if a majority party entrepreneur does not chair the relevant committee or subcommittee, one from his or her party will, and that situation facilitates cooperation. Also, the majority party's leaders—whether in the party or the committee structures—can control the chamber's agenda. When the majority party is also the nonpresidential party, both entrepreneurial opportunities and entrepreneurial incentives abound.

> *Hypothesis 7: Legislators from the majority party in the chamber engage in more entrepreneurial acts than minority party members.*

Another asset is serving in a *party leadership position* in the chamber (Smith 1994; Smith and Gamm 2001). Since the 1970s elected party

leaders have gained policy influence at the expense of the standing committee structure (Loomis and Schiller 2004; Sinclair 2000). Since the
mid-1980s "message politics" has given a policy voice to the elected leaders
of both parties in Congress (Evans 2001). When party leaders choose to
become foreign policy entrepreneurs, they bring considerably more resources (Krutz 2002) and visibility to their cause (Wawro 2000). For example, being the House Speaker helped Thomas "Tip" O'Neill (D-Mass.)
in his efforts to stop Americans from funding the Irish Republican Army
(Anonymous 2003d), and it helped Jim Wright to nurture his own Central
American peace plan after President Ronald Reagan distanced himself
from it (Wright 2001; Scott 1996). Similarly, serving as House Majority
Leader helped Dick Armey to get reforms of the International Monetary
Fund enacted (Scott and Carter 2005). Thus,

> *Hypothesis 8: Congressional foreign policy entrepreneurs who serve as
> elected party leaders are more likely to be successful in achieving
> their aims.*

A final advantage is *seniority*. Being more senior is not a necessity for
legislative influence (Mayhew 2000; Ehrenhalt 1991), and seniority's impact has diminished somewhat over time (Sinclair 2000). Nevertheless,
seniority still contributes to success (Ripley 1983). Seniority brings more
visibility, greater access to the media, and, all things being equal, more
influence in subcommittees, standing committees, and the chamber as a
whole (Schiller 2000; Ripley 1983). As their seniority increases, members
are more likely to obtain seats on their preferred committees and subcommittees, increase their opportunities to serve as chairpersons or ranking
minority members of those committees and subcommittees, and improve
their standing in their party caucus or conference (Loomis and Schiller
2004). As their seniority increases, the degree to which members are seen
as "experts" and are sought out by the media also increases—particularly
in the Senate (Schiller 2000, 1995). Seniority is often accompanied by a
"safer" seat in Congress, thereby freeing time otherwise spent on reelection efforts to devote to policy entrepreneurship (Wawro 2000). Greater
seniority makes it easier for MCS to act independently and to devote time
and attention to the issues they choose (Stratmann 2000). In short, seniority contributes to policy success (Hammond 2003). Thus two related
hypotheses regarding seniority can be suggested:

Hypothesis 9.1: Congressional foreign policy entrepreneurs who are more senior are more likely to be successful in achieving their aims.

Hypothesis 9.2: The degree to which seniority aids foreign policy entrepreneurship decreases over time.

Patterns of Entrepreneurship

In general, several patterns of action and activity can be expected from entrepreneurs. Instances of congressional foreign policy entrepreneurship should increase over time as a consequence of a number of factors. First, as the Cold War consensus unraveled and dissatisfaction with Cold War policies increased (Melanson 2005), policy disequilibria between MCs and the executive branch became more common, providing incentives for members to get involved (Hersman 2000; Carter 1998; Carter 1994). Additionally, foreign policy issues evolved and changed as interdependence and globalization deepened, prompting some MCs, formerly concerned only with domestic politics, to become increasingly involved in foreign policy because of its intermestic aspects. Also, MCs acquired greater resources for foreign policy concerns, including increased staff and institutional support, at the same time that Congress decentralized, allowing a greater number of foreign policy access points to develop in committees, subcommittees, and elsewhere. Concurrently, Congress became more partisan (Cooper and Young 1997), which also increased activity. These factors suggest that foreign policy entrepreneurship has increased over time since World War II. Thus,

Hypothesis 10: Since World War II, more members have chosen to become foreign policy entrepreneurs, particularly those from the nonpresidential party.

As noted, more access points are now available to MCs than before. The committee reforms of the 1970s created new subcommittees and eroded the power of the committee chairpersons over the policy agenda. The increasingly complex, overlapping committee and subcommittee jurisdictions over foreign affairs (which generate more "foreign policy" committee assignments) also contribute to this expectation (e.g. Sinclair 2000). An explosion in the number of policy and regional caucuses, many of which have foreign policy concerns, contributes to this expectation too (e.g. Hammond 1998). Finally, the more complex oversight issues and opportunities generated by committees and subcommittees, the reporting requirements and detailed appropriations that they specify, and the increasing pattern and acceptance of rank-and-file challenges to committee actions are important as well (e.g. Blechman 1990). Thus,

> *Hypothesis 11: Since World War II, entrepreneurs have used a greater variety of access points over time.*

With more access points for entrepreneurs, those wishing to set the agenda and influence policy face increasing competition from others. Relying on one or two preferred activities may not be enough to ensure success. Further, changes in the setting of congressional politics allow entrepreneurs more options. For example, foreign heads of state and foreign ministers now routinely seek out key MCs, there are far more media outlets than there were just ten years ago, and there are more registered foreign lobbyists than before. There are more ways to do more things to influence foreign policy (Burgin 1997). It is no longer sufficient merely to control the standing committee and subcommittee structure if one's desire is to control policy. In today's environment, those seeking to influence foreign policy need to engage in a greater variety of activities to shape policy. Thus,

> *Hypothesis 12: Since World War II, entrepreneurs have engaged in a greater variety of activities over time.*

Finally, not all issues should generate equal foreign policy entrepreneurship. MCs are often depicted as being primarily motivated by the concern for reelection, and believing that the way to get reelected is to bring home benefits for constituents (Arnold 1990; Mayhew 1974). To the extent that Americans vote their pocketbooks, MCs should seek to promote the economic development and well-being of key constituencies (Lindsay and Ripley 1993). Thus we can expect more entrepreneurship on economic and development issues, and less on war and peace issues that tend to favor the commander in chief (Hendrickson 2002; Hendrickson 2005).

However, chamber-specific differences can be expected in terms of the kinds of issues that entrepreneurs choose to address. The constitutional roles that the Senate enjoys (approval of treaties and ambassadorships, for example) might lead to more entrepreneurship than in the House on matters that Brecher, Steinberg, and Stein (1969) call political-diplomatic, or status, issues. Given the strong House role in appropriations as well as tighter links between its members and narrow constituencies, House members can be expected to be more active on issues of economic development, which often requires foreign aid. Finally, because of the close connection between representatives and their constituents, and the strong House role in appropriations, members of the House can be expected to be more active on issues of a structural nature, while members of the Senate should be more active on issues of a strategic nature, especially given the special Senate responsibilities in diplomacy. As Lindsay and Ripley (1993, 19) have noted, "strategic policy specifies the goals and tactics of defense and foreign policy. It encompasses much of what is commonly called foreign policy as well as those aspects of defense policy that govern the basic mix and mission of military forces. Structural policy governs how resources are used and most closely resembles decision making on domestic, distributive policies. In the defense realm, structural policy aims at procuring, deploying, and organizing military personnel and materiel. In foreign affairs, structural policy answers questions such as which countries will receive aid, what rules will govern immigration, and how much money will be given to international organizations." These observations suggest several related hypotheses.

> *Hypothesis 13: Overall, entrepreneurship is most common on economic-developmental issues.*

> *Hypothesis 14: Political-diplomatic and status issues are more prevalent among Senate entrepreneurs than House entrepreneurs.*

> *Hypothesis 15: Entrepreneurs from the House of Representatives focus more on structural foreign policy, while entrepreneurs from the Senate focus more on strategic foreign policy.*

Entrepreneurship Campaigns

Once the choice is made to engage in foreign policy entrepreneurship, a number of possible actions can be considered (Ripley 1998). MCS can choose to legislate, investigate, impeach or censure, make appointments, take stands, etc. By doing so, MCs can shape public opinion and mobilize the public. In his count of actions with significant implications for policy, Mayhew (2000, 103) finds that almost "a quarter of MC actions during the past two centuries have involved foreign or defense policy," and of these actions, only 40% involved legislating. Thus the majority of significant congressional actions to affect foreign and defense policy—the kinds of things congressional foreign policy entrepreneurs do—are such things as taking stands and educating the public. These actions often have significant policy impacts and yet are not to be found in analyses of roll-call votes (Burden 2007; Mayhew 2000). By operating below the radar of most congressional specialists (Mayhew 2000), congressional foreign policy entrepreneurs are likely to have an impact that is at best underestimated and at worst missed entirely.

The essential first step for entrepreneurs is *issue framing*—defining the issue in the most helpful way to get it on the governmental agenda (Mintrom 2000; Kingdon 1995; Baumgartner and Jones 1993). In their study of decisions to use force, Howell and Pevehouse (2007, 23) highlight the impact of framing and public appeals as a means to shape the policy debate and put the president on notice. Other observers argue that "how problems are defined or framed determines what factual evidence is relevant, which solutions or alternatives are considered effective and feasible, who participates in the decision process, and ultimately who wins and loses" (Jeon and Haider-Markel 2001, 227). According to Ripley (1998, 266), "Symbolic statements, and even confused statements, can also help set the terms of debate for an issue over time or can signal the president and foreign policy agencies in ways that alter their behavior incrementally." For example, in the mid-1970s Senator Frank Church (D-Idaho) created a public uproar and put the Nixon administration on the defensive when he publicly characterized the CIA as a "rogue elephant" (Daugherty 2004). As Jacoby (2000, 763) notes, "framing effects are extremely powerful— probably more so than previously recognized . . . Differing frames produce widespread *changes* in the ways that people respond to a single issue" (emphasis in original). As the literature on the "new institutionalism" stresses, Congress is adept at framing issues to favor congressional foreign policy initiatives rather than executive-branch ones (Lindsay 1994b).

Using the media is an important way to promote one's favored issue definition, particularly as one's seniority increases (Jeon and Haider-Markel 2001; Kedrowski 2001). Since the media tend to reflect congressional attention (e.g. Arnold 2004; Bennett 1990; Bermin 1999; Howell and Pevehouse 2007), this is a potential vital link between the entrepreneur's agenda and policy influence. Entrepreneurial members influence media attention and framing, which then influences public opinion and other policy makers.

As entrepreneurs persuade others to accept and use their preferred issue definitions, the possibility of getting the issue on the government's agenda increases dramatically (Sellers 2000; Riker 1997, Riker 1986; Cook 1989). Baumgartner and Jones (1993, 4) explain: "As disadvantaged policy entrepreneurs are successful in convincing others that their view of an issue is more accurate than the views of their opponents, they may achieve rapid success in altering public policy arrangements, even if these arrangements have been in place for decades. They need not alter the opinions of their adversaries; as new ways of understanding old political problems take hold, different policymakers and governmental institutions suddenly begin to claim jurisdiction over issues that previously had not interested them. The old policymaking institutions find themselves replaced or in competition with new bodies that favor different policy proposals. So agenda-setting has important policy consequences, and these are expected often to be dramatic reversals rather than only marginal revisions to the status quo."

Once issues are framed and the policy disputes are on the government agenda, entrepreneurs can then strategize, propose solutions, and "work the system" to organize others and provide leadership (Mintrom 2000). Every conceivable action available to MCs can be used, making an itemized inventory virtually impossible, but actions are typically taken in a particular sequence. Indeed, one staff aide to a congressional entrepreneur suggested a typical sequence in an interview with the authors (Anonymous 2001e):

1. Entrepreneurial activity usually begins with queries to executive branch officials to gather information and identify concerns and preferences;
2. Entrepreneurs then typically meet with (or write letters to) administration officials, make requests, and wait to see if action follows;
3. Hearings are often the next step, during which entrepreneurs get the

administration on the record and signal desired changes (this is, usually, the first point at which the attentive public becomes aware of the activity);

4. Depending on the administration's reactions, the next step is usually to introduce a bill or amendment, either in committee or on the floor.

In effect, the sequence described by this staff aide suggests that "working the system" comes down to three major steps. For many, the first step is to *contact the administration* to propose a new policy innovation. To maximize their chances of success, entrepreneurs seek administration support for their policy initiatives. As a number of congressional staff members emphasized, entrepreneurs may call officials in the White House or cabinet, seek personal meetings with them, or write them letters proposing the new policy position (e.g. Anonymous 2001c; Anonymous 2001d; Anonymous 2003d). Some entrepreneurs are comfortable contacting the administration regardless of their partisan affiliation. For example, when Congress was unwilling to bail out the Mexican peso in 1995, Jim Leach, a Republican, proposed the way to do so to a member of the Democratic Clinton administration (Leach 2001). Like many other policy entrepreneurs, he changed the policy venue to maximize his chances of success (Hunt 2002). However for many MCs it is far easier to work behind the scenes with the administration when entrepreneur and president are members of the same political party (Fulbright 1966c). As Representative Barney Frank (D-Mass.) stressed to the authors, being of the same party is critical in trying such informal routes. According to Frank (2001), members of the same party as the president "have more access and the threat of criticism of the administration's policy is more damaging."

One cost of this approach is that the administration may take credit for the initiative. Thus the peso bailout in 1995 was a "Clinton" victory, not a "congressional" victory or a "Leach" victory. Anecdotal evidence suggests that administrations often take credit for the ideas pressed by congressional foreign policy entrepreneurs. To the extent that this occurs, congressional initiative is a stealth phenomenon, escaping public awareness and reducing the perceived importance of members of Congress in foreign policy making.

When working with administrative officials proves unsuccessful, an entrepreneur's second major step in "working the system" is to *"go public."*

Just like presidents (Kernell 1997), congressional foreign policy entrepreneurs go public to mobilize support for their policy innovation or change.[8] In so doing, they use every conceivable means to get their message out and manipulate opinion, and to signal the administration of their preferences on policy, which can trigger adjustments to policy (Baumgartner and Jones 1993; Howell and Pevehouse 2007). At this stage, which is analytically distinct from the issue-framing stage, entrepreneurs feel that they have succeeded in defining the issue favorably and concentrate their efforts on getting their policy message out to the public. According to Representative Charlie Wilson of Texas (2008), the very threat of going public can sometimes push an administration to heed an entrepreneur's preferences to avoid unwanted negative publicity over a perceived policy failure.

One particularly powerful way to do this is to hold congressional hearings on the preferred issue (Mayhew 2000). Beyond the opportunity to articulate a favorable definition of the issue and advocate a preferred solution, hearings pressure administration officials to discuss the policy publicly on terms set by Congress, allow members to press ideas on the administration, and offer the opportunity to generate publicity for a desired policy shift (Anonymous 2001c; Anonymous 2003d). As congressional staff members have stressed (Anonymous 2003c), hearings "often influence policy without legislation. They can prod the administration to do more on an issue. They constitute informal means to . . . prod thinking on an issue. They are a pressure tactic in this sense, signaling preferences." The signals can be critical in producing "anticipated reactions"—adjustments of administration policy in the direction of congressional preferences to head off further policy-making efforts by members of Congress (e.g. Howell and Pevehouse 2007; Lindsay 1994a). Of course, employing this tactic through committees requires either membership on the appropriate standing committee or access to members of the committee. It also indicates the importance of structural components in congressional foreign policy entrepreneurship—both committee membership and sufficient seniority to influence committee and subcommittee operations.

The last major step in working the system is to *go formal* by introducing legislation or amendments to codify the entrepreneur's foreign policy preferences into law. This step is often a last resort, because of the many obstacles in the highly fragmented Congress that must be overcome for any initiative to become law (Loomis and Schiller 2004; Anonymous

2001c). Going formal means rounding up cosponsors; making statements or speeches in committee, on the chamber floor, or in other public forums; working within caucuses; and building winning coalitions (Koger 2003). One tactic frequently used by entrepreneurs at this stage is the use of "Dear colleague" letters. One congressional staff member (Anonymous 2001c) explained that such letters "explain why you care about an issue. These letters gain visibility for the issue and can help create circumstances for a future success." A good example of an entrepreneur who uses these letters is Senator Richard Lugar. According to a member of Lugar's staff, "If he thinks something's important enough he'll write them a little short note or pick up the telephone and call them. . . . He uses the 'Dear Colleagues' vehicle a lot. For example, on the Chemical Weapons Convention he sent out . . . 'Dear Colleagues' to every member of the Senate explaining how this treaty work[ed], why the critics [were] wrong, why President Bush should have signed this, why we should support [the treaty], and other points."[9]

When formal legislation is sought, the bill's referral to the appropriate committee will be aided if the entrepreneur is from the majority party (or, even better, an elected majority party leader), is more senior, sits on the referral committee, is closer ideologically to the committee chairperson, pushes hard for the bill, gives a pre-referral floor speech on behalf of the bill, and introduces the bill in the first rather than the second session of a Congress (Krutz 2005).

The final output of the process is a policy win or loss for the entrepreneur. Policy either changes, or fails to change, in the preferred direction. Successful policy shifts may be announced by the administration (in the case of the entrepreneurs working with the administration) or by Congress as it enacts the needed legislation. Whether successful or not, the results of one entrepreneurial campaign can feed back into the recognition of new problems and the development of new policy windows.

Our theory of congressional foreign policy entrepreneurship offers a starting point for understanding a body of congressional actions that (1) seem to have considerable policy impact and (2) are typically overlooked by many other observers of United States foreign policy making. In our view, some observers question the importance of Congress in the foreign policy–making process precisely because entrepreneurial actions have been overlooked. There are instances of significant congressional influence that are not the result of observable roll-call votes or even the passage of legislation and for which administrations take credit. To the extent that these behaviors can be identified and explained, a more sophisticated, nuanced understanding of the foreign policy–making process will result. Using the framework and theory discussed above to guide the inquiry, the following chapters provide the necessary empirical investigation of congressional foreign policy entrepreneurship, relying on both quantitative and qualitative methods.

3

SURVEYING THE LANDSCAPE

CONGRESSIONAL FOREIGN POLICY ENTREPRENEURS

SINCE WORLD WAR II

Since World War II congressional foreign policy entrepreneurs have become an increasingly important part of the foreign policy landscape. However, they are often overlooked by scholars, observers, and the media. As
we have suggested in the preceding pages, they have played key roles in
a wide range of cases. Over time, they have employed an expanded range
of approaches and instruments to engage issues of their preference. This
chapter begins the exploration into the empirical record by setting the
broad context of entrepreneurial characteristics and behavior. Subsequent
chapters examine key entrepreneurs during the Cold War Consensus, Cold
War Dissensus, and post–Cold War periods, and gauge their impact on
a variety of foreign policy issues. This overview surveys the post–World
War II era to explore identities, behavior, issue agendas, activities, and
trends. The broad empirical evidence presented here bears on a number of
the hypotheses discussed in chapter 2 and lays out many of the principal
features of this largely unexamined phenomenon.

Identifying the Contours of Entrepreneurship

What have been the basic features of congressional foreign policy entrepreneurship since World War II? This first pass at the entrepreneur phenomenon presents and assesses the overall evidence of the post–World
War II era to establish the empirical foundation and broad patterns of

entrepreneurship. Hence the focus at this stage of the investigation is at the aggregate level, with broad data presented on key entrepreneur characteristics (party characteristics, committee assignments, chamber membership), issue agendas (policy problems and issues to which attention is directed), behavior (activities and access points relied on by entrepreneurs), and impact (as gauged by the volume and frequency of entrepreneurship). Subsequent chapters delve deeper into the phenomenon, examining individual entrepreneurs, specific foreign policy periods since World War II, and more particular aspects of policy impact.

This chapter, and to a lesser extent those that follow, rely on an extensive database of entrepreneurship for the post–World War II era. To establish the broad empirical foundation, what is needed is a comprehensive, accessible, and consistent record of congressional foreign policy activity that will expose the entrepreneurial actions of individual members, while presenting the larger context of congressional activity. For such an empirical record, this study relies on an innovative investigation into the oft-used annual volumes of the *Congressional Quarterly Almanac* for the broad entrepreneur dataset (e.g. Carter 1986; Carter 1994; Carter 1998; Carter and Scott 2004; Scott and Carter 2002a; Smith 1994). The *CQ Almanac* presents an overview of annual congressional activity, drawing on the detailed *CQ Weekly Report*, and it reviews both legislative and nonlegislative activity.

The period 1946–2000 represents the universe under study. As noted earlier, this span of fifty-five years can be divided into three periods for comparative purposes. The Cold War began almost immediately after World War II ended, but with the Tet Offensive in early 1968, United States foreign policy changed. Policy makers sought ways to get out of the Vietnam conflict and to avoid being drawn into similar conflicts for the remainder of the Cold War. Then foreign policy dynamics changed again after the climactic events of 1989, which included the collapse of Soviet control over Eastern Europe and the demolition of the Berlin Wall. Based on these events, the post–World War II era can be divided into the *Cold War Consensus* period (1946–67), the *Cold War Dissensus* period (1968–89), and the *post–Cold War* period (1990–2000). In chapter 7 we discuss the years after the 2001 terrorist attacks on the United States as a *post-9/11* period.

To gain insight into congressional foreign policy entrepreneurs over this broad span, and the three periods into which it is divided, the over-view data were collected from a stratified random sample of the annual *CQ Almanac* volumes from 1946 to 2000. To ensure a proportional rep-resentation of their share of the entire post–World War II era, ten years from the Cold War Consensus period, ten years from the Cold War Dis-sensus period, and five years from the post-Cold War period were ran-domly selected.[1] The sections in each volume from this twenty-five-year sample dealing with foreign policy, defense policy, appropriations, interna-tional trade and finance, and agricultural trade were reviewed to identify instances of foreign policy entrepreneurship, as were any other sections found to reference foreign and defense policy coverage.[2]

The focus of the review was to identify and select those instances in which members of Congress introduced their own foreign policy issues rather than await action from the administration on those issues. As dis-cussed in chapters 1 and 2, the key to foreign policy entrepreneurship is the introduction of *new* issues. Thus incremental congressional changes in administration policy or spending requests did not fit the inclusion cri-teria. However, when members raised *new* issues in spending bills, those were coded as instances of entrepreneurship. For example, changing the spending totals for a weapons system that the administration desired, or raising or lowering foreign aid amounts to agreed-upon recipients, were not instances of entrepreneurship.[3] Instances such as injecting funding for a weapon system that the administration did not want, earmarking aid to a recipient not included in the administration's request, or delet-ing all requested aid for a recipient were seen as raising a new issue and were thus coded as entrepreneurial activity.[4] Each instance of entrepre-neurial behavior was coded separately. For example, if a senator wrote an op-ed piece and made three floor speeches to focus governmental atten-tion on the plight of refugees, these activities would have counted as four instances of entrepreneurial activity. The data collection produced a set of 2,621 cases of entrepreneurial activity conducted by 434 individuals across the 25 years of the sample. These data provide the basis for our description of congressional foreign policy entrepreneurship.

To gain insight into entrepreneurship, each instance of entrepreneurial behavior in this sample was coded for the year of the activity; the relevant page number of the *Congressional Quarterly Almanac*; the entrepreneur's name, party identification, and state; the substantive issue area involved;

the activity used by the entrepreneur; the access point used; and the avenue of influence used. Additionally, we included variables for the president's party at the time of the action; whether the member was in the majority or the minority party in Congress; whether the member was in the opposition party (relative to the president); whether the member was assigned to one of the traditional foreign policy–related committees, such as foreign relations, defense, or intelligence; and whether the action took place in a presidential or congressional election year.

To categorize the foreign policy issues address by entrepreneurs, the twenty-five substantive issue areas identified in the investigation were collapsed into the fourfold categorization offered by Brecher, Steinberg, and Stein (1969):

> The *Military-Security* issue area comprises all issues which focus on questions pertaining to violence, including alliances and weaponry, and those which are perceived by the foreign policy elite as constituting a security threat. The *Political-Diplomatic* issue area covers the spectrum of foreign policy interaction at each of the three levels of the external environment—global, subordinate, and bilateral—except for those dealing with violence, material resources, and cultural and status relations. The *Economic-Developmental* issue area comprises all those issues which involve the acquisition and allocation of resources, such as trade, aid, and foreign investment. The *Cultural-Status* issue area consists of those foreign policy issues involving cultural, educational, and scientific exchanges. It also contains status issues which relate primarily to self image, namely, the decision-makers' perception of their state's legitimate place in the global and/or subordinate systems (Brecher, Steinberg, and Stein 1969, 79).

Also, the issues were coded into the structural-strategic policy distinction employed by Lindsay and Ripley (1993). According to Lindsay and Ripley (1993, 19), "strategic policy specifies the goals and tactics of defense and foreign policy. It encompasses much of what is commonly called foreign policy as well as those aspects of defense policy that specify the basic mix and mission of military forces. Structural policy governs how resources are used and most closely resembles decision making on domestic, distributive policies. In the defense realm, structural policy aims at procuring, deploying, and organizing military personnel and materiel. In foreign affairs, structural policy answers questions such as which countries will receive aid, what rules will govern immigration, and how much money will be given to international organizations." In this categorization, the twenty-five foreign policy issues were recoded as strategic policy (thirteen issues) or structural policy (twelve issues). Finally, for the subset of issues that concern defense policy only, the issues were coded into defense strategic and defense structural policies.[5]

Because the behavior of entrepreneurs is also of interest, the data were coded by activities, access points, and avenues of influence as well. Thirteen activities and eight access points were identified. Activities included introducing legislation, making committee or subcommittee amendments or proposals, attending hearings, issuing reports, proposing floor amendments, making resolutions, making speeches or other public statements, making motions to recommit (or kill) a piece of legislation, citing someone for contempt of Congress, engaging in fact-finding missions, enacting procedures, consulting with others, or participating in lawsuits.

Access points included the House floor, the Senate floor, a committee, a subcommittee, the White House or other administration location, the public, congressional caucuses, and the courts. Avenues of influence were coded "1" for direct-legislative, "2" for indirect-legislative, "3" for direct-nonlegislative, and "4" for indirect-nonlegislative.[6] Intercoder reliability scores were more than acceptable.[7]

Post–World War II Entrepreneurs

As noted, the post–World War II sample identifies 2,621 instances of entrepreneurial behavior by 434 foreign policy entrepreneurs. Who are they? What do they focus on? What do they do? Here we discuss the aggregate profile of post–World War II entrepreneurship on these matters. In general, as described below, the data show that the *most likely member of Congress to become a foreign policy entrepreneur is a senator from the party opposing the president when that party is in the majority.* Such a member is likely to be increasingly active across different access points over time. The details supporting this generalized profile are given in the following pages.

Entrepreneur Characteristics

The initial set of features for the entrepreneur landscape since World War II concerns key identity characteristics of those who choose to take the lead on foreign policy issues.

1. *Chamber.* First, from which chamber are entrepreneurs most likely to arise? Although foreign policy entrepreneurs can be expected from either chamber of Congress, differences by chamber can be expected. First, the congressional policy literature suggests that foreign policy activism and assertiveness are generally more likely to be found in the Senate than in the House (e.g. LeLoup and Shull 1993). As Ross Baker (1995, 162) argues, "The Senate . . . has normally been the principal antagonist to the president on foreign policy and the focus of attention in clashes over the conduct of U.S. diplomacy." This greater likelihood is based on a number of factors. The Senate has some enumerated constitutional powers in foreign affairs not afforded to the House (such as the power to confirm treaties and ambassadorships). Since senators represent entire states, they may take broader and more cosmopolitan policy views than representatives with smaller districts. Given the Senate's constitutional foreign policy roles, this broader view might lead more senators than members of the House to get involved in foreign affairs. Political ambition may play a role as well. For those members of Congress who aspire to the presidency, a disadvantage often faced is a lack of foreign policy experience. Thus those hoping to gain the Oval Office may gravitate to foreign policy matters to get that experience; historically there seem to be more presidential hopefuls in the Senate than in the House.

At the same time, the Senate's greater involvement in foreign affairs relative to the House is declining over time (see LeLoup and Shull, 1993; Ripley and Lindsay 1993; Carter 1998). Again, multiple factors support this trend. In recent years the Senate Foreign Relations Committee lost much of its prominence and was eclipsed to some degree by the House Foreign Affairs and International Relations Committee. Moreover, in recent years more and more foreign policy issues have been resolved in appropriations, or even omnibus appropriations, bills rather than in authorization bills (the foreign aid budget being an excellent example). Such legislative tactics favor the House over the Senate because of its constitutional advantage in appropriations.

Table 2: Instances of Congressional Foreign Policy Entrepreneurship by
Chamber and Era, 1946–2000

Chamber	Overall, 1946–2000	Cold War Consensus, 1946–1967	Cold War Dissensus, 1968–1989	Post–Cold War, 1990–2000
House	40.2% (1,054)	41.4% (292)	36.8% (520)	48.2% (242)
	259 entrepreneurs	109 entrepreneurs	143 entrepreneurs	73 entrepreneurs
	10.4 per year	10.9 per year	14.3 per year	14.6 per year
Senate	59.8% (1,567)	58.6% (414)	63.2% (893)	51.8% (260)
	210 entrepreneurs	97 entrepreneurs	119 entrepreneurs	61 entrepreneurs
	8.4 per year	9.7 per year	11.9 per year	12.2 per year
Total	100.0% (2,621)	100.0% (706)	100.0% (1,413)	100.0% (502)

Since World War II the data on entrepreneurs are consistent with these
general expectations. As table 2 indicates, foreign policy entrepreneurship
across the board is more common in the Senate than in the House. Approximately 60% of entrepreneurial activity occurs in the Senate, and this
percentage holds for 1946–2000 as a whole, for the Cold War Consensus
years (1946–67), and for the Cold War Dissensus years (1968–89). During the post–Cold War years (1990–2000) entrepreneurial activity was still
more frequent in the Senate, but the gap narrowed appreciably (with the
numbers at approximately 52% for the Senate and 48% for the House).
So while entrepreneurship is most likely to occur in the Senate in all three
periods, by the post–Cold War years instances of entrepreneurship in the
House were almost as frequent as in the Senate. Hence, if the most recent
trend continues, the House may come to rival the Senate in terms of entrepreneurial activity.

Beyond counting entrepreneurial acts, table 2 also shows that the number of individuals acting as entrepreneurs also favors the Senate. During
the Cold War Consensus, about ten senators per year engaged in entrepreneurship. Since then, that number has increased to about twelve senators
per year (with the Senate's membership at one hundred for most of this
period, this means the proportion of the Senate's membership choosing
to be foreign policy entrepreneurs increased from 10% to 12%). There is
an increase in the House as well, from about eleven members per year in
the Cold War Consensus to almost fifteen per year in the post–Cold War
period. But with 435 members in the House, this means that only about

2.5% of House members chose to become foreign policy entrepreneurs in the Cold War Consensus years, while just over 3% chose to become foreign policy entrepreneurs in the Cold War Dissensus and post–Cold War years. Thus the Senate tops the House in both entrepreneurial activity and the proportion of the chamber engaging in entrepreneurship, but entrepreneurship in the House is growing over time in both dimensions.

2. *Party Characteristics.* It might be expected, at least initially, that Democrats would be more likely to engage in entrepreneurship than Republicans. Democrats are, after all, better known as policy activists and more associated with challenging rather than deferring to the White House on foreign policy. Entrepreneurshp data would seem to support this hunch at first glance. From 1946 to 2000 about 59% of entrepreneurship came from Democrats and almost 40% from Republicans. However, this is highly misleading. First, this difference varies from period to period, with Democrats exceeding Republicans in the Cold War Consensus and Dissensus periods, and Republicans exceeding Democrats in the post–Cold War period. Second, this difference is largely explainable as a consequence of two other factors. Once these are accounted for, the simple party identification distinction disappears.

As table 3 shows, the first factor is that *congressional foreign policy entrepreneurs are more likely to belong to the majority party than the minority party.* There is a robust relationship between control of Congress and entrepreneurship. Overall, nearly 64% of the instances of entrepreneurship were attributable to members of the majority party. Just as important, this linkage of majority party and entrepreneurship grows stronger over time, increasing from a low of 57% in the Cold War Consensus period to 71% in the Cold War Dissensus period and then 73% in the post–Cold War period.

Table 3: Foreign Policy Entrepreneurship by Party Characteristics and Era

Member	Cold War Consensus	Cold War Dissensus	Post–Cold War	Total
Majority party	57.2%	63.9%	71.1%	63.5%
	(404)	(903)	(357)	(1,664)
Opposition party	48.3%	71.2%	73.1%	65.4%
	(341)	(1,006)	(367)	(1,714)

The second factor is that *congressional foreign policy entrepreneurs are more likely to be members of the opposition party to the president.* Indeed, increasing partisanship is an extremely significant aspect of congressional foreign policy behavior, not only for entrepreneurship but more generally as well. Since Vietnam, partisanship has escalated in just about every way imaginable: among party leaders (Smith 1994); in congressional voting behavior on foreign and defense policy (e.g. Carter 1998; Delaet and Scott, 2006; McCormick, Wittkopf and Danna 1997; Rohde 1994; Sinclair 1993; Wittkopf and McCormick 1998); and among individual members of Congress who choose to make foreign policy a focus of their attention—that is, foreign policy entrepreneurs (Carter and Scott 2004).

Table 3 indicates that partisanship increasingly matters in foreign policy entrepreneurship in Congress. Simply put, being in the opposite political party from the president increases the likelihood that a member will be an entrepreneur (or, conversely, members of the president's party are less likely to be entrepreneurs). As indicated in the table, 65% of entrepreneurship originated with members of the opposition party, while 35% originated with members of the president's party. Again, partisanship has increased over time. During the Cold War Consensus years, less than half of entrepreneurship (48%) was attributable to members of the opposition party (which supports the idea of a bipartisan era). In the Cold War Dissensus, that figure grew to 71%. The partisan nature of entrepreneurship increased even more in the post–Cold War years, accounting for 73% of entrepreneurial activity.

There are some chamber-based differences in this pattern as well, which table 4 displays. In the House entrepreneurs are more likely to be members of the majority party. Nearly three-fourths of entrepreneurship in the House was by members of the majority party, compared to less than 60% in the Senate. Moreover, the data show a steady upward trend in this direction (in both chambers). Similarly, entrepreneurship would appear to be more partisan in the House than in the Senate. Almost three-fourths of entrepreneurship in the House was from members of the party opposite to the president, compared to about 60% in the Senate. It is noteworthy that the data show increasing partisanship in entrepreneurship in general, in both chambers, over the three periods.

Table 4: Instances of Entrepreneurship and Party Characteristics,
House vs. Senate, 1946–2000

Party Characteristic	Overall, 1946–2000		Cold War Consensus, 1946–1967		Cold War Dissensus, 1968–1989		Post–Cold War, 1990–2000	
	Senate	House	Senate	House	Senate	House	Senate	House
Democrat	56.7%	61.9%	57.7%	55.1%	61.9%	77.5%	37.3%	36.4%
	(889)	(652)	(239)	(161)	(553)	(403)	(97)	(88)
Republican	42.3%	37.8%	42.3%	44.9%	36.4%	22.5%	62.7%	62%
	(663)	(398)	(175)	(131)	(325)	(117)	(163)	(150)
Entrepreneurship by a member of majority party	58.3%	71.3%	54.6%	61%	58.1%	73.8%	64.6%	78.1%
	(913)	(751)	(226)	(178)	(519)	(384)	(168)	(189)
Entrepreneurship by a member of opposition party	61.1%	71.8%	46.4%	51%	65.4%	81.2%	69.6%	76.9%
	(957)	(757)	(192)	(149)	(584)	(422)	(181)	(186)

Entrepreneur Interests

To what issues do post–World War II entrepreneurs devote their attention? As suggested earlier, the entrepreneur dataset contains twenty-five issues receiving entrepreneurial attention. Table 5 shows the rank-ordered frequency of these issues. As the table shows, the most frequent targets of entreprenuerial attention since World War II have been military operations and war powers, diplomacy and the policies of the State Department, economic assistance, strategy for and control of nuclear weapons and other weapons of mass destruction, and defense procurement and spending. Hence in general, entrepreneurs were more concerned with security issues than any other concerns.

When these issue priorities are divided out by period, as in table 6, several interesting distinctions become apparent. First, during the consensus period of the Cold War, entrepreneurs devoted their primary attention to issues of aid and diplomacy. Second, as the consensus of the Cold War eroded after Vietnam, and with the end of the Cold War, entrepreneurs shifted their attention to shaping policy on the use of force, arms control, and the strategies for nuclear weapons. After Vietnam, reining in the imperial presidency on these issues was a major effort of foreign

Table 5: The Entrepreneur Issue Agenda, 1946–2000

Foreign Policy Issue	Frequency	Percent
Military operations, war powers	343	13.1
Diplomacy, State Department policy	246	9.4
Economic assistance	227	8.7
Nuclear weapons, weapons of mass destruction	207	7.9
Defense procurement, spending	190	7.2
Human rights, democracy promotion	172	6.6
General foreign assistance	165	6.3
Trade policy	149	5.7
Intelligence, paramilitary activities	149	5.7
Military assistance	142	5.4
Defense policy and process	140	5.3
General international economic policy	89	3.4
IGO reform and accountability	75	2.9
General oversight of executive branch	67	2.6
Population, refugees	53	2.0
Immigration	40	1.5
Other arms control	33	1.3
Drug trade	28	1.1
Personnel	25	1.0
Terrorism	23	0.9
Cultural exchanges	16	0.6
State Department spending	15	0.6
Global environmental policy	14	0.5
Transnational economic cooperation	8	0.3
Internal security and counterintelligence	5	0.2
Total	2,621	100.0

policy entrepreneurs. Third, the Cold War Dissensus period saw entrepreneurs attempt to play a much greater role in shaping intelligence activities, including covert action. Fourth, the post–Cold War period saw the rise of trade issues to the top of the entrepreneur agenda, as the security-dominant concerns of the Cold War abated. Finally, entrepreneurs in all three periods always devoted substantial attention to defense procurement and spending. These patterns strongly suggest that entrepreneurs respond to the foreign policy context and address themselves to issues of importance.

Table 6: Foreign Policy Priorities of Congressional Entrepreneurs, by Era

Cold War Consensus, 1946–1968			Cold War Dissensus, 1968–1969			Post–Cold War, 1990–2000		
Issue	Count	%	Issue	Count	%	Issue	Count	%
Economic assistance	129	18.3	Military operations, war powers	259	18.3	Nuclear weapons, weapons of mass destruction	61	12.2
Diplomacy, State Department policy	121	17.1	Nuclear weapons, weapons of mass destruction	132	9.3	Trade policy	56	11.2
General foreign aid	102	14.4	Intelligence, paramilitary activities	123	8.7	Military operations, war powers	55	11.0
IGO reform and accountability	51	7.2	Human rights, democracy promotion	107	7.6	Human rights, democracy promotion	41	8.2
Defense procurement, spending	47	6.7	Defense procurement, spending	106	7.5	Defense procurement, spending	37	7.4

In table 7 the twenty-five foreign policy issue areas are collapsed into four categories: military-security, political-diplomatic, economic-developmental, and cultural-status (Brecher, Steinberg, and Stein 1969). While one might expect economic-developmental issues to dominate congressional attention, as they would appear to be more connected to domestic concerns, this pattern holds only for the Cold War Consensus period. For both the Cold War Dissensus and post–Cold War periods, congressional foreign policy entrepreneurs are notably more interested in military-security issues than in other types. As a result, for the post–World War II era as a whole, military-security issues are most frequently addressed (52.5% of activity), followed by economic-developmental issues (26.4%), political-diplomatic issues (19%), and cultural-status issues (2%). After the downturn in the Vietnam War and the end of the Cold War, many entrepreneurs demanded input into military-security policy. Thus it appears that congressional foreign policy entrepreneurs are much more interested in military-security issues than conventional wisdom suggests.

However, examining these issues over the entire period and without distinction between the two chambers masks some important features. To bring even greater clarity to entrepreneurial interests, these policy categories can be examined for each chamber and each period. Doing so highlights some important aspects of the foreign policy agenda of congressional entrepreneurs.

Table 7: Foreign Policy Entrepreneurship by Issue Category and Era

	Cold War Consensus	Cold War Dissensus	Post–Cold War	Total
Political-diplomatic	27.2%	14.4%	20.7%	19.0%
	(192)	(203)	(104)	(499)
Military-security	30.9%	65.3%	46.8%	52.5%
	(218)	(923)	(235)	(1376)
Economic-developmental	37.1%	19.5%	31.1%	26.4%
	(262)	(275)	(156)	(693)
Cultural-status	4.8%	0.8%	1.4%	2.0%
	(34)	(12)	(7)	(53)
Total	(706)	(1413)	(502)	(2621)

Table 8: Instances of Entrepreneurship and Policy Category, House vs. Senate, 1946–2000

Policy Category	Overall, 1946–2000		Cold War Consensus, 1946–1967		Cold War Dissensus, 1968–1989		Post–Cold War, 1990–2000	
	Senate	House	Senate	House	Senate	House	Senate	House
Political-diplomatic	21% (329)	16.1% (170)	29.2% (121)	24.3% (71)	15.9% (142)	11.7% (61)	25.4% (66)	15.7% (38)
Military-security	52.9% (829)	51.9% (547)	30% (124)	32.2% (94)	65.2% (582)	65.6% (341)	47.3% (123)	46.3% (112)
Economic-developmental	24.3% (380)	29.7% (313)	35.7% (148)	39% (114)	18.4% (164)	21.3% (111)	26.2% (68)	36.4% (88)
Cultural-status	1.9% (29)	2.3% (24)	5.1% (21)	4.5% (13)	0.6% (5)	1.3% (7)	1.2% (3)	1.7% (4)
Total	100% (1,567)	100% (1,054)	100% (414)	100% (292)	100% (893)	100% (520)	100% (260)	100% (242)

The data show that entrepreneurs are driven not only by the context of the times but by the imperatives of their chambers. For example, table 8 indicates that in the wake of Vietnam, military security issues increased sharply in importance in both chambers. However, across the whole era, senators devoted more attention to political-diplomatic issues (21%) than their House counterparts (16.1%), while representatives focused on economic-developmental issues (29.7%) to a greater degree than their counterparts in the Senate (24.3%). The distinction is also clear in each time period as well, and grows in the post–Cold War period. In that last period, senators focused on political-diplomatic issues 61.8% more than members of the House did (25.4% versus 15.7%), while representatives focused on economic-developmental issues 38.9% more than senators did (36.4% versus 26.2%).

Table 9 presents the data with attention to strategic and structural policy types. As the data indicate, we examine this hypothesis against structural and strategic policy issues broadly conceived (i.e. both defense and broader foreign policy issues such as foreign aid, trade, terrorism, etc.), and against structural and strategic defense policy issues more nar-

Table 9: Instances of Entrepreneurship on Structural and Strategic Policy Issues, House vs. Senate, 1946–2000

Policy Type	Overall, 1946–2000		Cold War Consensus, 1946–1967		Cold War Dissensus, 1968–1989		Post–Cold War, 1990–2000	
	Senate	House	Senate	House	Senate	House	Senate	House
Structural policy	41.1%	49.3%	58.2%	67.5%	34.7%	41%	35.8%	45.5%
	(644)	(520)	(241)	(197)	(310)	(213)	(93)	(110)
Strategic policy	58.9%	50.7%	41.8%	32.5%	65.3%	59%	64.2%	54.5%
	(923)	(534)	(173)	(95)	(583)	(307)	(167)	(132)
Defense structural policy	27.4%	37.7%	44%	52.1%	25%	36.1%	24.3%	31.3%
	(175)	(157)	(37)	(38)	(112)	(88)	(26)	(31)
Defense strategic policy	72.6%	62.3%	56%	47.9%	75%	63.9%	75.7%	68.7%
	(464)	(259)	(47)	(35)	(336)	(156)	(81)	(68)

rowly defined. In terms of broad foreign and defense policy issues, for the overall post–World War II era, the Senate is more likely to attend to strategic policy (58.9%) than the House (50.7%), while the House is more likely to direct attention to structural policy (49.3%) than the Senate (41.1%).

Entrepreneur Behavior

The preceding discussion suggests that congressional foreign policy entrepreneurs address a broad range of issues and increasingly focus on policy rather than funding. How do they go about pursuing their policy interests? Entrepreneurs may engage in a variety of behavior, and employ a range of platforms or pivot points to press their policy preferences. Over time, as the following discussion details, these entrepreneurs have expanded their range of activities and avenues of influence through which they have attempted to influence foreign policy. The consequence has been an increasingly formidable set of foreign policy players vying for influence in an increasingly varied fashion.

1. *Activities and Access Points.* One straightforward way to assess how entrepreneurs pursue their policy agendas is to examine their use of different access points and their engagement in different activities. The post–World War II data on entrepreneurs shows a widening use of both. Table 10

Table 10: Access Points and Activities Used by Year and Era

Year	Number of Access Points Used	Number of Activities Used
1946	3	3
1950	5	8
1954	4	5
1958	5	4
1959	4	4
1960	3	5
1961	4	5
1962	5	8
1963	4	6
1965	6	9
Average, Cold War consensus	4.3	5.7
1968	5	9
1970	6	8
1972	4	7
1973	5	7
1975	6	9
1979	6	7
1984	5	7
1985	6	7
1986	6	9
1987	7	10
Average, Cold War dissensus	5.6	8.0
1992	5	8
1994	5	8
1996	5	6
1997	6	5
1999	7	5
Average, post–Cold War	5.6	7.2

shows the number of activities in which entrepreneurs engaged to address foreign policy each year. Again, a trend toward a greater range of activities is generally present. During the Cold War Consensus, an average of *5.7 types of activities* were used per year. In the Cold War Dissensus period, an average of *8.0 types of activities* were used per year. In the post–Cold War era an average of *7.2 types of activities* were used per year. It appears that the use of different types of entrepreneurial activities increased sharply from the Cold War Consensus to the Cold War Dissensus. However, at that point the number of types of activities used leveled off and slightly declined.

In terms of access points, table 10 also shows expanded use by entrepreneurs. Table 10 shows the number of access points used in each of the years of the sample (House floor, Senate floor, committee, subcommittee, White House or other executive-branch location, the public, congressional caucuses, and the courts). During the Cold War Consensus an average of *4.3 types of access points* were used by entrepreneurs per year. In both the Cold War Dissensus and post–Cold War periods, an average of *5.6 types of access points* were used per year. Thus on average foreign policy entrepreneurs relied on more access points in the Cold War Dissensus period than in the Cold War Consensus period, and they continued to use this broadened range of access points in the post–Cold War period.

2. *Committees*. Another way to explore the behavior of entrepreneurs is to examine their reliance on committees and subcommittees for their activities and access points as they pursue their policy agendas. Here one might expect to find chamber-specific differences in tactics. Given that the House has a larger membership than the Senate, the influence of its standing committees and subcommittees is greater (see e.g. Fenno 1973). As Baker (1995, 62) summarizes, "the House member is more a creature of his committee assignment than is the senator. The life-and-death nature of committee-assignment decisions in the House has no parallel in the Senate." Thus, because of its larger size and more complex structure and rules, entrepreneurs in the House should rely on their committee assignments to a greater degree than their counterparts in the Senate.

Table 11 shows the general picture regarding the use of committee and subcommittee assignments. The results are somewhat mixed. For both chambers since World War II, entrepreneurs are just about as likely as not to be members of the foreign relations, armed services, and intelligence committees. When the data are broken down by historical period, it appears that entrepreneurs were considerably more likely to be members of the traditional foreign policy committees during the Cold War Dissensus and post–Cold War period than during the Cold War Consensus (43.3%). This seems to suggest that access points are not broadening as much as might have been expected.

Table 11: Entrepreneurship and Committee Assignments by Era

Member	Cold War Consensus	Cold War Dissensus	Post–Cold War	Total
Traditional foreign policy committees	43.3% (320)	57.7% (816)	54.4% (273)	53.8% (1,409)
Other committees	54.7% (386)	42.3% (597)	45.6% (229)	46.2% (1,212)
Total	(706)	(1,413)	(502)	(2,621)

When chamber differences are examined, as in table 12, the results are similarly mixed. On the one hand, and contrary to expectations, entrepreneurship in the Senate was more likely than in the House to have been engaged in by members of the foreign policy committees or appropriations committee. Overall, about 58% of Senate entrepreneurship was generated by members of the foreign policy committees (Foreign Relations, Defense, Intelligence), compared to only about 47% of House entrepreneurship. Moreover, the gap actually grows across the three historical periods, from about 47% in the Senate to 44% in the House during the Cold War Consensus, compared to over 63% in the Senate and 45% in the House in the post–Cold War period. Similarly, about 22% of entrepreneurship in

Table 12: Instances of Congressional Foreign Policy Entrepreneurship and Committees, House vs. Senate, 1946–2000

Entrepreneur Committee Connection	Overall, 1946–2000		Cold War Consensus, 1946–1967		Cold War Dissensus, 1968–1989		Post–Cold War, 1990–2000	
	Senate	House	Senate	House	Senate	House	Senate	House
Member of foreign policy–related committee	58% (909)	47.4% (500)	46.6% (193)	43.5% (127)	61.8% (552)	50.8% (264)	63.1% (164)	45% (109)
Member of appropriations committee	22.1% (346)	15.4% (162)	23.7% (98)	15.4% (45)	20.2% (180)	15.2% (79)	26.2% (68)	15.7% (38)
Entrepreneurship occurring in committees	23.8% (373)	24.4% (268)	17.9% (74)	17.8% (52)	24.6% (220)	23.1% (120)	30.4% (79)	39.7% (96)
Committee activities as source of entrepreneurship	13.1% (205)	16.1% (169)	10.6% (44)	13.3% (39)	12.9% (115)	15.3% (80)	17.8% (46)	20.7% (50)

the Senate was generated by members on the Appropriations Committee, compared to a little over 15% by House members of the counterpart committee.

However, when committees in general are considered (as points of access and as generators of activities), the expected pattern emerges. Committees are somewhat more likely to be the point of access of House entrepreneurship, especially in the post–Cold War period, and members of the House are more likely to use committees for their activities. Hence, while particular foreign policy committee assignments are not used for entrepreneurship in the House more often than the Senate, committees are more often the access point and the source of entrepreneurial activity in the House—which suggests the growing intermestic nature of foreign policy, as the so-called non–foreign policy committees are getting increasingly involved in foreign policy making.

3. *Avenues of Influence.* Finally, the data on the use of different avenues of influence by entrepreneurs can be seen in table 13. The data show that entrepreneurs focus the majority of their activity on direct legislative efforts, such as issue-specific legislation, appropriations, and treaties. In general, however, indirect legislative, direct nonlegislative, and indirect nonlegislative avenues are typically relied on more by entrepreneurs after the Cold War Consensus period. As the table indicates, during the Cold War Consensus period, 75 percent of all entrepreneur activity was direct-legislative. In subsequent periods use of the other avenues generally increased, indicating a diffusion of activity, although use of the direct legislative avenue crept back up somewhat in the post–Cold War period, though not to Cold War Consensus levels. Particularly interesting is the steady increase over time in the reliance on indirect-legislative tools such as nonbinding resolutions, confirmations of appointments, and procedural legislation.

There are some chamber differences as well, as can be seen in the same table. While the data show that entrepreneurs devote most of their effort to direct-legislative avenues of influence, entrepreneurs in the Senate are somewhat more likely than their counterparts in the House to rely on indirect avenues (whether legislative or nonlegislative). Across the entire post–World War II era, almost 30% of the activities of Senate entrepreneurs occurred through these avenues, compared to less than 25% in the House.

Table 13: Entrepreneurship and Policy Avenues of Influence,
House vs. Senate, 1946–2000

Policy Avenue of Influence	Overall, 1946–2000		Cold War Consensus, 1946–1967		Cold War Dissensus, 1968–1989		Post– Cold War, 1990–2000	
	Senate	House	Senate	House	Senate	House	Senate	House
Direct-legislative	64.6%	67.6%	72%	78.1%	60.2%	60.8%	68.1%	69.4%
	(1,013)	(712)	(298)	(228)	(538)	(316)	(177)	(168)
Indirect-legislative	3.4%	1.8%	1.0%	1.7%	3.9%	1.5%	5.4%	2.5%
	(53)	(19)	(4)	(5)	(35)	(8)	(14)	(6)
Direct-nonlegislative	5.9%	7.7%	7%	6.8%	5.9%	8.8%	3.8%	6.2%
	(92)	(81)	(29)	(20)	(53)	(46)	(10)	(15)
Indirect-nonlegislative	26.1%	23.0%	20%	13.4%	29.9%	28.8%	22.7%	21.9%
	(409)	(242)	(83)	(39)	(267)	(150)	(59)	(53)
Total	100%	100%	100%	100%	100%	100%	100%	100%
	(1,567)	(1,054)	(414)	(292)	(893)	(520)	(260)	(242)

Note: Because of rounding, percentages may not add to 100.

Entrepreneur Impact I

In this overview chapter, the discussion of impact chiefly concerns entrepreneur efforts and activities. Subsequent chapters—which rely on case studies—explore impact in terms of policy influence and the degree to which entrepreneurs shaped outcomes and decisions. Figure 4 displays a series of data on the growing significance of congressional foreign policy entrepreneurs in the post–World War II era.

1. *Increasing Entrepreneurship.* Our data show substantial variance in entrepreneurship from year to year, as might be expected given what would appear to be a link between entrepreneurs and the issues of the times. When considered by historical period, it is clear that entrepreneurship increased dramatically during the Cold War Dissensus, from 70.6 instances of entrepreneurship per year to over 140 instances per year. While it receded somewhat in the post–Cold War period, falling to about 100 instances per year, it remained higher than during the Cold War Consensus.

2. *Increasing Entrepreneurs.* Perhaps more importantly, however, there

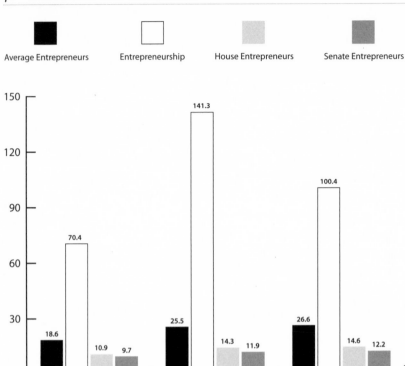

Figure 4: Entrepreneurs and Entrepreneurship

has been a significant increase in the number of members of Congress choosing to become foreign policy entrepreneurs across these time periods. As figure 4 indicates, during the ten Cold War Consensus years in the sample, there were 186 congressional foreign policy entrepreneurs, or an average of *18.6 different entrepreneurs per year.* During the ten Cold War Dissensus sample years, there were 255 entrepreneurs, or an average of *25.5 per year.* In the five post–Cold War years in the sample, there were 131 entrepreneurs, or an average of *26.6 per year.* Therefore, on average, more congressional foreign policy entrepreneurs are found in each era over time.

The last two bars on the series show the entrepreneurs per year by chamber. Again, there is a steady increase in both chambers, across the eras. For the House of Representatives, the increase is from 10.0 to almost 15 (or from 2.5 percent of the members to 3.4 percent). For the Senate, the increase is from 9.7 to 12.2 (or from 9.7 percent of the members to 12.2 percent).[8]

Key Trends and Conclusions

Not only is Congress as an institution becoming more assertive in foreign policy (Scott and Carter 2002a), but individual foreign policy entrepreneurship in Congress is also becoming more common. The overview data presented here on the characteristics and behavior of congressional foreign policy entrepreneurs offer a useful profile of the increasingly important element of congressional foreign policy activism. As figure 4 shows, over time more members of Congress are choosing to become foreign policy entrepreneurs. Overall, individual entrepreneurs are becoming more active, from more access points, and generally in more varied ways, on foreign policy issues. Strategic, not structural, policy and military-security issues, not economic-developmental ones as expected, motivate entrepreneurs most. Senate foreign policy entrepreneurs gravitate more to political-diplomatic and strategic foreign policy issues than their House counterparts do, and House entrepreneurs gravitate toward economic-developmental and structural issues more than Senate entrepreneurs do. The bottom line is that congressional foreign policy entrepreneurs represent an increasingly significant foreign policy phenomenon across the entire post–World War II era.

What accounts for this bottom-line assessment? First, foreign policy entrepreneurship is growing over time in each chamber, especially as measured by the increasing number of members engaging in entrepreneurship per year. While entrepreneurship is more common in the Senate, inter-chamber differences have dramatically narrowed in the post–Cold War period. This trend reinforces those who argue that the bipartisan notion of "politics stopping at the water's edge" is less true with every passing year. While presidents have obvious advantages, the "presidential preeminence" model of United States foreign policy making cannot be assumed, and other models involving power sharing must be considered (Scott 1997).

Second, in both chambers the greatest number of foreign policy entrepreneurs comes from the majority party, and that pattern is particularly strong in the House. In both chambers these activists rely on the committee and subcommittee structures to which they belong or which they control to advance their preferred foreign policy agendas. Thus which party controls Congress makes a significant difference in the foreign policy process.

Third, partisanship now matters every bit as much in foreign policy as in domestic policy, and it has for some time. As one recent study of Congress concluded, "congressional-executive relations have been marked by greater discord since the Cold War's end, thus undermining bipartisanship in the conduct of American foreign policy" (Wittkopf and McCormick 1998, 10). Our study confirms that pattern as it relates to congressional foreign policy entrepreneurs. Entrepreneurship rises consistently through each time period, and by the post–Cold War period *almost three-fourths* of it originates with members of the opposition party, with the vast majority of that occurring when the opposition party is also in the majority. Significantly, while partisanship is most pronounced as a presumptive motivating force among House foreign policy entrepreneurs, the amount of entrepreneurial activity arising from the party in opposition to the president increases over time in each chamber of Congress.

While a few may disagree (Krehbiel 1998; Mayhew 1991), most observers seem to accept the premise confirmed by these findings: that divided government affects policy. Across a variety of largely domestic policy issues, studies show that divided government affects the policy direction and productivity of Congress (Edwards, Barrett, and Peake 1997; Sundquist 1992; Cox and McCubbins 1991; McCubbins 1991; Kernell 1991; Burns 1990; Burns 1963). This study extends the policy significance of divided government further into the various realms of foreign policy, in terms of both ends and means. Now presidents must expect that entrepreneurs from the opposition party in Congress will introduce issues from their own foreign policy agendas. In the Senate those agendas will typically feature strategic foreign policy challenges concerning politics and diplomacy. In the House those agendas will typically emphasize structural foreign policy challenges involving economic and developmental issues. It seems little exaggeration to say that future presidents will increasingly face Senate challenges over the basic ends of foreign policy and House challenges about the means to achieve those ends.

The finding about the importance of indirect nonlegislative means also bears attention. Most of the activities falling under this heading involve some form of issue framing. The importance of these activities should not be minimized. While senators have long used their access to the media to frame foreign policy issues in ways helpful to their policy agendas, now entrepreneurs from the House increasingly rely on them as well. While there may be a numerical disadvantage to being one of 435 members as opposed to one of 100, there is still only one chairman of a House standing committee or subcommittee relevant to foreign policy. Thus well-situated House entrepreneurs find that they can reach out to the media seemingly as well as senators can, and foreign policy entrepreneurs from both chambers of Congress rely on such efforts. When congressional foreign policy entrepreneurs get to frame important policy issues, administrative officials find themselves in a reactive mode, playing catch-up in a game they no longer control. Congressional imperatives forced on George W. Bush and his administration, like the creation of a Department of Homeland Security and of a bipartisan task force to investigate the operations of the intelligence community before the invasion of Iraq, show the power of this issue-framing role, as will any congressionally imposed timelines to withdraw from Iraq.

At the same time, this overview indicates that at the heart of congressional foreign policy entrepreneurship is a focus on direct legislative action, in the form of issue-specific legislation, appropriations, and other such activity. Congressional activism may well encompass a wider range of activity, as some suggest (e.g. Burgin 1997; Carter 1998; Lindsay 1993; Scott 1997), but entrepreneurs generally seek to enact their preferences through the more direct route.[9]

Additionally, while congressional foreign policy activism is probably becoming more widely dispersed as members from more and more committees and subcommittees and the rank and file address foreign policy issues (see Lindsay 1994a; McCormick 1993; Ripley and Lindsay 1993; and Sinclair 1993), entrepreneurs seem to have gravitated over time to the traditional foreign policy committees. This trend is consistent with their interest in and commitment to foreign policy and the opportunities for sustained attention offered by membership in these committees. The apparently anomalous result also distinguishes between general foreign policy activism, which as Hersman (2000) notes is increasingly likely to come from anywhere, and congressional foreign policy entrepreneurship, which is increasingly likely to come from the foreign policy committees. The importance of these committees is also seen in the steady rise of activities falling into the indirect legislative avenue. These committees are the ones most likely to deal with nonbinding resolutions, confirmations of appointments, and procedural legislation, and they are typically the "home court" for the activities denoted by the "new institutionalism" concept (see Lindsay 1994b).

Thus from the perspective of the White House, control of the foreign policy–making process is becoming more challenging as congressional foreign policy entrepreneurs pursue their own policy opportunities and create obstacles for the administration to accomplish its goals in its desired ways. As President Bill Clinton noted in 1995, "The more I stay here and the more time I spend on foreign policy . . . the more I become convinced that there is no longer a clear distinction between what is foreign and what is domestic" (quoted in Spiegel 1997, 296). However from the perspective of Capitol Hill, foreign policy making is becoming more representative of the will of the people, whether primarily motivated by idiosyncratic, partisan, constituency-based, or public opinion concerns. As long as members of Congress perceive their greater involvement in foreign policy making as a public service virtue, with the political rewards outweighing the political risks, they will continue to increase their foreign policy engagement. Any foreign policy embarrassments suffered by an administration, such as the failure to find weapons of mass destruction in Iraq after making the presence of these weapons a centerpiece of the case for going to war in 2003, will only encourage more congressional foreign policy entrepreneurship from members of the opposition party. Over time, and particularly in cases such as those noted above, opportunities for assertive congressional foreign policy involvement will expand, as will the foreign policy obstacles faced by presidential administrations.

4

THE RISING TIDE

ENTREPRENEURSHIP IN THE COLD WAR
CONSENSUS PERIOD, 1946–1967

Some of the most enduring images of the United States foreign policy-making process come from the early Cold War period. Whether described as "concentric circles of decision making" (Hilsman 1967), "the president proposes and Congress disposes" (Robinson 1962), or "the two presidencies" (Wildavsky 1966), the idea of the preeminent presidency and a marginalized Congress was seemingly accepted as fact by a generation of scholars. "The early Cold War, accordingly, is not remembered as a period of intense congressional activism" (Johnson 2006, xvi).

As Wildavsky later acknowledged, the Cold War period that he characterized (1948–64) did not produce a typical foreign policy relationship between the president and Congress (Oldfield and Wildavsky 1989). Others came to agree (see Fleisher, Bond, Krutz, and Hanna 2000). But were such depictions accurate for the period 1946–67? According to the historian Robert Johnson (2006, xvi), "the reality was considerably more complex."

Even when policy makers and the public shared a Cold War consensus about the need to contain the spread of communism along Soviet lines, Congress played a *more* significant role in foreign policy making than many realize. While MCs conceded some power over warmaking and treaties, during this early Cold War era others aggressively used committees and subcommittees to influence foreign policy by introducing legislation (direct legislative means), holding hearings (direct nonlegislative means), creating bonds with foreign policy officials (direct nonlegislative means), and using the appropriations power (direct legislative means). There were only seven foreign policy subcommittees in the Senate when this Cold War Consensus period began; there were over thirty when it ended in 1967 (indirect legislative means) (Johnson 2006), and that predates the explosion of House subcommittees after the subcommittee bill of rights of 1973 (Rohde 1974)!

Contrary to the conventional wisdom, an increased congressional willingness to challenge the president in foreign policy making dates from at least the mid-1950s (Marshall 2005; Carter 1986). A focus on congressional foreign policy entrepreneurs from 1946 to 1967 also reveals a surprising level of assertiveness. To examine the nature and impact of congressional foreign policy entrepreneurship in the Cold War Consensus years, this chapter begins with an overview of entrepreneurial activity for the period, followed by examples of specific entrepreneurs in action, and more detailed case studies of three significant foreign policy entrepreneurs in this period.

A Quantitative Overview

Those anticipating a preeminent presidency will be surprised at the significant level of foreign policy entrepreneurship in Congress during the height of the Cold War. As table 14 shows, more than a quarter of all the entrepreneurial activity from 1946 to 2000 came before 1968.[1] In this period like others, more entrepreneurs tend to be senators than representatives.

Some interesting differences reflect the era's bipartisan nature. The largest share of entrepreneurial behavior was engaged in by the majority party as expected, but there was room for minority party members to engage in significant efforts to shape foreign policy as well; apparently majority party members relied less on their structural advantages in the chamber to squelch input from minority party entrepreneurs than majority members would later. However, another partisan pattern is found. Unlike later years when most entrepreneurs were members of the non-presidential party, *most entrepreneurs in the Cold War Consensus era were from the president's party.* Presidential preeminence is hard to sustain when members of the president's party choose to act on their own foreign policy agendas.

Table 15 shows other interesting differences for entrepreneurs in the

Table 14: Foreign Policy Entrepreneurship by Chamber, Party Characteristics, and Era

	Cold War Consensus, 1946–1967	Remaining Post–World War II Era, 1968–2000	Total, 1946–2000
Senate	58.6% (414)	60.2% (1,153)	59.8% (1,567)
House	41.4% (292)	39.8% (762)	40.2% (1,054)
Member of majority party	57.2% (404)	65.8% (1,260)	63.5% (1,664)
Member of opposition party	48.3% (341)	71.7% (1,373)	65.4% (1,714)
Total	26.9% (706)	73.1% (1,915)	100% (2,621)

Table 15: Foreign Policy Entrepreneurship by Issue Category and Era

	Cold War Consensus, 1946–1967	Remaining Post–World War II Era, 1968–2000	Total, 1946–2000
Political-diplomatic	27.2% (192)	16.0% (307)	19.0% (499)
Military-security	30.9% (218)	60.5% (1,158)	52.5% (1,376)
Economic-development	37.1% (262)	22.5% (431)	26.4% (693)
Cultural-status	4.8% (34)	1.0% (19)	2.0% (53)
Total	26.9% (706)	73.1% (1,915)	100% (2,621)
Structural policy	62% (438)	37.9% (726)	44.4% (1,164)
Strategic policy	38% (268)	62.1% (1,189)	55.6% (1,457)
Defense structural policy	47.8% (75)	28.6% (257)	31.5% (332)
Defense strategic policy	52.2% (82)	71.4% (641)	68.5% (723)

Cold War Consensus. Reflecting the shared values of the consensus, these entrepreneurs were far less likely to focus on military-security issues than were entrepreneurs in later years. Instead they focused more on political-diplomatic, economic-developmental, and cultural-status issues. Before 1968 entrepreneurs were more likely to focus on the means by which to address shared foreign policy goals (for example, by political-diplomatic and economic-developmental means) than on the shared goals themselves.

However, early Cold War entrepreneurs tended to devote their attention to structural policy more often than entrepreneurs of later periods. Overall, entrepreneurs devoted over 60% of their efforts to issues of how to use resources (structural policy) rather than the broad goals of policy (strategic policy). In the defense policy subset, entrepreneurs' attention was almost evenly split between defense structural concerns (e.g. procurement) and defense strategy concerns (e.g. force mix and mission). Again, however, attention to defense structural issues was considerably higher for early Cold War entrepreneurs than for their counterparts from later periods. In effect, entrepreneurs of the Cold War Consensus were more engaged on means than ends.

Another feature of the times is that entrepreneurs were four times more likely than later entrepreneurs to deal with cultural-status issues. These issues relate to policy makers' views of their own state and its status in the international system, and were more common in the Cold War days, when policy makers sought to portray the United States as the leader of the free world and the model for all nonaligned states to follow.

Table 16 shows another aspect of shared values during the height of the

Table 16: Entrepreneurship and Committee Assignments by Era

Member	Cold War Consensus, 1946–1967	Remaining Post–World War II Era, 1968–2000	Total, 1946–2000
Traditional foreign policy committees	45.3% (320)	56.9% (1,089)	53.8% (1,409)
Other committees	54.7% (386)	43.1% (826)	46.2% (1,212)
Total	26.9% (706)	73.1% (1,915)	100% (2,621)

Table 17: Access Points and Activities Used by Year and Era

Year	Number of Access Points Used	Number of Activities Used
1946	3	3
1950	5	8
1954	4	5
1958	5	4
1959	4	4
1960	3	5
1961	4	5
1962	5	8
1963	4	6
1965	6	9
Average, Cold War Consensus	4.3	5.7
1968	5	9
1970	6	8
1972	4	7
1973	5	7
1975	6	9
1979	6	7
1984	5	7
1985	6	7
1986	6	9
1987	7	10
1992	5	8
1994	5	8
1996	5	6
1997	6	5
1999	7	5
Average, Remaining Post–Second World War Era	5.5	7.5

Cold War. Unlike later years, most entrepreneurs during this period were *not* members of the traditional foreign policy committees. Members of the Foreign Affairs, Foreign Relations, and Armed Services Committees were less motivated to act on their own agendas than they would be in later years, suggesting a greater similarity between their agendas and those of the administrations at the time.

In line with expectations, two key differences in this earlier period are displayed in table 17. First, after 1967 MCs benefited from having more potential access points from which to shape policy. Subcommittee reforms in the 1970s and the increasing presence of the mass media (and later the Internet) provided more access points for entrepreneurs to exploit in seeking to put their stamp on foreign policy. Second, with more access points came more types of activities to use. After the end of the Cold War Consensus period, entrepreneurs had more tools in their policy-making toolbox. C-SPAN and cable television transformed televised hearings from a rarity to a commonplace occurrence. The same can be said for floor speeches. During the Cold War Consensus one did not see MCs making televised floor speeches to an empty chamber, but now they are a widely used tactic to get one's message out. Sending e-mails to other policy makers was also unknown before the establishment of the Internet and the World Wide Web. In many ways, the changing nature of the times provided later entrepreneurs more different ways to communicate their policy agendas than were available during this earlier period.

Table 18 further illustrates these differences. Much of what is described above reflects indirect ways to influence policy or the policy context. During the Cold War Consensus entrepreneurs relied more on direct avenues of influence, whether direct legislative or direct nonlegislative, than their later counterparts. From 1968 onward entrepreneurs could rely more on

Table 18: Entrepreneurial Uses of Avenues of Influence by Era

	Cold War Consensus, 1946–1967	Remaining Post–World War II Era, 1968–2000	Total, 1946–2000
Direct-legislative	74.5%	62.6%	65.8%
	(526)	(1,199)	(1,725)
Indirect-legislative	1.3%	3.3%	2.7%
	(9)	(63)	(72)
Direct-nonlegislative	6.9%	6.5%	6.6%
	(49)	(124)	(173)
Indirect-nonlegislative	17.3%	27.6%	24.8%
	(122)	(529)	(651)
Total	26.9%	73.1%	100%
	(706)	(1,915)	(2,621)

both indirect legislative avenues (like subcommittee hearings and subcommittee reports) and indirect nonlegislative avenues (like televised speeches before friendly groups, public demonstrations, and so on).

In short, there was more entrepreneurial foreign policy activity during the Cold War Consensus than most observers would expect. The nature of that activity seems to have been somewhat more concerned with the means of foreign policy than with the ends, and military-security issues were less a concern than other types. A variety of ways existed to initiate and influence foreign policy, but fewer ways than would exist later. Congressional foreign policy entrepreneurs shaped policy during this era, and it is to examples of their influence that we now turn.

Entrepreneurs in the Cold War Consensus

In politics, timing can be everything. Just a month after the bombing of Hiroshima, Brien McMahon (D-Conn.) introduced a bill to create what would become the Atomic Energy Commission (AEC) to oversee the new atomic energy industry. By doing so, this freshman senator tried to preempt the more senior chairmen of the House and Senate Military Affairs Committees (Andrew May, D-Ky., and Edwin Johnson, D-Colo.), who later introduced a bill to create an AEC dominated by the military. With the help of others more interested in civilian control of atomic energy, McMahon persuaded the leadership to establish a special committee to investigate the issue, which he would chair as a freshman! By interviewing more than seventy witnesses, producing a voluminous report, and cultivating members of the media élite like Drew Pearson, Joe Alsop, Walter Lippmann, and others, McMahon framed the issue in such a way that his bill seemed like the only way to avoid the complete military control of atomic energy. Thus the Atomic Energy Act (1946) not only established an AEC where the civilian commissioners could not automatically be outvoted by their military counterparts, it also created a new congressional Joint Committee on Atomic Energy that would have both substantive and procedural powers over the industry (Johnson 2006).

Similarly, the creation of the National Aeronautics and Space Administration (NASA) was an entrepreneurial success. Like many other Americans, Senate Majority Leader Lyndon Johnson (D-Texas) was shocked by the Soviet launch in 1957 of Sputnik—the first earth satellite. This new Soviet capability challenged the United States in terms of technological status and a potential military threat. Johnson used his chairmanship of the Armed Services Preparedness Investigating Subcommittee to hold hearings from November 1957 to January 1958 on the need for an appropriate response. In February 1958 the Senate responded by creating the Special Committee on Space and Aeronautics, which Johnson chaired. When the Eisenhower administration resisted the idea of a new civilian space agency, Johnson and Styles Bridges (R-N.H.) introduced a bill on 14 April 1958 to create NASA. The House counterpart legislation was introduced the same day by House Majority Leader John McCormack (D-Mass.). To overcome administrative opposition, the bill created an organizational framework by which civilian and military space applications would be coordinated, but it left considerable flexibility to the new NASA director to decide exactly what projects would be pursued by the civilian agency (NASA 2006). Despite the administration's opposition, the result was a new civilian space agency that was an unequivocal response to the challenge of the Soviet space program.

As suggested by the overview data earlier in this chapter, entrepreneurs devoted considerable attention to structural policy issues such as defense spending and procurement. For example, in the late 1950s Stuart Symington (D-Mo.) devoted substantial efforts to increasing United States defense spending, employing a variety of strategies and tactics to do so, including hearings, reports, amendments, and the like (e.g. Johnson 2006; McFarland 2001). In contrast, George McGovern (D-S.D.) introduced an amendment in 1963 to reduce defense spending by 5%, gathering thirty supporters for the idea (Johnson 2006, 90). While McGovern failed, Kennedy's aide Theodore Sorensen recalled a successful effort by Rep. Carl Vinson (D-Ga.), chairman of the House Armed Services Committee, to keep the B-70 bomber alive. Vinson included Kennedy's request for the bomber three times, and his amendment "directed, mandated, and required" that the money be spent. The amendment also stated that "if the language constitutes a test as to whether Congress has the power to so mandate, let the test be made . . . [for] the role of the Congress in determining national policy, defense or otherwise, has deteriorated over the years" (quoted in Sorensen 1965, 347). The administration negotiated a compromise with Vinson that preserved some funding, initiated a new study of the bomber, and prompted Vinson to withdraw the harsh language (Sorensen 1965, 347).

Other instances of congressional foreign policy entrepreneurship during the Cold War Consensus also exist. Some were successful; others were not. The year 1948 provides an example of each. That year Congress successfully passed legislation circumventing immigration rules to assist United States farmers hiring temporary agricultural workers from Western Hemisphere countries under what became known as the *bracero* program. The entrepreneurs behind the legislation were Senators George Aiken (R-Vt.) and Edward Thye (R-Minn.) and Representative Clifford Hope (R-Kan.). This type of temporary worker program, successful from the farmers' point of view, was resuscitated in the immigration reform proposals of George W. Bush's administration. However that same year Representatives Emmanuel Celler (D-N.Y.), Walter Lynch (D-N.Y.), and Abraham Multer (D-N.Y.) unsuccessfully tried to penalize the British for their perceived anti-Jewish Palestine policy by introducing floor amendments cutting off their Marshall Plan aid (*Congressional Quarterly Almanac* 1948).

After Israel's independence others sought to protect the new state. One of the most active in this regard was Representative Jacob Javits (R-N.Y.), who saw the protection of Israeli Jews as a human rights issue after the Holocaust. His impact on policy regarding Israel and the Middle East began immediately upon his election to the Senate in 1956, when he went to Israel and met with Prime Minister David Ben-Gurion after the Suez Crisis ceasefire. Ben-Gurion told him that Israel would not permit Egyptian troops to return to the Sinai Peninsula, just captured by the Israelis. Javits cabled a report of his conversation to the White House immediately after the meeting. In it he stated, "There are deep misunderstandings as to the effect of United States policy here which ought to be dispelled urgently . . . The prime minister equates Nasser [president of Egypt] directly with the Communist penetration of the African continent and the Middle East. Our policy is being read as building up Nasser so as to enable him to realize all his ambitions and to dominate the Arab and perhaps the Moslem world" (Javits 1981, 274). Upon his return Javits gave several speeches on the Senate floor advocating military involvement by the United States if further hostilities threatened the security of Israel (Javits 1981). Thereafter "Nasser made some conciliatory gestures, and United States and United Nations officials began to come forward with the assurances and promises that Israel had demanded" (Javits 1981, 274). With a changed policy environment, the Israelis pulled back from the Sinai.

In the 1960s Javits proposed several measures to ensure that the United States, Britain, and France would join in a mutual defense treaty with Israel, but none were successful. Additionally, he worked to raise money through the Carnegie Endowment for International Peace to assist economic development plans to integrate Israel and Palestinian refugees into the Middle East (Javits 1981).

In the later years of the Cold War Consensus congressional foreign policy entrepreneurs took advantage of the policy window offered by the annual foreign aid authorization cycle to try to shape the broad contours of foreign assistance policy. As Secretary of State Dean Rusk (1990, 402) remembered, "During the sixties, Congress really dug its heels in on foreign aid, with people like Bill Fulbright leading the way. Congress disagreed with the administration on how much foreign aid we should give, the priorities we should focus on, and whether foreign aid had to be used to buy American products." Key entrepreneurs including Senators Fulbright, Wayne Morse (D-Ore.), Ernest Gruening (D-Alaska), and Symington, and a handful of others, were the leaders of this "foreign aid revolt" (Johnson 2006, 94–104). These entrepreneurs initiated an effort to recast foreign aid away from military aid and to place restrictions on it (especially to dictators). Morse was the key leader who "left his mark on foreign aid for all the world to see" (Johnson 2006, 101).

These entrepreneurs began their efforts early in Kennedy's administration. As Kennedy's aides Arthur Schlesinger and Theodore Sorensen recalled, the entrepreneurs' initial efforts involved prohibiting long-term financing of aid, and serious cuts (more than 20%) and restrictions on aid packages (Schlesinger 1965; Sorensen 1965). Morse and Gruening in particular were "alienated by the persistent emphasis on military aid" and "began to fight against the program" (Schlesinger 1965, 595). Symington, for instance, held hearings on aid to Iran, Pakistan, and India aimed at the military aid program (Johnson 2006). Later in the 1960s Fulbright led a fight to scale back and restrict the Foreign Military Sales program (Johnson 2006).

Indeed, entrepreneurs worked to place a variety of restrictions on aid. For example, Bourke Hickenlooper (R-Iowa) introduced a successful amendment to prohibit foreign aid for any country expropriating property owned by United States individuals or entities (Johnson 2006). It passed

Congress handily, and was still in effect when Jesse Helms (R-N.C.) used it to block aid to Nicaragua after Violeta Chamorro's electoral victory in the early 1990s (see chapter 6).

In a similar fashion, Gruening led an effort to curtail aid to Egypt in the early 1960s. While the Kennedy administration was attempting to woo the Egyptian leader Gamel Abdel Nasser, Gruening had other ideas. First, he wrote a letter to Kennedy objecting to aid to Egypt and urging a different approach. When that letter failed to elicit the desired response, Gruening introduced a successful amendment to the Foreign Assistance Act barring aid to countries planning to commit aggression against the United States or a recipient of its aid (clearly targeted at Egypt for its hostility toward Israel). According to Bass (2003), Gruening's entrepreneurship annoyed Kennedy and prompted a visit by Dean Rusk to Fulbright to complain. It also closed the possibility of "wooing" Nasser. Referring to Gruening's actions, as well as others from this period, Kennedy complained of the "worst attack on foreign aid that we have seen since the beginning of the Marshall Plan" (quoted in Bass 2003, 139).

Another entrepreneur took aim at what he regarded as the self-defeating and dangerous policy of supporting authoritarian leaders in Latin America. With support from Gruening and Hubert Humphrey (D-Minn.), Wayne Morse, who chaired the Foreign Relations Latin America subcommittee, advocated an end to military aid to Latin America, and sponsored an amendment barring aid to countries whose governments came to power through a coup d'état (Martin 1994). According to the assistant secretary of state for Latin America, Edward Martin, these actions caused the administration to withhold aid to Honduras and Dominican Republic for fear of congressional backlash (Martin 1994) and "were a major factor" in its "inability to continue to fund" several elements of the "Alliance for Progress" aid program (Martin 1994, 179). Moreover, as Martin recalled, the administration used the threat of Morse's amendment to press for early elections in various countries, including the Dominican Republic and Honduras (Martin 1994).

By 1964 their campaign had been relatively successful. Having taken office after Kennedy's assassination and left with little choice, President Lyndon Johnson accepted the latest round of restrictions and signed the foreign aid bill protesting "the growing tendency to hamstring Executive flexibility with rigid provisions wholly inappropriate and potentially dangerous in a world of rapid change" (Johnson 2006, 102). According to one observer, "The foreign aid revolt had succeeded beyond anything . . . Morse or Gruening could have imagined. In the process a new era in executive-legislative relations was inaugurated" (Johnson 2006, 104).

Senator Mike Mansfield (D-Mont.) led another important entrepreneurial effort in the 1960s targeted at the NATO alliance and relations among its members, especially concerning "burden sharing." After pressing the idea behind the scenes, in 1966 Mansfield sponsored a successful resolution in favor of a major withdrawal by the United States of troops from Europe (e.g. Priest 2006). As President Johnson recalled in his memoir, Mansfield's efforts and his resolution had a dramatic impact on the administration's discussions with France and Britain. In particular, the administration implemented a new "dual basing" option to assuage Mansfield and his allies. This policy provided for troop rotation in which two of three brigades moved to the United States while one stayed in Germany, and applied to both air and ground units (Johnson 1971, 307).

These examples of the broad impact of congressional foreign policy entrepreneurs highlight the range of issues to which their attention was directed, the scope of their activity, even during a period of so-called presidential preeminence, and the magnitude of their impact on foreign policy. Additionally, these examples display the range and combination of activities across the avenues of influence. As described, these entrepreneurs relied on direct legislative (e.g. legislation), direct nonlegislative (e.g. hearings), indirect legislative (e.g. procedural legislation), and indirect nonlegislative (e.g. agenda setting, issue framing, foreign contacts) avenues to place their stamp on foreign policy in these important instances. We now turn to case studies for a more in-depth examination of entrepreneurship in the Cold War Consensus period.

McCarran, Reuss, and Fulbright in the Cold War Consensus

The remainder of the chapter focuses on three case studies of prominent entrepreneurs in the Cold War Consensus period—Pat McCarran, Henry Reuss, and William Fulbright—to highlight their motives, actions, strategies, and impact.

Pat McCarran: Protecting the U.S. from "Them"

Born in 1876 to Irish immigrants, Pat McCarran grew up on a ranch near Reno, Nevada. Because of the remote location of the ranch, he did not begin school until he was ten years old. He later moved to Reno to graduate from public high school at the age of twenty-one. He attended the University of Nevada in Reno but left school during his senior year to run the family ranch after his father's death (Ybarra 2004). After his election to the state legislature as a Democrat in 1903, he studied law and was admitted to the bar in 1905 at the age of twenty-nine. McCarran then began a career in Nevada politics during which he served as a district attorney, supreme court justice, member of the boards of pardons and paroles, and chairman of the state board of bar examiners. Elected to the U.S. Senate in 1932 on his third try, he served there until his death in 1954. In the Senate, he chaired the Committee on the District of Columbia, the Appropriations Subcommittee dealing with the State Department, the Judiciary Committee, and the Joint Committee on Foreign Economic Cooperation (Congressional Biographical Directory 2006; Ybarra 2004). During his career "McCarran built his influence by placing his supporters in various executive agencies and through the operations of his staff," which had few rivals in terms of intelligence gathering in the Congress (Johnson 2006, 35).

McCarran's worldview saw America and its way of life threatened by "them." "They" included foreign communists, their domestic allies in the United States, immigrants in general, and Jews in particular (Ybarra 2004). His xenophobic and largely isolationist worldview generated three major themes: aid to anticommunist regimes, protecting the United States from domestic communist subversion, and protecting Americans from a tidal wave of immigrants, particularly those who seemed "different."

Theme 1: Helping anticommunist regimes. To McCarran, containing communism meant helping anticommunist regimes. Two in particular seemed natural allies: Francisco Franco's fascist regime in Spain and Chiang Kai-shek's Nationalist Chinese regime in Taiwan.

Franco's anticommunist and Catholic credentials appealed to McCarran, himself a Roman Catholic with two daughters who became nuns. After a personal meeting with Franco in Spain in 1949, McCarran decided that Franco had been unfairly maligned in the American press (Ybarra

2004). President Harry Truman could not forgive Franco's fascist ideology or his tilting toward Hitler during World War II. Truman's position was to isolate Spain by not sending an ambassador to Madrid and having no dealings with the regime (Lowi 1963). McCarran's self-appointed task was to reverse Washington's policy toward Spain. He began in 1949 by inserting a $50 million loan for Spain into the Marshall Plan appropriation and using a subcommittee hearing to berate Secretary of State Dean Acheson for United States policy failures toward Spain. The loan was defeated on the Senate floor (Ybarra 2004).

In April 1950 McCarran reintroduced the $50 million loan for Spain. After the outbreak of the Korean War, he held a clandestine meeting in his office. Invited senators met with military officers who were frustrated by Truman's "hands-off" policy toward Spain and felt that United States military bases in Spain were necessary to contain the Soviet Union. McCarran told those attending of his plan to escalate his loan request to $100 million and his goals to make Spain a NATO member and give Spain enough military aid to transform its army into one of the leading military forces in Europe. For him, the meeting served two purposes. The military officers convinced the senators of the need for bases in Spain, and McCarran encouraged the officers to organize and press the Truman administration to change its Spanish policy. The Senate subsequently passed the $100 million loan, but the House-Senate conference committee reduced it to $62.5 million. Under pressure from both outside and inside the administration, Truman reluctantly agreed to exchange ambassadors with Spain in December 1950 (Lowi 1963).

McCarran kept pushing. In May 1951 he invited the deputy undersecretary of state and the chairman of the Export-Import Bank to a meeting in his office. In front of Spain's ambassador to the United States, he castigated them for the administration's Spanish policy and asked why Spain had not yet seen more of the $62.5 million loan. McCarran subsequently introduced another $100 million loan to Spain as part of the Mutual Security Act of 1951. In the Mutual Security Act of 1952, McCarran helped to secure for Spain an additional $25 million loan (Ybarra 2004). In 1952 the Truman administration reversed its long-standing policy and began negotiating for bases in Spain. The result in 1953 was the Madrid Pact, by which the United States acquired air and naval bases in Spain and the Spanish received $226 million in direct and indirect military assistance

(Lowi 1963; Ybarra 2004). McCarran thus achieved his goal, having played a key role in placing United States policy toward Spain on the agenda and in shaping the alternatives.

On the other hand, McCarran's efforts to help Nationalist China were unsuccessful in forcing a policy shift on the administration. In early 1949 the State Department distanced itself from the Nationalist Chinese regime, which it viewed as a corrupt lost cause (Ybarra 2004). In February 1949 McCarran introduced the China Aid Act, which provided for a $1.5 billion loan to the Nationalists. At the administration's urging the Foreign Relations Committee killed the bill, but the fight over China policy had just begun (*Congress and the Nation* 1965).

Like Franco, Chiang Kai-shek offered the appeal of both anticommunism and Christianity. In June 1949 McCarran used a testimonial dinner for the archbishop of Nanking to attack what he saw as the State Department's pro-communist tilt in China. Although Communist Chinese forces already controlled Beijing and Chiang had taken his Nationalist regime to Taiwan, McCarran said that State had not supported Chiang enthusiastically enough. Because of such pressures, State was forced to respond in 1949 with a controversial White Paper explaining the inevitability of the communist victory in China (Ybarra 2004). McCarran tried to help again in 1951, when he unsuccessfully proposed a $1 billion military aid package to finance a Nationalist invasion of the Chinese mainland (Johnson 2006). However, events in the region combined with other factors to block McCarran's efforts on this issue.

Theme 2: Protecting the United States against domestic communist subversion.   Although Senator Joseph McCarthy (R-Wis.) is the political figure most closely associated with the hunt for communist subversives in the 1950s, McCarran did the legislative work necessary to put anticommunist restrictions into law.[2] His position in the majority party helped so much that the *Washington Post* called him the most important member of Congress in 1952 (cited in Johnson 2006). McCarran's anticommunist concerns were of long standing. In 1935 he toured the country, calling on Americans to stamp out the domestic communist threat. On Armistice Day 1939 McCarran used a speech in Las Vegas to proclaim that domestic communist subversion was a greater danger than Hitler to the United States. He railed against domestic communist subversion in radio addresses during his reelection campaign in 1944. In that election and again in 1950, McCarran claimed that communists had targeted him for defeat (Ybarra 2004).

In 1946 an informer told FBI agents of a communist spy ring in Washington which included senior administration officials like the State Department's Alger Hiss. When Truman failed to act on the threat, the FBI director, J. Edgar Hoover, authorized leaking this information to friendly members of Congress. One was McCarran. In June 1946 McCarran used his chairmanship of the Appropriations Subcommittee for the State Department to insert an amendment giving the secretary of state the authority to fire any department employee, without due process, in the name of national security. Three months later he pressed the same theme in a speech before the San Francisco Bar Association. With additional critics pressing the administration from outside and the FBI pressing it from within, Truman reluctantly approved a government loyalty program in 1947 that allowed the investigation of current and future federal workers (Ybarra 2004).

McCarran's search for subversives widened. In 1948 the immigration subcommittee of his Judiciary Committee investigated how the State Department issued visas, particularly to diplomats from communist regimes. In 1949 the subcommittee subpoenaed the attorney general and assistant secretary of state to provide security files on 168 employees of the UN suspected of being communist spies. When the administration refused, McCarran leaked testimony that had been given to his subcommittee in closed session, including names of UN employees suspected of espionage. At this point, the editorial page of the *Washington Post* referred to McCarran as "a one-man Un-American Activities Committee in the Senate" (Ybarra 2004, 451).

In February 1950 Hoover told McCarran's Appropriations Subcommittee that there were 53,000 communists currently in the country, as well as half a million "fellow travelers" ready to do their bidding. The outbreak of the Korean War in June further fueled the fears of internal subversion. In August 1950 McCarran introduced his Mutual Security Act (the McCarran Act),which combined in omnibus form a wide array of security provisions from virtually all the thirty-two internal security bills then before Congress. Not unlike the more recent laws passed in reaction to 9/11, the legislation provided for restrictions on immigration rules and on civil rights and liberties (including preventive detention of suspects without trial).

Because of its timing (after the Korean attack and McCarthy's sensational charges), the legislation easily passed. Truman vetoed it, but his veto was overridden (Ybarra 2004).

To ensure that the act was fully implemented, McCarran engineered the establishment of a subcommittee on internal security in the Judiciary Committee. He became its chairman, packed it with archconservative members and staff, and launched a series of both closed and open hearings lasting eighteen months. The purpose of these efforts was to demonstrate that communist successes were due to the combined efforts of communist subversives and disloyal State Department officials (Ybarra 2004). As he told an audience in Denver in 1952, a global communist conspiracy was intended to weaken the United States both externally and internally (McCarran 1952).

McCarran took his hearings on the road to publicize alleged communist infiltration of organized labor, the movie industry, the military, and the UN, and then introduced an unsuccessful resolution that called for breaking off diplomatic relations with the Soviet Union (*Congressional Quarterly Almanacs* 1953, 1954; Ybarra 2004). Only his death in 1954 stopped his anticommunist efforts. The McCarran Act's provisions forcing communists to register with the government and denying them passports were later ruled unconstitutional, but the provision allowing preventive detention, although never used, was not repealed by Congress until 1971 (Doyle 1989).

Theme 3: Protecting the United States from "Dangerous" Immigrants. McCarran's fears of "them" extended beyond communists and subversives to immigrants—particularly displaced persons (DPs) in Europe after World War II. The administration wanted to assist displaced persons immigrating to the United States. McCarran's position was the opposite. Most DPs were Jews and McCarran was an anti-Semite.[3] Reinforcing his anti-Semitism was his fear of communist spies smuggled into the country as Jewish refugees (Ybarra 2004). While McCarran was unsuccessful in his legislative efforts to prevent all displaced persons from reaching the United States, he limited their numbers as much as possible and minimized the number of Jews among them. McCarran's Internal Security Act of 1950 tightened immigration rules regarding DPs. When the DP program ended in 1952, nearly half a million refugees had come to the United States. Jews accounted for fewer than 100,000 of them (Ybarra 2004).[4]

McCarran's Internal Security Act of 1951 also successfully limited immigration by denying visas to anyone who had been a member of a totalitarian group. This restriction prevented the entry of those who had joined Communist, Nazi, or Fascist parties in Europe, even if their membership had been legally required to apply for jobs, housing, or food. It also kept 47,000 refugees out of the United States by facilitating their resettlement in Europe (*Congress and the Nation* 1965).

McCarran's Immigration and Nationalities Act of 1952 (the McCarran-Walter Act) made it easier to ban subversives from the country (Ybarra 2004). Although it removed the last color bar on citizenship by allowing the naturalization of Asians and continued the *bracero* program, Truman vetoed the bill, calling it "worse than the infamous Alien Act of 1798" (*Congress and the Nation* 1965, 223). Congress overrode the veto (Ybarra 2004), but its limits on refugees only lasted one year. McCarran lost his chairmanship of the Judiciary Committee when a Republican majority in the Senate was elected in 1952. With a new Republican president seeking new legislation, Congress responded by passing a bill allowing 214,000 refugees to enter the country over three years without regard to the restrictions in McCarran-Walter (*Congressional Quarterly Almanac* 1953). McCarran could not stop immigration, but he did limit the total number of refugees and other immigrants and made it more difficult for Eastern Europeans and Jews to enter the country.

In summary, along with others Pat McCarran succeeded in reversing United States policy from one of isolating Spain to integrating Spain into the western alliance and ultimately into NATO. Lowi (1963, 669) captures the direct legislative, direct nonlegislative, indirect legislative, and indirect nonlegislative approaches used by McCarran to reverse Washington's policy toward Spain: "Congress, led by Senator McCarran, brought the entire spectrum of political techniques successfully to bear on the Truman Administration. Large sums of money were voted gratuitously to Spain; strong public pronouncements were registered in favor of Generalissimo Franco and Spain; the spokesmen of the Administration were consistently badgered in public hearings; officers and civilian officials of all branches of the armed services were encouraged in hearings and meetings to publicize the tactical and strategic importance of Spain; and the issue was surcharged with the growing fears of the Communist threat. With the support of key members of the two houses of Congress, the Spanish issue was placed upon the political agenda and was kept there until action was taken."

United States policy toward China was another arena where McCarran had a policy impact. Relying on direct legislative means such as committee hearings and indirect nonlegislative means such as speeches and foreign contacts, McCarran helped frame the debate and set the agenda for tightening the relationship between Washington and Taipei, thus making necessary the current policy of "one China, two systems."

McCarran's efforts helped intensify and potentially prolong the Cold War. His actions to root out communist subversives at home made any conciliatory gestures by policy makers toward the Soviets or Communist Chinese seem like political suicide. He used direct legislative means to make it easier for the government to identify domestic subversives and to chill policy debate by muzzling domestic critics of Cold War policies. He also relied on direct nonlegislative means such as hearings and oversight of the State Department to drive "suspect" policy makers from positions of influence, and he created his own internal security subcommittee to ensure that the McCarran Act was faithfully implemented. He also relied heavily on public speeches about the domestic communist threat to frame the debate and set the agenda.

Finally, McCarran shaped immigration policy by limiting the number of immigrants who could enter the country, Jewish immigrants in particular. He did this through direct legislative means such as the McCarran-Walter Act. He also relied on hearings as a direct nonlegislative means to highlight the threats posed by "suspect" immigrants, and he worked to set the agenda and frame the debate on immigration as a threat to the American way of life. In short, McCarran was able to nudge United States foreign policy in a more anticommunist, xenophobic direction.

Henry Reuss: Promoting the Practices of a Peaceful World

In 1912 Henry Reuss was born into the German-American community of Milwaukee. Although the son and grandson of banking executives Henry chose a legal career, graduating from Cornell University in 1933 and Harvard Law School in 1936. After private practice and then a civil service judgeship in Milwaukee, in 1941 he moved to Washington to begin work as the counsel for the U.S. Office of Price Administration (OPA). In 1943 he enlisted in the Army, rising to the rank of captain and serving in both staff and combat positions in the European theater. Based on his OPA experience, he spent the first six months after the German surrender as the price controls officer for the military government in Germany (Reuss 1999; Congressional Biographical Directory 2006).

After two years of private practice in Milwaukee, Reuss went to Paris for a year as part of the legal team for the Economic Cooperation Administration coordinating aid under the Marshall Plan (Reuss 1999). In December 1949 he returned to Milwaukee, where he became a special prosecutor investigating corruption in local government. Although unsuccessful in campaigns for state attorney general in 1950 and for the Democratic senatorial nomination to oppose Joseph McCarthy in 1952, he was elected as a Democrat to the House in 1954, where he served until 1983. In the House he served on the variously named banking committees and the Joint Economic Committee, at times chairing each of them (Congressional Biographical Directory 2006). He also served on the Government Operations Committee and its Foreign Operations Subcommittee (Reuss 1999). Reuss wrote that he believed in "peace, national independence, humane institutions and civil liberties, equality and civil rights—both here and abroad" (Reuss 1964, 15). In short, he wanted to build a more peaceful world.

Theme 1: Creating more person-to-person contact.   One way of promoting a more peaceful world was more person-to-person contact. In 1955 Reuss introduced a bill to expand cultural exchange programs with other countries, establishing them at the state, not the federal, level (*Congressional Quarterly Almanac* 1955). While not successful at the time, the effort was an early example of the kind of local-international outreach that is now commonplace, and the forerunner of Reuss's most lasting legacy: the Peace Corps.

The origins of the Peace Corps show how congressional entrepreneurs promoted American values to developing countries while improving the quality of life. Most people associate the Peace Corps with President John Kennedy; he proposed its creation on the campaign trail in October 1960 and created it by executive order in March 1961. However, the idea had been floating through the problem and policy streams throughout the 1950s in the United States, the United Kingdom, Australia, and West Germany (Wright 2001; Coyne 1999).

The idea for the Peace Corps came to Reuss on a trip to Cambodia in

1957. There he saw government economic aid wasted on big projects that did not improve average people's lives (like superhighways in countries where most residents did not have cars), while a small four-person team from International Volunteer Services went around building schools in rural areas where educational opportunities were previously unknown. As he stated, "I made my youth corps proposal the subject of dozens of my speeches and articles, and I convened a series of meetings with leaders in business, labor, the clergy, and various voluntary organizations to hammer out a proposal for a more person-to-person approach to our foreign aid activities" (Reuss 1999, 59). Reuss thus relied on indirect nonlegislative means to set the agenda for a civilian service corps. His efforts shaped both the definition and awareness of the problem, and provided an appealing alternative for addressing it.

In January 1960 Reuss introduced a bill to study creation of a "Point Four Youth Corps." Richard Neuberger (D-Ore.) introduced the companion bill in the Senate. The study authorization passed (Reuss 1999). In May, Reuss described his proposal in an article in *Commonweal*. He envisioned a youth corps ten thousand strong, paid at military wage rates, to undertake civilian public service projects that would improve lives in developing countries (Reuss 1960). In the article he also suggested that such civilian service could be substituted for compulsory military service, which led Vice President Richard Nixon to denounce the proposal as "a haven for draft dodgers" (quoted in Reuss 1999, 59). Because of sentiments like Nixon's emanating from the administration, Reuss feared a veto if a bill authorizing the youth corps actually passed during the last year of Eisenhower's presidency. Faced with this inopportune political context, he limited his efforts to getting the study funded. By agreeing to support the earmarking of funds for a major concern of Representative Otto Passman (D-La.)—removal of the pesky water lotus from waterways in Louisiana—Reuss secured an appropriation for the study in the summer of 1960. When the study was published in 1961 it credited Reuss for having brought the first meaningful governmental attention to the idea of a civilian youth service corps (Albertson, Rice, and Birky 1961). In June 1960 Senator Humphrey joined in the effort. He took over Senate sponsorship of the idea after Neuberger's death and introduced a bill to create a "Peace Corps." This was the first time that name was used for the program (Reuss 1999).

In the early fall of 1960 Tris Coffin, the editor of the *Washington Spec-*

tator, took Reuss's idea of a youth corps and pitched it to Jack Kennedy. In Coffin's words, "One day in 1960 Henry Reuss told me of his idea for an overseas service corps. I thought the idea was so good that it needed a national forum and debate. So I went to another friend, Senator Jack Kennedy, whom I had known ever since he was a lonely freshman congressman, and who was running for the presidency. He listened thoughtfully and when I had finished my spiel he said, 'That's an interesting idea.'" Ten days later Kennedy gave his Peace Corps speech (quoted in Reuss 1999, 60). In effect, a dramatic shift in the political stream provided a window of opportunity. Shortly after Kennedy's inauguration, he preempted Congress by creating the Peace Corps by executive order. Thus Kennedy may have formally created the Peace Corps (Coyne 1999), but the entrepreneurial groundwork for this new initiative was laid by Reuss and, to a lesser degree, Humphrey (Polsby 1984).

Another way of promoting more person-to-person contact was to make it easier for immigrants and refugees to enter the United States—thereby reversing some of McCarran's efforts. In 1955 Reuss introduced a bill to make it easier for some aliens currently in the United States to gain permanent residency status (*Congressional Quarterly Almanac* 1955). In 1957 he introduced bills to amend and revise the McCarran-Walter immigration act and to amend the Refugee Act of 1953 by extending the period during which refugee visas could be granted (*Congressional Quarterly Almanac* 1957). While these direct legislative efforts were unsuccessful, they kept a spotlight on restrictive refugee and immigration laws that were later changed.

A final example of promoting more person-to-person contact occurred in 1961. President Kennedy asked Reuss, who had served as an informal adviser in reaching out to German-Americans during the 1960 campaign, for advice concerning a forthcoming trip to Germany. Reuss suggested that Kennedy go to West Berlin and give a speech to the German people while standing near the new Berlin Wall (Reuss 1999). Thus one of the hallmark moments of the Kennedy administration may well have been due to the background prompting by a House member.

Theme 2: Reforming foreign aid.   Like other entrepreneurs discussed earlier in this chapter, Reuss tried to reduce what he saw as an overemphasis on military aid and to reform the economic aid program. In one article

Reuss proposed that foreign aid be redirected away from military purposes and toward economic development, both to better help the recipient countries and to compete better with the impressive Soviet aid program (Reuss 1958). He elaborated this argument further in 1961 in an article published in the *Annals of the American Academy of Political and Social Science*. Reuss objected to the current levels of military aid and to the tendency of economic assistance, which in any case was insufficient in amount, to be overwhelmingly directed to security allies of the United States rather than being disbursed on the basis of need. He advocated more coordination of economic aid, greater oversight of the program, and more care that aid went to the truly needy—including those in neutralist countries (Reuss 1961). In 1964 he reiterated these ideas in his book *The Critical Decade: An Economic Policy for America and the Free World*.

Beyond such indirect nonlegislative attempts to shape the problem and policy contexts, Reuss also tried direct nonlegislative means. For example, in 1965 he was a co-author of a report of the Joint Economic Committee that recommended expanding economic assistance to developing countries (Associated Press 1965a). In 1967 he publicly decried the fact that United States arms sales and grants to developing countries far outstripped its economic assistance to those countries. Reuss argued that providing munitions to developing countries in such volume made the recipients less safe—as it prompted their neighbors to increase their supply of arms as well (Reston 1967). He threatened to lead a revolt by House liberals against a sale of supersonic jets to Latin American states, thereby prompting Secretary of State Dean Rusk to promise in a letter that the United States would halt sales to any countries spending so much on defense that they hurt their own economic development. Reuss also persuaded the undersecretary of the treasury to write a letter stating that no funds from the Inter-American Development Bank had been, or would be, used directly or indirectly to buy military equipment (*Congressional Quarterly Almanac* 1967).

Theme 3: Promoting free or freer trade.   The Reuss family's background in banking and Reuss's experience in price control surely helped generate his interest in promoting a more prosperous world economy. As noted earlier, serving on the House banking committee and Congress's Joint Economic Committee gave him structural forums from which to work in this regard. He began traveling to Europe on behalf of the Joint Economic Committee in 1959 and continued on fact-finding trips for the rest of his career (*Congressional Quarterly Almanac* 1959; Reuss 1999).

Reuss was an early champion of a free trade agreement with the European Common Market countries, seeing it as a potential win for both sides. He wrote a paper for the Joint Economic Committee paper suggesting such an agreement in 1961, and subsequently Treasury Secretary Douglas Dillon endorsed the idea of gradually reducing the tariffs on trade between the United States and Europe (UPI 1961). In 1962 Reuss gave a House floor speech in which he called for the United States to drop tariff levels for non–Common Market European states, thereby forcing the Common Market to drop its tariffs. He also proposed dropping United States tariffs for all developing countries to promote their economic development and reduce the gap between rich and poor states (Reuss 1962). The next year he wrote an article for *Harper's Magazine* advocating the abolition of tariffs on major commodities, thereby promoting developing countries' exports (Reuss 1963).

In *The Critical Decade* Reuss proved to be ahead of his time. He predicted European protectionism directed at American exports (particularly in the agricultural sector). So he championed free trade as the ideal and global tariff reductions as a practical first step. Should the Common Market countries not be willing to enter into a free trade agreement with the United States, he proposed that the government should pursue free trade agreements with others (Dale 1964; Reuss 1964). By doing so he contributed ideas to the problem and policy streams that in later years led to the World Trade Organization and a series of free trade zones like NAFTA and CAFTA.

Theme 4: Strengthening the world monetary system.　In his book Reuss envisioned a new international monetary mechanism which would stabilize the world economy by providing more capital reserves to the International Monetary Fund (IMF) or another like body, thereby giving borrowers more available credit to work out of temporary cash flow problems (Reuss 1964). His ideas came to fruition thirty years later through reform of the International Monetary Fund. Reuss's concerns about the value of global currencies, particularly the dollar, were enough to cause him to ask for the creation of a new Joint Economic Committee Subcommittee on International Exchange and Payments. In 1965 he was successful: the subcommittee was created, and he was named as its chairman (Reuss 1999), placing him in a good position to seek stronger measures.

One of those stronger measures was freeing the dollar from the gold standard. Reuss pressed President Johnson on the issue, and in 1965 the administration announced its support of the basic concept (Associated Press 1965c). The House passed a bill supported by the administration to lessen the reliance on gold, but Reuss objected, saying it did not go far enough to remove the country from the current international payments system (Associated Press 1965b). In 1967 he introduced a bill to repeal the gold standard, but it went nowhere because of the crisis-like atmosphere following devaluation of the British pound (Reed 1967). Despite his lack of success during the Johnson administration, Reuss had to be pleased when President Nixon repealed the gold standard in 1971.

Theme 5: Reducing the emphasis by the United States on the use of military force.   As noted in the discussion of military and economic assistance, Reuss came to believe that the government overrelied on military means to address foreign policy goals. One way to minimize this unilateral trend was to rely more on the United Nations. In 1957 Reuss introduced bills to create a permanent UN emergency force and a permanent UN police force (*Congressional Quarterly Almanac* 1957). Three years later he wrote a letter to the director of the U.S. Information Agency, requesting cancellation of a planned cruise of five warships to West Africa intended to "show the flag." Reuss argued that the military cruise sent the wrong message when African states were emerging from colonial rule (UPI 1960). These efforts were unsuccessful, but others were not.

Reuss was an early, albeit moderate, opponent of the Vietnam War. In an article in *Commonweal* in 1965 he called for a UN debate on the Vietnam War, which he hoped would lessen the perception that the United States was acting in an imperialist fashion in its unilateral support of South Vietnam, and would revitalize the UN's peacekeeping role as a result (Reuss 1965). He was also one of the first MCs to support a draft lottery, so as to offset the draft's class and race bias (Reuss 1967). More broadly, Reuss's concern was that Vietnam represented a political problem, not a security problem. In 1966 he was one of seventy-eight House Democrats to sign a letter expressing their support for United States troops but also supporting a negotiated political settlement of the Vietnam conflict with no further escalation of the war (*Congressional Quarterly Almanac* 1966). Like some other House Democrats, he viewed the National Liberation Front as a necessary participant in any peace negotiations (UPI 1966).

In 1967 Reuss joined a congressional group of self-professed "owls." They were described as neither hawks nor doves on the Vietnam War but desiring a negotiated political settlement. In the House, Reuss introduced an amendment to a supplemental Vietnam defense authorization calling for a negotiated settlement, but it was ruled nongermane and stricken from consideration (UPI 1967). Six years later a political settlement was reached.

In summary, Henry Reuss was a good example of an entrepreneur who largely flew below the radar. He wanted to see a more peaceful world in which people learned about and interacted with each other, so he pushed for the Peace Corps, economic assistance programs that addressed the recipient's needs rather than United States security needs, free and "freer" trade, a stronger international economy and monetary system, and a decreased reliance on military means to accomplish foreign policy goals. To press his policy agendas he relied on means that were direct legislative (legislation), indirect legislative (procedural legislation), direct nonlegislative (consultations, oversight), and indirect nonlegislative means (agenda setting, issue framing, foreign contacts).

J. William Fulbright: Resisting the Arrogance of Power

J. William Fulbright ranks second only to Jesse Helms (R-N.C.) as the most active congressional foreign policy entrepreneur in the post–World War II era. Like Reuss he had an internationalist worldview, rejecting McCarran's anticommunist, xenophobic isolationism (Woods 1998). Fulbright grew up in Fayetteville, Arkansas, and attended the experimental grammar and secondary schools run by the College of Education at the University of Arkansas. He earned his undergraduate degree at Arkansas and, after graduation in 1925, was a Rhodes Scholar. Impressed by the environment of students consumed with learning about other cultures and committed to making a difference in the world, he was also greatly influenced by the Oxford professor Robert McCallum, a Liberal Party member who shared Woodrow Wilson's ideas about the practical importance of an international collective security organization. After receiving his Oxford undergraduate degree in modern history in 1928, Fulbright went to Vienna and immersed himself in continental café society. He also toured Sofia, Belgrade, and Athens, where he interviewed prime ministers and other high government officials (Woods 1998).

After returning home, Fulbright graduated second in his law school class at George Washington University in 1934. After a stint in the Justice Department's Antitrust Division, he returned to George Washington University as a law school instructor in 1935. The next year he returned home to Fayetteville to become a member of the law school faculty at the University of Arkansas. After the death of the university president in 1939, Fulbright was appointed to succeed him, at the age of thirty-four. In 1942 Fulbright won election to the House of Representatives as a Democrat, serving one term before successfully running for the U.S. Senate, where he served until 1974 (Congressional Biographical Directory 2006). Fulbright's entrepreneurship in the Cold War Consensus period was guided by his cosmopolitan worldview and life experiences, and encompasses five themes.

Theme 1: Strengthening international organization and promoting multilateralism. Fulbright was an advocate of international organizations, even at the expense of national sovereignty, and he regularly peppered the policy stream with his preferred alternatives. During World War II he introduced a successful resolution supporting the "creation of appropriate international machinery with power adequate to prevent future aggression and to maintain lasting peace, and as favoring participation by the United States therein" (Woods 1998, 80). In 1946 he wrote in the *New York Times Magazine* that an excessive emphasis and reliance on national sovereignty inevitably led to war, and he recommended a stronger United Nations and more deference by the major powers to UN collective security efforts (Fulbright 1946b). He also introduced a successful amendment to the Foreign Economic Assistance Act requiring recipients of Marshall Plan funds to use their counterpart funds (local currencies) to promote economic integration of Western Europe. That principle became a hallmark of the European Recovery Program (*Congressional Quarterly Almanac* 1946).

One of Fulbright's signature pieces of entrepreneurship soon followed. In 1946 Fulbright introduced a bill "authorizing the use of credits established through the sale of surplus properties abroad for the promotion of international good will through the exchange of students in the fields of education, culture, and science" (Johnson and Gwertzman 1968, 128).

This act established the well-known Fulbright exchange program that continues today (see also Vogel 1987).

In 1947 Fulbright cosponsored a bill favoring the creation of a United States of Europe within the framework of the UN (Fulbright 1947b), further defending the concept at an address at the University of Toronto (Fulbright 1947a). His speech suggested that a federation was the best means of preventing the Soviets from gaining control of Western Europe, Africa, the Near East, and the Middle East (Woods 1998). The next year he wrote an article in the *Annals of the American Academy of Political and Social Science* defending his idea of a United States of Europe as an appropriate bulwark against the spread of communism (Fulbright 1948). He also introduced a Senate floor amendment to make political union one of the goals of Marshall Plan aid. Although the amendment did not go forward, Fulbright again returned to this theme in a speech on the Senate floor in 1949 (Fulbright 1949). Despite his efforts and those of his cosponsor (Elbert Thomas, D-Utah), the amendment failed (Woods 1998).

In 1950 Fulbright introduced a resolution in favor of an immediate special session of the UN General Assembly to deal with disarmament and atomic weapons control issues (*Congressional Quarterly Almanac* 1950). That opportunity was lost as the UN's susceptibility to Cold War deadlock soon became apparent. In the early 1960s Fulbright gave up on the UN's ability to be a force for peace, but he did not give up on multilateralism. In a speech at the University of Wisconsin in 1960, he urged the coordination of the free world's military, economic, and political activities to compete with the Soviet Union by creating a Common Market for free world states (Fulbright 1960).

In *Foreign Affairs* the next year Fulbright set forth his ideas for a new "Concert of Free Nations" to supplant the efforts of the UN (Fulbright 1961a). These ideas were expanded in his book *Prospects for the West* (Fulbright 1963b). He later went out of his way to criticize France for its Gaullist policy of distancing itself from the western alliance, saying that France needed to be an active partner in the alliance. This point was made both in a Senate floor speech and in an article in the *Saturday Evening Post* (Fulbright 1963a; Fulbright 1964b). He returned to these themes in 1966, when he had the Foreign Relations Committee conduct hearings as part of a study of the role of the United States in NATO (*Congressional Quarterly Almanac* 1966).

Theme 2: Tempering anti-Sovietism and anti-communism.   Fulbright was uncomfortable with rigid ideological thinking, and thus he challenged the Cold War consensus. He believed that states were neither good nor evil but actors with their own interests that warranted reasonable accommodations. In an address in 1946 to a joint meeting of the American Academy of Arts and Letters and the National Institute of Arts, he argued that the United States should recognize and address Russia's legitimate interests rather than let a dissatisfied Russia undermine the status quo (Fulbright 1946a). Twelve years later he called for the United States to find new areas of agreement with the Soviet Union and to explore the feasibility of Soviet proposals (Fulbright 1958b).

A more forceful repudiation of ideologically driven foreign policy came after Senator Barry Goldwater (R-Ariz.) in 1961 expressed support for "total victory" over communism. On the Senate floor, Fulbright said that the historical record of "total victories" was not promising, and added: "We are neither omniscient nor omnipotent, and we cannot aspire to make the world over in our image. Our proper objective is a continuing effort to limit the world struggle for power and to bring it under civilized rules" (Fulbright 1961c, 217). He further developed this idea in a speech at the National War College and the Industrial College of the Armed Forces (Fulbright 1961e) and in his book *Prospects for the West* (1963). In a speech at the University of Connecticut in 1966 (Fulbright 1966e), he contrasted an ideological America that lurched from one intervention to the next with a more practical and humane America that avoided problems and crises.

Fulbright spoke out on the misperceptions that seemed to guide United States foreign policy (Fulbright 1958a, 1959a), a message he formalized in 1964 in a Senate floor speech entitled "Old Myths and New Realities." In this speech, and at greater length in a book with the same title, he expounded on a number of myths built into the Cold War consensus that he felt mistakenly guided foreign policy makers: that communism was a global monolithic force, that the Cold War could either be unilaterally won or unilaterally ended, and that Castro and Communist China would somehow go away. Since these notions were false, Fulbright believed that the country should deal with these realities in a sensible, non-ideological fashion. He also wanted the country to stop defending the status quo and reach out to nationalist revolutions and progressive groups in the developing world (Fulbright 1964a; Fulbright 1964c).

As early as 1959 Fulbright began advocating less confrontational policies toward communist states (Fulbright 1959a). His Senate floor speech
in March proposing negotiations on the future of Berlin was brought to the
attention of the Soviet premier Nikita Khrushchev and helped make possible Khrushchev's visit to the United States in September 1959 and the accompanying, brief Cold War "thaw" (Fulbright 1959b). Fulbright endorsed
cooperative overtures toward Communist China in the Senate in 1959 and
1964, and before outside groups in 1966 (Fulbright 1959a; Fulbright 1964a;
Fulbright 1966e; Fulbright 1966a). In 1966 he used hearings of the Foreign
Relations Committee to study foreign policy toward China (*Congressional
Quarterly Almanac* 1966), thereby helping to set the agenda for the later
recognition of the People's Republic of China.

Theme 3: Addressing the real problems of the developing world.   Like
Reuss and the other entrepreneurs who participated in the "foreign aid
revolt" of the 1960s, Fulbright believed that the United States overrelied
on military instruments of foreign policy and needed to promote financial and economic growth and reform in the developing world. In 1948 he
introduced a bill to create a revolving fund to purchase agricultural commodities for occupied Europe and Asia, and an amended form of the bill
passed (*Congressional Quarterly Almanac* 1948). In an address at Columbia University in 1959 he called for the United States to help developing
countries by exporting more capital to them and making it easier for them
to sell their products in the United States (Fulbright 1959c). In speeches
in the late 1950s he favored a reduction in United States military aid to
other countries and an increase in economic and cultural aid (Fulbright
1958b; Fulbright 1959c). He repeated this theme in a Senate floor speech
in 1961 (Fulbright 1961d), and expanded on it in 1965. In an article for the
New York Times Magazine, Fulbright wrote that the foreign aid program
needed fundamental reform. He proposed the separation of military from
economic aid, funding foreign aid on a long-term basis rather than an annual appropriation, and making foreign aid multilateral rather than unilateral (Fulbright 1965a).

Theme 4: Opposition to the Vietnam War.   Entrepreneurs such as
William Fulbright were the center of opposition to the Vietnam War.
Early in the Kennedy administration, key entrepreneurs had significant
impact in a number of ways. For example, according to Lawrence Freedman (2000, 332), as he made his decisions about Vietnam, "Kennedy was

also aware of the need to sell any policy to Congress and the American people. He was well aware of the limited appetite for a major commitment to Vietnam in Democratic Party circles, made clear by such influential figures as Senators Mansfield and Russell." Mansfield traveled to Vietnam in 1962 and returned with a report highly critical of United States policy and the likelihood that incremental escalation would simply "trap" the United States in a growing conflict. Instead, Mansfield believed, the administration should avoid the trap of unwanted commitments and negotiate the neutralization of all of Indochina (Giglio 1991; Dallek 2003).

What effect did Mansfield's report have? First, the damning report and recommendation that the administration should deescalate rather than escalate persuaded Kennedy to reassess American policy. As Kennedy's aide Kenneth O'Donnell (O'Donnell and Powers 1970, 15) recalled, the president told O'Donnell: "I got angry with Mike for disagreeing with our policy so completely, and I got angry with myself because I found myself agreeing with him." According to Halberstam (1972, 207–8), Kennedy soon "dispatched two of Harriman's people in late December to make their own check, Roger Hilsman of State and Michael Forrestal of the White House." They returned with another pessimistic report. Consequently, in May 1963 Kennedy initiated planning for the possible withdrawal of American military advisers (Dallek 2003).

In the summer of 1963 Mansfield was joined by Morse and Gruening, who advocated a complete American withdrawal, and Fulbright, who warned against escalation and an open-ended commitment to Vietnam (Reeves 1993). In August, Mansfield urged the withdrawal of 10% of United States forces by the end of the year (Dallek 2003). Under this pressure, Kennedy confided in Mansfield and O'Donnell that he "now agreed with the Senator's thinking on the need for a complete withdrawal from Vietnam. But I can't do it until 1965—after I'm reelected" (O'Donnell and Powers 1970, 16). In late August the military aide Maxwell Taylor was instructed to prepare plans to withdraw a thousand advisers by January 1964, and later that fall Kennedy aides further advanced that idea in policy memoranda (e.g. Dallek 2003). It is hard to argue that pressure from congressional entrepreneurs was not a major factor in these actions.

Until late in the conflict, entrepreneurs such as Mansfield and Russell stayed mainly behind the scenes, offering their counsel and warning against the perils of escalation. Mansfield, for instance, regularly coun-

seled LBJ against escalation in face-to-face meetings and long personal letters (Barrett 1993). Johnson's memoirs are replete with references to conversations and meetings with Mansfield and others. Barrett (1993) shows
the extent of the conversations that Johnson had with key members of
Congress, especially Mansfield, Fulbright, and Richard Russell.[5] It demonstrates how anxious LBJ was to gain and keep their support, and how
much he worried over their opposition. It is noteworthy that Johnson almost always chose a middle or moderate option, to assuage critics and re-
sist full-on intervention. But accounts such as these also show that entrepreneurs do not always succeed when they opt for giving informal advice
and consultation.

By contrast, Fulbright is perhaps best known for his increasingly public
opposition to the Vietnam War. Over time, Fulbright came to see Washington's Vietnam policy as the most compelling illustration of the failed logic
of the Cold War consensus, with rigid ideological thinking leading to mis-
calculation, misperception, and the misapplication of policy. As early as
1961 Fulbright was telling his Senate colleagues that United States policy
toward South Vietnam relied far too heavily on military means and failed
to address the economic and social concerns of the Vietnamese people
(Fulbright 1961d). He saw the Vietnam conflict as a nationalist movement
rather than an effort to establish a pro-Soviet government and warned
the Kennedy administration against an open-ended commitment. Later,
in 1965, he used a Senate floor speech to call for the United States to support the national aspirations of the Vietnamese people (Fulbright 1965b).

To be sure, Fulbright's attention evolved from such concerns to outright opposition. Indeed, in 1964 Fulbright was the Senate floor manager
for the Tonkin Gulf Resolution, which authorized "all necessary measures"
to repel attacks against the United States and its allies in Southeast Asia
(Tonkin Gulf Resolution 1964). The resolution passed the House 416–0
and the Senate 88–2 (with Senators Morse and Gruening the lone dis-
senters). However, Fulbright's concerns grew and his role soon shifted. By
1965 he began to oppose United States intervention, and his initial criticism grew into outright dissent as intervention deepened. Key administration advisers recount Fulbright's efforts to redirect American policy
in the fateful first seven months of 1965, when the decision to escalate
took shape.[6] According to Barrett (1993, 44), "In the first half of 1965 . . .
Fulbright tried earnestly to convince the president that a commitment to

defend South Vietnam with combat troops would be a mistake." At first Fulbright avoided public criticism of President Johnson, noting: "I kept thinking that I could influence him privately" (Barrett 1993, 45).

Fulbright secured lengthy, private visits with the president in February, June, and July, and he wrote numerous letters and memos to him. In one he warned that "it would be a disaster for the United States to try to engage in a massive ground and air war in Southeast Asia" (Barrett 1993, 45). On 5 April 1965 Fulbright sent a memorandum to President Johnson laying out six points concerning the Vietnam intervention:

1. It was a costly and grave mistake;
2. Chinese imperialism, not communism, stood as the real threat to Asia;
3. fearful of Chinese domination, independent Asian nations would bring about stability and security in the region;
4. the United States should declare a moratorium on bombing, clarify aims, and use a campaign of persuasion to bring about an open and more democratic Vietnam;
5. the United States should support an independent Vietnamese regime, as long as it recognized individual rights and was not directly connected to a great power;
6. it was more advantageous for the country to have an Asian regime friendly to the Soviet Union than one controlled by the Chinese.

Fulbright also participated in a key meeting on escalation in July 1965, again counseling alternatives (Ball 1982, 403).

In the summer of 1965 Johnson decided to escalate. Although Fulbright had been initially optimistic about the effect of his letters, memos, and advice on President Johnson's thinking, the escalating intervention soon persuaded him otherwise (Johnson and Gwertzman 1968, 205–6), as did his subsequent disenchantment with Johnson over the Dominican intervention (Johnson 2006). He then abandoned his informal, behind-the-scenes efforts.

In 1966 Fulbright went public with what was then the highly unusual step of holding televised hearings of the Foreign Relations Committee to study United States foreign policy in Vietnam. The hearings focused on the shortcomings of that policy and on reasons to oppose United States participation in the war. Fulbright objected to the administration's depiction of the Vietnam War as North Vietnamese aggression, questioned the lack of clarity regarding United States diplomatic goals, criticized the military escalation of the war, and noted his regret at having introduced and supported the Tonkin Gulf Resolution, which he had come to view as sanctioning a misuse of presidential power (*Congressional Quarterly Almanac* 1966). Fulbright sponsored a Senate floor motion to repeal the resolution in March 1966. The motion was rejected by a vote of 95–5 (Powell 1984). That same month Fulbright inserted into the *Congressional Record* a petition opposing the war signed by eight hundred Peace Corps volunteers (Woods 1998).

In an article in the *Saturday Evening Post* in 1996, Fulbright described the South Vietnamese government as an "unstable and intransigent regime" and called on the United States to propose peace talks to end the Vietnam conflict (Fulbright 1966f, 10). In the article he criticized both the executive and legislative branches of government for the military escalation in Vietnam, and he was openly critical of Congress, and particularly of the Senate, for its failure to hold the executive branch to account.

Fulbright expanded his critique of Vietnam policy in remarks entitled "The Arrogance of Power," first delivered in 1966 as a speech to the School of Advanced International Studies at Johns Hopkins University and reprinted in both *U.S. News and World Report* and the *New York Times Magazine*. Fulbright charged: "We are trying to remake Vietnamese society, a task which certainly cannot be accomplished by force and which probably cannot be accomplished by any means available to outsiders. The objective may be desirable, but it is not feasible" (Fulbright 1966a, 117; Fulbright 1966b). In these remarks, and in the book, Fulbright called for peace through the neutralization of both Vietnam and the entire Southeast Asian region under the protection of the great powers, including China (Fulbright 1966a; Fulbright 1966c). He also sought to influence women by speaking out in *Redbook*, defending both critics of the war and the hearings on it that he had conducted as head of the Senate Foreign Relations Committee (Fulbright 1966d).

By 1967 Fulbright led a growing number of MCs in proposals to halt the bombing, begin negotiations, reduce military appropriations, and restrict military operations. The growing opposition persuaded the administration to call a bombing halt in 1967 and seek negotiations. By the end of 1967, on the eve of the Vietnamese Tet Offensive, Fulbright's efforts had dramatically affected the problem and political streams, and had introduced alternatives to what was increasingly regarded as a failed and costly policy. Thus Fulbright set the agenda for the successful effort to end United States participation in the Vietnam War in 1973.

Theme 5: Preserving the integrity of democratic foreign policy making. For Fulbright a final overarching theme was his concern for the nature and processes of foreign policy in a democracy. This concern manifested itself in a variety of ways. One had to do with the integrity of the players and processes involved. In 1961 Fulbright learned that under directives issued during the Eisenhower administration and still in force, uniformed military officers were promoting what he saw as a radical right-wing view of the dangers of the Cold War, a view that contradicted the policies of the new Kennedy administration. He sent a memorandum to the secretary of defense requesting an end to this practice and assurances that military propaganda programs, the National War College, and the Joint Chiefs of Staff would remain under civilian control (Fulbright 1961b). Fulbright also responded to scandals regarding former government officials acting as lobbyists for foreign governments. In 1964 he introduced legislation to close loopholes in the Foreign Agents Act, and in 1966 he sponsored a new Foreign Agents Registration Act that passed Congress (*Congressional Quarterly Almanac* 1964; *Congressional Quarterly Almanac* 1966).

Another example of this theme was Fulbright's willingness to challenge Democratic and Republican presidents alike on the basis of policy ideas rather than partisanship. In the 1950s he challenged both Truman and Eisenhower. He once demanded Truman's resignation and challenged his actions in South Korea, even supporting a withdrawal of forces from Korea to avoid igniting a third world war (Johnson and Gwertzman 1968). In challenging the intervention in the Middle East in 1957, he questioned the Eisenhower Doctrine and unsuccessfully tried to require the administration to produce a White Paper explaining the events leading up to and including the Suez Crisis (Woods 1998). As previously discussed, Fulbright was more than willing to challenge the Johnson administration over Vietnam policy.

A third example was Fulbright's growing concern over the reconciliation of democratic values with United States foreign policy. In 1946 he introduced a "sense of the Senate" resolution providing that the promotion of democracy was a foreign policy priority (*Congressional Quarterly Almanac* 1946). In his book *Prospects for the West* (1963) he wrote: "the future of the Western nations depends more on the shaping of their own community and on the character and quality of their own free societies than on their confrontations with those who threaten them from outside" (Fulbright 1963b, vii–viii). He repeated these concerns in *The Arrogance of Power* (1966). In an article in the *New York Times Magazine* in 1967 he disagreed with the former CIA director Allen Dulles's recommendation to "fight fire with fire," noting that mimicking the communists' methods risked the values that the United States was trying to protect (Fulbright 1967b).

A final and perhaps the most significant example of the theme was Fulbright's concern over the balance of power between the president and Congress (especially the Senate), and the proper role and authority of each. Undue congressional deference, he believed, had led to administrative missteps in foreign policy that went uncorrected. For example, how could the Senate oversee covert intelligence operations if denied knowledge of them? As early as 1954 Fulbright and Representative Mansfield attempted to expand the so-called Secret Seven, a group in the Senate Armed Services Committee to which the CIA reported, into a joint committee of the House and Senate. Although that effort failed, in 1966 Fulbright, Mansfield, and Eugene McCarthy (D-Minn.) persuaded the Foreign Relations Committee to report out a measure that would transform the subcommittee into the Full Committee on Intelligence Operations, with nine members drawn equally from the Foreign Relations, Armed Services, and Appropriations committees (Woods 1998). Shortly thereafter Fulbright used the pages of the *New York Times Magazine* to press for better congressional oversight of the intelligence community (Fulbright 1967b). Thus his efforts helped prepare the stage for the intelligence reform efforts of the 1970s.

The refusal of Congress to accept its responsibilities was particularly seen in the escalation of the Vietnam War, which Fulbright noted in an article in the *Saturday Evening Post* (Fulbright 1966f) and in his "Arrogance of Power" works (1966a; 1966b; 1966c). Fulbright was trying to prevent future Vietnams by prompting more assertive congressional oversight of the administration's foreign and defense policy.

In summary, Fulbright had a powerful impact on United States foreign policy. His entrepreneurship prompted "anticipated reactions" by the executive branch as the White House accommodated his concerns. Examples include his advocacy of integration in Europe and conditionality for aid under the Marshall Plan. His entrepreneurship often drove the congressional agenda. Examples include his questioning of Vietnam War policy and undue congressional acquiescence in executive power. Fulbright often went public by mobilizing support within the institution and among the public for various policy ideas, including disengagement from Vietnam, détente with the Soviets and the Chinese, arms control, and UN reform. His entrepreneurship developed and presented new policy options and alternatives. Examples include Vietnam policy, détente, arms control, reform of aid programs, and European integration. Fulbright helped to establish and reshape programs and policy initiatives through legislation, such as the provisions creating and later reforming the United Nations and that creating the Fulbright exchange program. Thus Fulbright's entrepreneurship was instrumental in setting the stage to end the Vietnam War, building momentum for détente with the Soviet Union, generating support for more productive relations with China, making adjustments to foreign aid, and driving the congressional foreign policy assertiveness that would follow the Vietnam War, not to mention the array of more specific, if limited, initiatives for which he was responsible.

Fulbright's brand of entrepreneurship relied on all avenues of influence. Direct legislative efforts included legislation and amendments. Indirect legislative efforts included nonbinding "sense of the Senate" resolutions and procedural legislation regarding interbranch relations. His direct nonlegislative efforts included attempts to change administration policy by communicating directly with the president and other administrative policy makers, holding committee hearings, and using the Foreign Relations Committee for oversight of the administration's foreign policy. His many speeches inside and outside the Senate, as well as his voluminous body of writings, were indirect nonlegislative attempts to set the government's foreign policy agenda and frame the terms of policy debate.

The Cold War Consensus of 1946–67 was marked by a surprising amount of significant congressional foreign policy entrepreneurship. To promote and maintain peace, some entrepreneurs pushed for greater international cooperation. Some envisioned stronger roles for international organizations like the UN and the forerunners to the EU. Some endorsed Third World outreach through the Peace Corps, economic assistance, and new international monetary mechanisms. Still other entrepreneurs preferred a more confrontational approach in the Cold War, pushing a more robust form of containment and an aggressive hunt for communist subversives at home. At least initially, the last group seems to have had the greatest impact, but the less confrontational entrepreneurs prepared the ground for changes that occurred in the Cold War Dissensus period.

It would be hard to imagine presidents during the Cold War Consensus accepting the premise that Congress routinely provided what the administration wanted in foreign policy. During Truman's administration, entrepreneurs institutionalized Cold War policies both at home and abroad that he actively opposed. These policies would delay détente for another twenty years. During Eisenhower's administration, the space race was forced upon a reluctant president through the creation of NASA. Also, entrepreneurs pushed a more supportive relationship with Israel that helped offset Eisenhower's perceived "tilt" toward Arab oil-producing states. During Johnson's administration, the groundwork was laid to later force the termination of the Vietnam War, and the seeds of both détente and reform of the UN and IMF were planted. In short, both major and minor foreign policy shifts by the United States were preceded by efforts on behalf of these shifts by congressional foreign policy entrepreneurs. From 1946 to 1967 presidents clearly led the country in foreign policy, but they were also forced to react to the domestic pressures created by foreign policy entrepreneurs on Capitol Hill.

As the historian Robert Johnson (2006, xxiii) notes, "Understanding the congressional response to the Cold War, however, requires looking beyond instances where Congress did (or did not) declare war or approve treaties to examine three other facets of legislative power: the use of spending measures; the internal workings of a Congress increasingly dominated by subcommittees; and the ability of individual legislators to affect foreign affairs by changing the way that policymakers and the public thought about international questions." Entrepreneurs like Pat McCarran, Henry Reuss, and William Fulbright, along with the others in this period, used all three of these direct and indirect means to shape foreign policy in important ways.

5

PLAYERS IN THE GAME

ENTREPRENEURSHIP IN THE COLD WAR
DISSENSUS PERIOD, 1968–1989

Even the most diehard proponents of the "preeminent presidency" acknowledge that interbranch relations changed after the downturn in
American involvement in the Vietnam War. The resulting congressional
resurgence in foreign policy making was seen as a "revolution that will
not be unmade" (Franck and Weisband 1979, 6). In this period the highest
priorities on the foreign policy agenda for many MCs were ending the Vietnam War and ensuring that Congress played a meaningful role in future
warmaking decisions. Responding to continuing revelations about the activities of the Nixon administration, MCs also tried to ensure that they were
informed of covert operations or other ongoing foreign policy initiatives
often conducted through secret executive agreements with other regimes.
Watergate revelations further spurred MCs to enact procedural legislation
to restrict the president's freedom of action in foreign policy making where
possible. Not surprisingly, congressional foreign policy entrepreneurs were
at the forefront of these activities.

A Quantitative Overview

Given these challenges, it is unsurprising that the bulk of the entrepreneurship in the period 1946–2000 should have occurred in the twenty-one
years from 1968 to 1989. As table 19 shows, over half of the entrepreneurial
activity in the data set comes from these years.

Table 19 shows some of the notable changes in this period. The Senate was much more active in entrepreneurship than the House, while both chambers saw entrepreneurship become more common from the majority party. Finally, entrepreneurship became more common from the opposition party to the president. Thus foreign policy entrepreneurship took on a much more partisan tone than it had previously. The politicization of foreign policy had begun.

Table 20 shows that key foreign policy issues revolved around warmaking and war powers. Entrepreneurial behavior focusing on political-diplomatic, economic-developmental, and cultural-status issues sharply decreased compared to the rest of the post–World War II years, and entrepreneurial behavior focusing on military-security issues sharply increased. Compared to other years, the amount of entrepreneurial activity devoted to military-security issues nearly doubled in this period (65.3% compared to 37.5%). In terms of policy type, entrepreneurship in the Cold War Dissensus years was dramatically more likely to be targeted at broader goals and strategies (strategic policy) than to focus on the means and allocation of resources (structural policy). In this period 63% of overall entrepreneurship and 71% of entrepreneurship on defense policy was strategic rather than structural. As described in chapter 4, during the preceding

Table 19: Foreign Policy Entrepreneurship by Chamber, Party Characteristics, and Era

	Cold War Dissensus, 1968–1989	Remaining Post–World War II Era, 1946–1967, 1990–2000	Total, 1946–2000
Senate	63.2%	51.8%	59.8%
	(893)	(674)	(1,567)
House	36.8%	48.2%	40.2%
	(520)	(534)	(1,054)
Member of majority party	63.9%	63.0%	63.5%
	(903)	(761)	(1,664)
Member of opposition party	71.2%	58.6%	65.4%
	(1,006)	(708)	(1,714)
Total	53.9%	46.1%	100%
	(1,413)	(1,208)	(2,621)

Table 20: Foreign Policy Entrepreneurship by Issue Category and Era

	Cold War Dissensus, 1968–1989	Remaining Post–World War II Era, 1946–1967, 1990–2000	Total, 1946–2000
Political-diplomatic	14.4% (203)	24.5% (296)	19.0% (499)
Military-security	65.3% (923)	37.5% (453)	52.5% (1,376)
Economic-development	19.5% (275)	34.6% (418)	26.4% (693)
Cultural-status	0.8% (12)	3.4% (41)	2.0% (53)
Total	53.9% (1,413)	46.1% (1,208)	100% (2,621)
Structural policy	37% (523)	53.1% (641)	44.4% (1,164)
Strategic policy	63% (890)	46.9% (567)	55.6% (1,457)
Defense structural policy	28.9% (200)	36.4% (132)	31.5% (332)
Defense strategic policy	71.1% (492)	63.6% (231)	68.5% (723)

period, those numbers were 38% and 52%. In effect, entrepreneurship in the Cold War Dissensus years was more likely to take the shape of fundamental challenges to the direction of foreign and defense policy.

Table 21 shows another fundamental difference with other periods. During these twenty-one years a strong majority of the entrepreneurial challenges to the president's foreign policy agenda came from MCs on the traditional foreign policy committees. That was not so in other years when a narrow majority of entrepreneurial activity arose from MCs on non–foreign policy committees. Those with the most expertise were challenging presidential foreign policy agendas in this period.

Another difference is seen in table 22. Tactical changes are found in the ways MCs chose to undertake their entrepreneurship during this time as well. MCs used more access points to pursue their entrepreneurial activity,

Table 21: Entrepreneurship and Committee Assignments by Era

Member	Cold War Dissensus, 1968–1989	Remaining Post–World War II Era, 1946–1967, 1990–2000	Total, 1946–2000
Traditional foreign policy committees	57.7% (816)	49.1% (593)	53.8% (1,409)
Other committees	42.3% (597)	50.9% (615)	46.2% (1,212)
Total	53.9% (1,413)	46.1% (1,208)	100% (2,621)

Table 22: Access Points and Activities Used by Year and Era

Year	Number of Access Points Used	Number of Activities Used
1968	5	9
1972	4	7
1973	5	7
1975	6	9
1979	6	7
1984	5	7
1985	6	7
1986	6	9
1987	7	10
Average, Cold War Dissensus	5.6	8.0
1946	3	3
1950	5	8
1954	4	5
1958	5	4
1959	4	4
1960	3	5
1961	4	5
1962	5	8
1963	4	6
1965	6	9
1992	5	8
1994	5	8
1996	5	6
1997	6	5
1999	7	5
Average, Remaining Post–World War II Era	4.7	5.9

Table 23: Entrepreneurial Uses of Avenues of Influence by Era

	Cold War Dissensus, 1968–1989	Remaining Post–World War II Era, 1946–1967, 1990–2000	Total, 1946–2000
Direct-legislative	60.4%	72.1%	65.8%
	(854)	(871)	(1,725)
Indirect-legislative	3.0%	2.4%	2.7%
	(43)	(29)	(72)
Direct-nonlegislative	7.0%	6.1%	6.6%
	(99)	(74)	(173)
Indirect-nonlegislative	29.5%	19.4%	24.8%
	(417)	(234)	(651)
Total	26.9%	73.1%	100%
	(1,413)	(1,208)	(2,621)

and they relied on a wider range of means to push their foreign policy agendas than in other years. These changes are not surprising. During the early part of this period, the "Subcommittee Bill of Rights" dramatically expanded the number of subcommittees of congressional standing committees (Rohde 2005). More subcommittees meant more access points for entrepreneurs, whether as subcommittee members or chairpersons. More subcommittee power meant that it was harder for standing committee chairpersons to limit what entrepreneurial MCs on those subcommittees could do, which meant that more means were available to those MCs. With the explosive rise of cable television during these years, there were more venues for entrepreneurs to publicize and press their foreign policy agendas. As the former secretary of state Dean Rusk (1990, 542) commented, "Now no individuals or small groups can speak for Congress. . . . As a result, executive-legislative consultations have been greatly complicated."

This last point is further illustrated in table 23. During the Cold War Dissensus, entrepreneurs relied less on direct legislative avenues of influence and more on the other avenues. Both indirect legislative and direct nonlegislative avenues were used a bit more than in the rest of the post–World War II era, but the biggest change was seen in the growing use of indirect nonlegislative avenues of influence. These methods, which include the use of the media to frame issues and foreign contacts, were approximately 50% higher for this period than for the rest of the post–World

War II years (29.5% versus 19.4%). Thus entrepreneurial MCs responded to the changing nature of the policy-making environment in rational ways to pursue their goals. But were they successful? To that question we now turn.

Entrepreneurs in the Cold War Dissensus

The greatest challenge to presidential prerogatives came with the congressionally forced termination of the Vietnam War, and entrepreneurs led this effort. As noted in chapter 4, William Fulbright played an important role in legitimating opposition to the war, thereby shaping the political stream, redefining the problem, and introducing alternatives into the policy stream (Kingdon 1995). In 1969 he led the Senate effort to forestall future undeclared wars by sponsoring the National Commitments Resolution, a nonbinding declaration that commitments to other states had to be approved by both the legislative and executive branches (Small 1999). In an attempt to head off a full-scale debate on the Vietnam War led by Fulbright the following year, the Nixon administration persuaded Senator Bob Dole (R-Kan.) to introduce an amendment to repeal the Tonkin Gulf Resolution. The administration's hope was that such a symbolic action would gut Fulbright's efforts to force more substantive efforts to end the war (Bundy 1998). The administration's goal was not met. In later hearings further discrediting the American effort in Vietnam, Fulbright prodded the director of central intelligence (DCI), William Colby, to admit that Operation Phoenix had resulted in the assassination of thousands of suspected Viet Cong leaders in South Vietnam, a finding that helped lead to the later investigation of intelligence activities under Frank Church (Szulc 1978).

While the Nixon administration focused on Fulbright, other entrepreneurs like Senator Javits took up the Vietnam issue. In 1969 Javits introduced a bill with Senator Claiborne Pell (D-R.I.) requiring the withdrawal of United States forces from Vietnam by the end of 1970 (Kissinger 1979). The measure failed, but Javits kept the pressure on the administration by framing the debate in more sweeping terms. In an article in *Foreign Affairs* in 1970 he challenged the preeminent presidency on constitutional grounds (Javits 1970). After taking part in an antiwar rally in Washington that same year (Javits 1981), he introduced his first War Powers Resolution as a Senate floor amendment imposing a thirty-day time limit on the ability of presidents to put United States troops into combat without congressional approval (Bundy 1998). The amendment was unsuccessful (*Congressional Quarterly Almanac* 1970). The next year, he introduced a more comprehensive War Powers bill. After discovering that both Senators John Stennis (D-Miss.) and Thomas Eagleton (D-Mo.) were already at work producing similar legislation, Javits incorporated some of their preferences into his bill. His bill passed the Senate easily but died when the House preferred a weaker bill (Javits 1981).

The narrower issue of stopping the war in Vietnam was addressed in early 1973, when Fulbright sponsored a successful amendment prohibiting the use of funds for any United States combat activity in Southeast Asia after 15 August 1973. This forced the Nixon administration to stop the bombing of Cambodia and accept the final termination of the Vietnam War. According to his aides, "Nixon . . . was livid with rage. He felt Congress was betraying him" (Szulc 1978, 708).

The continuing Watergate scandal provided more evidence of White House misdeeds, which altered the political context and made it politically more difficult to oppose restrictions on the president's claims of unilateral executive powers. Consequently, House opponents also became more receptive to establishing stronger constraints on the broader issue of presidential warmaking abilities (Javits 1973). A compromise between Senate and House leaders was finally reached in late 1973, which stipulated that presidents could only send troops into hostilities, or circumstances where hostilities appear imminent, by virtue of a declaration of war, a congressional authorization, or an attack on United States territories or troops (Javits 1981). When President Nixon vetoed this measure, Javits rallied the opposition to override the veto, and the War Powers Resolution became law on 7 November 1973. According to the historian Melvin Small (1999, 244), this measure has been called "Congress's greatest triumph against the imperial presidency."

Fulbright and Javits were not the only active congressional foreign policy entrepreneurs during this twenty-year era, and Vietnam was not the only important issue. In the later years of the Cold War Dissensus, examples of significant entrepreneurs are numerous. They include people like Senator William Proxmire (D-Wis.), whose persistence in advocating United States ratification of the genocide convention included 3,211 speeches on behalf of the treaty, beginning in 1967 and ending with the treaty's successful ratification in 1987 and passage of the implementation legislation in 1988 (Shields 2005; Wisconsin Historical Society 2006).

A splendid example of the creativity, wide-ranging actions, and policy impact of Cold War Dissensus entrepreneurs is provided by Representative Charlie Wilson (D-Texas), who took it upon himself to ensure that the mujahheddin in Afghanistan were well armed in their fight against Soviet occupiers in the 1980s. As Scott (1996, chap. 3), Coll (2004), and especially Crile (2003) detail, Wilson used his committee assignment (Appropriations), ties to key bureaucrats in the CIA and the Department of Defense, threats of public criticism, and foreign travel (through which he cultivated ties to foreign leaders in Saudi Arabia, Egypt, and Pakistan) to build and expand support for Afghan rebels fighting the Soviet Union in Afghanistan (Wilson 2008). Wilson was directly responsible for dramatic increases in aid to the rebels after 1982, for securing advanced surface-to-air-missiles for them in the mid-1980s, and for keeping their aid alive for several years after the Soviet withdrawal.

Wilson was not alone in his entrepreneurship on Afghanistan. As Rodman (1994, 330) recalled, Senator Paul Tsongas (D-Mass.) and Representative Don Ritter (R-Pa.) "bombarded" the administration, calling on it to do more to "render effective material aid to the freedom fighters." Wilson and Senator Gordon Humphrey (R-N.H.) "were the most active in harassing the administration to provide more aid. In 1985, Humphrey created a congressional task force, with 26 members from both parties, which conducted public hearings on political, strategic, and other aspects of the war. . . . Congressional pressures and backing ensured more than doubling of the covert military assistance, from a reported $250–$280 million in fiscal year 1985 to $630 million in fiscal year 1987" (Rodman 1994, 330).

But it was Wilson who was the prime mover. When asked to explain the Soviet defeat, the former Pakistani president Zia ul-Haq said simply, "Charlie did it" (Crile 2003, 4), and in 1989, when Wilson visited Saudi Arabia, he was housed in lavish quarters and treated as a guest of honor. An aide to the Saudi defense minister, Prince Sultan, explained: "We want you to know, Mr. Congressman . . . that these are larger quarters than we provided for George Bush. Mr. Bush is only the Vice President. *You won the Afghan war*" (quoted in Crile, 2003, 510, emphasis added). From the vantage point of the post-9/11 years, aid to the rebels in Afghanistan takes on a different look. However, those who make the argument that President Reagan's policy of arming the Afghans led to a "blowback" against the United States should also include Wilson in their critique.

Representative Steven Solarz (D-N.Y.) provides another good example. As Scott (1996, chap. 4) describes it, Solarz was a prime mover behind the decision to provide nonlethal and then lethal aid to the noncommunist resistance in Cambodia. Solarz used his assignment to the House Foreign Affairs subcommittee on East Asia to hold hearings and direct attention to the Cambodian conflict. By raising the profile of the problem and redefining alternatives, Solarz prepared the groundwork for legislation authorizing assistance. Then, taking advantage of the policy window provided by the annual budget authorization and appropriation cycle, he introduced his measure, built support for it, and persuaded both his colleagues and the administration to endorse it. Peter Rodman (1994, 269), a State Department official during the Reagan administration, noted Solarz's impact on moving the United States into more aggressive efforts to aid the non-Khmer opposition and seek a diplomatic solution.

Late in the 1980s Solarz, working directly with the Australian minister of foreign affairs Gareth Evans, promoted the idea of a UN body to administer and enforce a settlement in Cambodia. As Rodman (1994, 468–69) characterized it, "the idea filled the policy vacuum to such a degree that by January [1990] it already had the backing of all five permanent members of the UN Security Council." Hence, Solarz provided the formula for the settlement that resolved the conflict, which by that time had ground on for more than twelve years.

Another key entrepreneur of the period initiated a campaign during the Reagan administration to align the United States with the Mozambique National Resistance, known as RENAMO. Sen. Jesse Helms (R-N.C.), a prolific entrepreneur discussed in detail in chapter 6, used a multi-pronged strategy to achieve his goals, with elements that were legislative, procedural (blocking the nomination of Melissa Wells as ambassador to Mozambique), foreign (contacts with RENAMO, UNITA, and South African security forces), and bureaucratic (alliances with hard-liners in the White House, Defense, and the CIA) (Scott 1996, esp. chap. 7). The State Department officials Chester Crocker (1992) and George Shultz (1993) both discussed Helms's efforts to secure aid for RENAMO, noting that while he was ultimately unsuccessful, his efforts held up diplomacy for several years.

Not surprisingly, the conflict in and controversy over Central America in the 1980s attracted many entrepreneurs. Among the many entrepreneurs seeking to define American policy in the region, Christopher Dodd is a leading example.[1] In 1981 he offered a successful bill tying United States military aid to El Salvador to a presidential certification that El Salvador was meeting human rights standards (*Congressional Quarterly Almanac* 1981). In 1983 he introduced a stronger version of the Salvadoran certification bill and traveled to San Salvador to endorse multilateral peace talks (Dickey 1983, § A, 1). As the Reagan administration official Peter Rodman (1994, 247) put it, Dodd and other Democrats in Congress "continued to fight against any, especially military, aid to El Salvador and relented only on condition that the aid be formally linked to the United States president's ability to certify on a regular basis that progress was being achieved in such areas as human rights, economic reform, free elections, peace negotiations, and the investigation of the murders of the American nuns in 1980."

Dodd persuaded the Senate Foreign Relations Committee to send a letter to Secretary of State Shultz requesting that the United States promote Salvadoran peace talks. The letter also endorsed a cap on the number of United States military advisers in El Salvador and restrictions on their activities, reform of the Salvadoran judiciary, and efforts to make the Salvadoran government assign a high priority to prosecuting those responsible for the murders of eight Americans in El Salvador (*Congressional Quarterly Almanac* 1983). Seeking to redefine and frame the issue, in 1983 Dodd gave the Democratic response to President Reagan's speech on 27 April on United States policy toward Central America and was highly critical of military aid to El Salvador (and the contras) (*Congressional Quarterly Almanac* 1983). As he explained in an interview after delivering the response, his experience with the Peace Corps in the Dominican Republic showed him that the problems in the region were economic and social, not ideological as the Reagan administration believed (Broder 1983, § A, 1). In the end the administration was forced to accept a certification process that required elections and progress on human rights as conditions for American assistance. As Shultz (1993) notes, this formula was attributable to Congress and entrepreneurs such as Dodd.

A cluster of entrepreneurs including Dodd engaged with, and had substantial impact on, policy toward Nicaragua in the 1980s as well. For example, concerns over administration actions led Representative Edward

Boland (D-Mass.) to attach an amendment to the defense appropriations bill in 1982 prohibiting aid to groups for the purpose of overthrowing the government of Nicaragua. In the Senate Dodd took similar action, introducing a floor amendment barring the use of any funds after 20 January 1983 for the direct or indirect support of irregular military or paramilitary groups in Central America. Despite his public statements calling for congressional approval of military and covert operations in Central America (Chapman 1982) and a floor speech contending that United States support for contra groups based in Honduras was expanding Central American conflicts into other countries, Dodd's amendment was rejected (*Congressional Quarterly Almanac* 1982). By contrast, Boland's succeeded, and this and subsequent amendments like it fundamentally shaped the landscape for Nicaragua policy. According to Rodman (1994, 239), Boland's amendment and its successors kept the contra aid program covert, and "the administration paid a price . . . for the covert nature of the program." Boland's efforts were at the root of the aid cutoff in 1984, aided by the negative publicity surrounding revelations of the administration's mining of Nicaraguan harbors (Shultz 1993).

In the mid-1980s entrepreneurs again shaped United States policy. One State Department official credited pressure from MCs such as Dodd for forcing the administration into opening a diplomatic track on Nicaragua (Rodman 1994, 246). According to Shultz (1993, 955), Dodd "conducted his own negotiations, making suggestions that undercut" the administration positions, and encouraged the Contadora talks much more than the administration desired. While some entrepreneurs such as Dodd were attempting to end contra aid completely, making media appearances and offering one amendment after another, others were pushing a two-track strategy that combined some aid and diplomacy. Representative Dave McCurdy (D-Okla.), for example, was central to developing the two-track alternative in Congress. McCurdy negotiated with members of the administration and his colleagues in the House to forge an alternative. To secure aid in 1985 President Reagan had to write a letter to McCurdy assuring him and other centrist Democrats that the administration favored negotiated solutions in Central America and that its overriding goal was to promote democracy. Interestingly, this letter had been drafted by McCurdy himself (Rodman 1994), and his efforts to forge an alternative were successful: aid was provided in 1985 and 1986.

According to James Baker, then secretary of state, in the wake of these bruising clashes over Nicaragua, he met privately in 1989 with a group of entrepreneurs that included Lee Hamilton (D-Ind.), Bob Michel (R-Ill.), Joe Biden (D-Del.), John Kerry (D-Mass.), and Dodd, who counseled against aid to the contras. These entrepreneurs urged a centrist, largely political resolution. Their efforts led the administration to change its policy. As Baker recalled, "Look, I told Dodd, I'd actually prefer military aid to the contras. But we realize that's not in the cards, so I'm not even going to ask for it" (James Baker 1995, 56). Ultimately David Obey (D-Wis.) was the entrepreneur who provided the compromise proposal that established a new approach, in which nonlethal aid would be authorized, but withheld for eight months until the appropriations and foreign policy committees of both houses reviewed the situation. Subsequent contra funding would require approval from all four committees. In the meantime the administration would endorse negotiations leading to elections. The administration accepted the new entrepreneur-led policy (James Baker 1995).

Finally, entrepreneurs were instrumental in redefining and redirecting foreign policy toward the countries of Eastern Europe at the end of the Cold War Dissensus period as well. According to President Bush and his national security adviser Brent Scowcroft (Bush and Scowcroft 1998, 138–39), pressure from George Mitchell (D-Maine), who denounced the tentative administration approach to Eastern Europe in 1989 and 1990 as "almost nostalgic about the Cold War," was important. So was the leadership of entrepreneurs such as Senator Claiborne Pell (D-R.I.) in proposing aid to Eastern Europe, which eventually prompted the enactment of the Support for Eastern European Democracy (SEED) act in 1989. Other entrepreneurs developed the Freedom Support Act in 1992, which we discuss in chapter 6.

These examples nicely illustrate the military-security, political-diplomatic, economic-developmental, and cultural-status issues to which entrepreneurs attended in the Cold War Dissensus. They further show the accelerated use and interweaving of direct legislative, indirect legislative, direct nonlegislative, and indirect nonlegislative activities in pursuit of their agendas, and the collaboration and alliances forged between entrepreneurs. Entrepreneurs' influence on United States foreign policy is readily apparent from these seminal examples. The next few pages provide more in-depth examination of three entrepreneurs— Frank Church

(D-Idaho), Edward Kennedy (D-Mass.), and Jim Wright (D-Texas)—and their activities, roles, and impact in the Cold War Dissensus.

Frank Church: Building Structures of Accountability

Frank Church grew up in Boise. As a sickly child, Church spent much of his time reading and listening to the radio. He particularly enjoyed the radio speeches of the noted orator and Republican senator William Borah of Idaho, chairman of the Foreign Relations Committee. At fourteen Church declared his career goal to become a senator and chair the Foreign Relations Committee himself (Church 1985). In high school Church won the American Legion's national oratory contest, and the prize was a scholarship to Stanford University, which he left during his freshman year in 1943 to enlist in the Army. After military intelligence and officer candidate schools, Lt. Church was off to China, where he won a Bronze Star for the quality of his intelligence reports. With the war's end he returned to Stanford, graduating Phi Beta Kappa in 1947. He went home to Boise, married the daughter of a former governor, and returned to Stanford for law school (Church 1985).

At twenty-three Church was diagnosed with terminal cancer. However, extensive surgery followed by experimental radiation treatment cured him, and he finished his law studies in 1950 and began legal practice in Boise. In 1956 he unexpectedly announced a run for the U.S. Senate and was elected at the age of thirty-two. He later said that beating cancer changed his outlook on life. In his view life was risky and might be short, so he might as well aim high. Within two years he was appointed to the Foreign Relations Committee (Johnson 1985), and he served in the Senate until his defeat for reelection in 1980.

Church's policy impact can be seen as a product of the times. He helped limit and then end the Vietnam War, redress the imbalance of war powers between the branches, and restrict the influence of multinational corporations, and he led the effort to investigate and curb abuses by intelligence agencies.

Theme 1: Ending the Vietnam War and rebalancing interbranch war powers. Church's antiwar stances predated the Cold War Dissensus. As early as 1965 he began to frame the Vietnam conflict in a way that would support his entrepreneurial efforts to redirect United States policy. For example, he said in a Senate floor speech that the Vietnam War involved two dictatorial regimes fighting for control of the country. He also rejected the idea that United States military security in Asia required a victory in Vietnam (Church 1969b). According to President Nixon's domestic affairs adviser John Ehrlichman (1982), Church's opposition to the war (along with that of others in Congress) pushed the new president to nominate a long-time House member, Melvin Laird (R-Wis.), as secretary of defense. The administration hoped that his congressional experience would enable Laird to neutralize congressional opponents of the war like Church. Their hope was not fulfilled.

To the contrary, Church and other entrepreneurs stepped up their efforts. In a Senate floor speech in 1969, Church likened the Vietnam War to the American Revolution, with the South Vietnamese guerrillas playing the role of the American colonists. Calling the war unnecessary and unsuccessful (Church 1969b), Church built on his efforts to define the problem as one of providing alternatives, introducing a bill with Mark Hatfield (R-Ore.) calling for the immediate withdrawal of United States forces from Vietnam (Kissinger 1979).

Although that bill failed to gain sufficient Senate support to pass, Church also worked to prevent the war from spreading by sponsoring an amendment barring the introduction of United States ground forces into Laos or Thailand. This effort was more successful, as the amendment passed the Senate, and the House accepted it in conference committee (*Congressional Quarterly Almanac* 1969). Building on this success, the next year he sponsored amendments with John Sherman Cooper (R-Ky.) to restrict military operations in Thailand, Laos, and Cambodia (*Congressional Quarterly Almanac* 1970; Johnson 2006). When these amendments passed they constituted "the first occasion since before the Second World War in which Congress had controlled military operations through the appropriations power" (Johnson 2006, 164). President Nixon castigated the Cambodia amendment as "the first restrictive vote ever cast on a president in wartime" (Wicker 1991, 586). As Nixon knew, its passage meant that not just Democrats but influential Republicans as well would no longer unquestioningly accept his Indochina policy (Wicker 1991). As a result of the Cooper-Church amendments Nixon announced a policy shift, ending military activities in Cambodia (Mason 2004; Szulc 1978).

In late 1970 Church defended war protesters in a speech at Washington University in St. Louis, saying that they recognized what their leaders could not: Vietnam had nothing to do with American security, Ho Chi Minh was no Hitler, and the United States had no business intervening in someone else's civil war. Further he argued that communism was not monolithic and that misplaced fears had driven the United States to support "despotic governments that are the very antithesis of all we stand for as a nation" (Church 1970b, 172).

Church remained instrumental in ending the Vietnam War. In April 1972 he cosponsored the Church-Case amendment that would have "prohibited the use of U.S. funds to maintain or support U.S. forces in hostilities in Indochina after Dec. 31, 1972, subject to agreement for release of all U.S. prisoners of war and accounting for those missing in action" (*Congressional Quarterly Almanac* 1972, 325). Although his version of that amendment did not survive the Senate floor, others, including Fulbright's, later did, and the United States military presence in Vietnam ended as a result.

Church also redirected attention to the broader issue of war powers. In the Senate debate on the National Commitments Resolution in 1969, he chastised the Senate for allowing presidents to usurp Congress's constitutional roles in warmaking. He believed that no one person should hold the fate of 200 million Americans in his hands (Church 1969a). Church repeated this refrain the next year on the Senate floor as well as at Stanford University (Church 1970a). Church was thus an early leader in the national debate that led to the passage of the War Powers Resolution in 1973, and an active supporter of the efforts led by Jacob Javits discussed earlier in this chapter.

Theme 2: Investigating the abuses of the intelligence community. Church is best remembered for his chairmanship of the Senate Select Committee on Intelligence Activities and its investigation into intelligence abuses. Key events and developments helped to drive this problem to the foreground, including concerns over the abuses of the Nixon administration in the Watergate scandal. More specifically, though, in September 1974 press reports linked the CIA to the Chilean military coup of 1973 that overthrew President Salvador Allende's regime and resulted in Allende's death. And in December press reports alleged that the Nixon administration had conducted illegal *domestic* intelligence operations on a massive scale. Even President Gerald Ford's attempt to allay the growing concerns backfired; although he created a commission headed by Vice President Nelson Rockefeller to investigate CIA activities, in January 1975 the Senate created its own Select Committee to Study Government Operations with Respect to Intelligence Activities to ensure a thorough inquiry. Church aggressively sought the chairmanship of the select committee from the Senate majority leader, Mike Mansfield (D-Mont.). Church reminded Mansfield that despite his nineteen years in the Senate he had not held the chairmanship of a major committee, and he was named to the post (Johnson 1985).

To capitalize on the opening window of opportunity, Church was determined to conduct a balanced investigation. He did not think that the executive branch could credibly investigate itself, and he vowed not to repeat Congress's prior lax congressional oversight of the intelligence community. Perhaps owing to his military intelligence background, he acknowledged that the intelligence community had legitimate tasks to perform. He started his tenure as committee chairman by telling the press that he wanted to protect legitimate national security interests, but he would not overlook abuses of power that could help create an American police state. Appearing on the CBS television show *Face the Nation*, he said that his task was to reform but "not to wreck" the intelligence community (Johnson 1985, 15). As he told a dinner party, he took the chairman's role knowing that it could hurt the presidential bid he was considering for 1976 (Johnson 1985).

Once the committee began working Church engaged in an array of entrepreneurial activities to gather information, shape the debate, and develop solutions to the problem.[2] When the administration balked at providing requested information, he had committee staff members cleared to handle classified materials. When that did not speed the flow of information to his committee, he wrote multiple letters requesting the documents to President Ford, Vice President Rockefeller, and the director of central intelligence, William Colby. He met with the president in the Oval Office to request the information. When it was not forthcoming, Church had two meetings with the vice president and many with the director of central intelligence (Johnson 1985).

Church also kept up the public pressure with persistent issue framing. In almost daily press briefings, Church told reporters that the Select Committee would stay in business as long as it took to get the information it needed, and that the administration needed to understand this. As the administration stonewalled and delayed, Church's requests eventually turned to demands and his public statements became more assertive (Johnson 1985). In a magazine interview in March 1975, he was asked about reports of assassination attempts by the CIA. His memorable response was: "In the absence of war, no Government agency can be given license to murder. The President is not a glorified Godfather" (*Time*, 24 March 1975, 26).

Church began holding closed committee hearings by late spring 1975. After two days of testimony by Colby in May, Church told reporters that murder by government agencies was "simply intolerable" (Johnson 1985, 46). In July, when former President Dwight Eisenhower's brother gave assurances that Eisenhower had known nothing of assassination plots, Church gave reporters a quote that became infamous: "The CIA may have been behaving like a rogue elephant on a rampage" (Johnson 1985, 57).

By September 1975 Church accelerated his efforts to define the problem, gather information, and soften the ground for his preferred alternatives. For example, to highlight his claim that the CIA was out of control, he told reporters and a local television program in Washington that the CIA had refused direct presidential orders to destroy stockpiles of lethal biological toxins. He also moved from closed to open hearings, increasing the public pressure. Beyond the issue of illegal toxins, the public hearings also dealt with domestic intelligence abuses by both the FBI and the CIA: Church revealed campaigns of illegal opening of mail by the CIA (including releasing the names of prominent Americans whose mail had been opened) and burglaries by the FBI (at least 238 from 1942 to 1968) to learn more about alleged subversive activities by American citizens. Church also revealed that intelligence officials did not inform each other or the president of their illegal activities.

Church turned his attention in October to the illegal investigation by the Internal Revenue Service of prominent Americans thought to be subversive, and he again read names into the record. He also appeared on the ABC program *Issues and Answers* to further discuss the alleged political assassinations. While all these efforts highlighted the problem, Church also pressed his preferred policy solution, telling a reporter in October that he favored the creation of a joint congressional intelligence committee as a permanent oversight body (*Congressional Quarterly Almanac* 1975; Johnson 1985).

In late October Church began a new round of public hearings on the activities of the National Security Agency, at the time a highly secret operation. Questioning the legality of its activities, he said that new legislation might be necessary to protect the constitutional rights of all Americans (*Congressional Quarterly Almanac* 1975). When Colby and Secretary of Defense James Schlesinger were unexpectedly fired by President Ford in early November, Church told reporters that the administration's efforts at concealment would not disrupt the committee's investigation (Johnson 1985).

In November 1975 Church issued a report that detailed a twenty-year effort by the FBI to disrupt, discredit, and undermine protest groups and movements in the United States. In the accompanying hearing Church told the FBI's deputy assistant director for intelligence that federal law enforcement officers should not break the law. Church also released the committee report on CIA efforts to assassinate five foreign leaders (Castro in Cuba, Lumumba in the Congo, Trujillo in the Dominican Republic, Diem in South Vietnam, and General Rene Schneider in Chile) (*Congressional Quarterly Almanac* 1975). By releasing the report on his own authority as committee chairman, Church angered many senators. A closed session of the Senate was consumed with denunciations of the committee for the decision to release the report without seeking the entire chamber's approval (Johnson 1985).

In December 1975 Church began to shift his emphasis from framing and information gathering to advocacy of his preferred policy alternative, although he continued to hold hearings and frame issues in the press and to the public. For example, that month there were hearings on the use of the FBI for political purposes (*Congressional Quarterly Almanac* 1975), a speech on covert action to an academic forum at the Sheraton Park Hotel in Washington (Johnson 1985), and the release of his committee's report confirming the role of the CIA in trying to influence Chilean elections and in overthrowing President Allende (*Congressional Quarterly Almanac* 1975). He also called Secretary of State Henry Kissinger a "compulsive interventionist" and denounced the administration's use of interventions into the Angolan civil war and in Italian elections (Johnson 1985, 170). Church appeared on the *Today* show, defending the Select Committee's work from criticism that it went either too far or not far enough.

Church used his committee position and agenda-setting power to change the focus from abuses to procedural intelligence reform. In mid-January 1976 Church briefed the press about the nature of reforms being considered. Then on 21 January he testified before the Senate Government Operations Committee, calling for the creation of a permanent Senate Intelligence Committee. On 29 January he introduced a bill to create such a committee (Johnson 1985).

With his policy alternative prominently injected into the policy stream, Church accelerated his efforts on the public stage. In February 1976 he published "Covert Action: Swampland of American Foreign Policy" in the *Bulletin of the Atomic Scientists*. Church argued that intelligence gathering and analysis were necessary, but that there was no statutory authorization to conduct covert operations. Citing troubling covert operations in Guatemala, Indonesia, Iran, Cuba, Laos, Congo, the Dominican Republic, Vietnam, and Chile, he argued that even when successful, such covert operations cost the United States "its good name and reputation" and led to a "startling decline in American prestige" (Church 1976, 11). He followed the article's publication with a speech to the Reverend Jesse Jackson's congregation in Chicago, in which he castigated the CIA for forgetting that the United States was a Christian country, for conspiring to assassinate the leaders of small countries whose actions could not harm the United States, and for its current intervention into Angola. At a press conference in Los Angeles he warned that the CIA had a powerful bureaucratic interest in creating a need for and carrying out covert interventions (Johnson 1985).

In the spring of 1976 Church began releasing to the public the documents that the Select Committee had used in its investigation, and he announced his candidacy for the Democratic presidential nomination. He made campaign stops in Idaho, California, Oregon, and Nebraska, pressing for reform of the intelligence community and restraints on interventionism at each stop in an appearance on the *Today* show. In a nationally televised fund-raising appeal in April, he called it a mark of weakness to betray our own values by trying to imitate the Soviet KGB.

Finally, in April, the Select Committee began issuing its multivolume final report. The committee's work was praised by the *Washington Post*: "The Senate, by this report, has earned the public's confidence in its capacity to join in the shaping of national intelligence policy" (quoted in Johnson 1985, 228). The committee report called for a new Senate intelligence committee with subpoena power that would oversee activities and authorize all spending by the intelligence community, a ban on United States support for police or internal security forces that systematically violate human rights, advance notification of covert operations to the appropriate congressional committees, and an annual national intelligence budget, with the total amount of expenditures made public. All these major recommendations were later enacted, many in the Intelligence Oversight Act of 1980 (*Congressional Quarterly Almanac* 1976; Johnson 1985).

Theme 3: Addressing American economic health and the power and influence of transnational business. Church used his position on the Foreign Relations Committee's Subcommittee on Economic Policy to call for a substantial reduction in United States funds going abroad. Although unsuccessful, his efforts included a suspension of the foreign aid program until the Vietnam War ended and the return of at least half the United States troops in Europe (*Congressional Quarterly Almanac* 1968), the termination of aid to OPEC nations after the oil embargo (*Congressional Quarterly Almanac* 1974), and a requirement that the executive branch annually report to Congress on its efforts to control and monitor loans by the International Monetary Fund (*Congressional Quarterly Almanac* 1978).

Based on the role of United States multinationals in Chile, Church was especially concerned with the impact of the corporations at home and abroad. He employed a number of weapons to try to control multinational corporations, linking hearings, public statements, and legislative instruments. In 1974 he used his position as chairman of the Foreign Relations Subcommittee on Multinational Corporations to hold hearings on the multinational oil industry, especially concerning its profits and taxes (or, better, its tax evasion). Later that year he proposed in committee and on the Senate floor to restrict funding of transnational activities by the Overseas Private Investment Corporation. In a conference committee he also tried to limit funding by the Export-Import Bank of fossil fuel projects in the Soviet Union by multinational oil corporations (*Congressional Quarterly Almanac* 1974).

Church sustained this interest through the remainder of his congressional career. In 1976 he began a new investigation of multinationals in his subcommittee. The Senate passed one of his efforts requiring United States corporations with overseas dealings to disclose their gifts, contributions, taxes, and commissions (*Congressional Quarterly Almanac* 1976).

In 1978 he unsuccessfully sought to add reservations to a treaty that restricted the ability of the United States to tax British multinationals (*Congressional Quarterly Almanac* 1978). Throughout, his overriding concern was to control the ability of transnationals to harm United States interests or unduly influence United States foreign policy.

In summary, Church relied on all four entrepreneurial avenues. He used direct legislative avenues like introducing bills, sponsoring amendments, and defending them on the Senate floor, indirect-legislative avenues like holding hearings, issuing reports, and testifying before other committees, direct nonlegislative avenues like meeting personally with the president and other top administration officials and sending them letters, and indirect nonlegislative avenues when he issued press releases, briefed reporters, gave interviews, appeared on television, and made public appearances all over the country.

In terms of policy impact, his efforts helped end the use of force in Cambodia, end the Vietnam War, led to the nomination of Secretary of Defense Laird, focused public attention on the broader war powers issue, and held the intelligence community's activities up to scrutiny. Church's efforts to create a new permanent Senate intelligence committee are a textbook example of the power of procedural innovations to control policy. Indeed, the Intelligence Oversight Act of 1980 not only created permanent oversight committees but also required, for the first time, prior notification of covert activities in most circumstances. This result had important effects on intelligence activities in the 1980s and laid the groundwork for legislation enacted in 1991, after the Iran-contra affair (as part of the intelligence authorization bill), that finally defined covert actions, required written findings in all cases, and banned retroactive findings. Finally, Church's efforts to reduce United States foreign aid and reform the IMF may have helped lay the groundwork for the substantive changes of the 1990s. Thus Church's entrepreneurship at times drove the congressional agenda, mobilized support within the institution and among the public for various policy ideas, and developed and presented new policy options and alternatives.

Edward Kennedy: Pursuing Justice and Restraint

Edward M. Kennedy was born in 1932. Educated in Britain during his father's tenure as United States ambassador to the Court of St. James's, he returned to the United States in 1940 to attend a series of exclusive schools in New York and Massachusetts. After entering Harvard in 1949, he enlisted in the Army in 1951, serving two years, returned to Harvard, and earned his degree in 1956. He then earned a law degree from the University of Virginia in 1959 (*Congressional Directory* 2002).

After helping his brother John win the presidential election in 1960, Kennedy was appointed assistant district attorney in Suffolk County, Massachusetts. In 1962 he won a special election to fill John's seat in the Senate. He was reelected in 1964 and in seven subsequent elections. During more than forty years in the Senate, he has held leadership positions on the Judiciary Committee and the Labor and Human Resources Committee. He also served on the Armed Services Committee.

Early on, Kennedy's high profile as the sole remaining Kennedy brother and potential rival to Richard Nixon gave him considerable leverage. For example, Kennedy is credited with keeping Senator Henry Jackson (D-Wash.) from serving as President Nixon's first secretary of defense. Jackson had agreed to accept the job, but Kennedy's threat to make Jackson's life miserable each time he had to appear before the Senate caused Jackson to change his mind (Evans and Novak 1971; Klein 1980). Kennedy's public call in March 1969 for China to be admitted to the United Nations, and for ending travel and economic restrictions on China, smoothed the way for Nixon's relaxation of those travel and economic restrictions in July 1969 (Small 1999).

Indeed, Nixon paid considerable attention to Kennedy, as he saw the various Kennedy brothers as his rivals throughout his political career. He expected Edward to be his opponent in 1972, and so often tried to match what Kennedy did. For instance, when Kennedy said "he would have 'crawled' to Hanoi to get prisoners-of-war released, the president showed up at a conference on POWs . . . When the senator went to India and Pakistan to study the refugee problems, Secretary of State Rogers addressed the United Nations on the refugee problem" (Matthews 1996, 309). Kennedy was capable of that kind of impact, and he directed his efforts toward a broad range of concerns that cluster around the themes of anti-intervention, arms control, and human rights and humanitarianism.

Theme 1: Anti-interventionism (military and paramilitary). Kennedy worked against American military and paramilitary interventions. Many of these efforts reflected his concern for the effects of these actions on civilians. Two examples from different periods highlight both this area of concern and the range of activities in which Kennedy engaged to press his preferences: Vietnam and Central America.

Human costs led Kennedy to oppose the Vietnam War. Building on his prior efforts to provide for Indochinese refugees (Burner and West 1984; Clymer 1999; Galloway 1971), in 1970 Kennedy was an enthusiastic supporter of the Cooper-Church amendment to force the withdrawal of United States forces from Cambodia. In 1972 he met with Secretary of State Rogers, urging that a medical delegation be sent to North Vietnam to assess its needs when the war ended (Haldeman 1994). The next year Kennedy led the Senate Democratic Caucus to attempt to end the war by cutting off its funding once United States military personnel and prisoners were out. Those ideas formed the basis of the McGovern-Hatfield amendment. The amendment did not pass, but it kept pressure on the Nixon administration to end the war (Lippman 1976; Clymer 1999). Kennedy also proposed to offer reconstruction aid to both South and North Vietnam to improve chances of a peaceful settlement of the conflict (Burner and West 1984). Later, in 1973, he supported the War Powers Resolution against President Nixon's veto and led efforts to block continued aid to South Vietnam after the United States withdrawal (Lippman 1976). In these roles he was an active entrepreneur seeking an alternative course for United States policy in Southeast Asia.

A decade later Kennedy again sought an alternative approach to a presidential policy. The focus was the Reagan administration's Central American anticommunist agenda, especially in El Salvador and Nicaragua. United States policy toward Central America resonated in his home state of Massachusetts, a base for Maryknoll nuns, who were embroiled in Central American conflicts. Further, two of Kennedy's fellow Massachusetts Democrats, Speaker Tip O'Neill and the chairman of the House Intelligence Committee, Edward Boland, cared about these causes, as did his friend and fellow senator Chris Dodd (Clymer 1999).

On El Salvador, Kennedy used floor amendments to try to block the aid package the administration sought and later to bar United States troops (*Congressional Quarterly Almanac* 1984). In the end Congress tied aid to progress on human rights, forcing the administration to press for elections and curbs on human rights abuses by security forces and death squads. Once Napoleon Duarte won the elections in 1984, the Salvadoran issue was relegated to the background because of concerns over neighboring Nicaragua.

Kennedy's approach to Nicaragua ratcheted into high gear in 1984 and 1985. Kennedy told his colleagues on the chamber floor that American policy was "a case of see no evil, hear no evil, speak no evil while doing evil" (*Congressional Record* 1984, 7705). That same year Kennedy offered several amendments to end aid to the Nicaragua contras entirely (which were defeated), and to prohibit the use of American troops in Nicaragua (also defeated). After revelations that the United States had mined Nicaraguan harbors, Kennedy offered an amendment to a tax bill that condemned the actions, which ultimately passed the Senate (*Congressional Quarterly Almanac* 1984).

Kennedy believed that diplomacy was needed in the region (Dale 1984a). In an op-ed piece in the *New York Times* in November 1984, he urged a diplomatic approach to Nicaragua rather than a paramilitary intervention (Kennedy 1984). In 1985 he offered a floor amendment requiring direct, bilateral negotiations between the United States and Nicaragua (*Congressional Quarterly Almanac* 1985). Because of the insistence of Kennedy and other opponents, the administration was forced to open a diplomatic track that eventually contributed to resolution of the conflict (Scott 1996, esp. chap. 6).

Theme 2: Arms control and disarmament.   A second major aim of Kennedy's entrepreneurship was to find an alternative to the nuclear arms race and to promote arms control in general (Lippman 1976). Several salient examples drawn from his career highlight this concern.

An early example can be seen in Kennedy's response to plans to develop an antiballistic missile system in the late 1960s. His entrepreneurship was innovative and offers one of the first examples of an MC acting independently to develop the expertise necessary to challenge the executive branch on defense matters. Kennedy collaborated with another entrepreneur engaged on this issue—Senator Symington (D-Mo.). Along with his fellow senators Cooper and Philip Hart (D-Mich.), Symington led "the first sustained congressional debate about a weapons system since before World War II" (Johnson 2006, 148). In parallel, Kennedy assembled a team of experts to study the ABM system so that senators would not be dependent on the Defense Department or the Armed Services Committee for information. Kennedy's initiative provided a powerful impetus and support for the Foreign Relations and Armed Services Committees to hold additional hearings. Kennedy's study group published its findings in a well-respected book, *ABM: An Evaluation of the Decision to Deploy an Antiballistic Missile System*, edited by Jerome Wiesner and Abram Chayes (Clymer 1999; Lippman 1976).

Ultimately the Cooper-Hart amendment, which would have prevented expenditures on the ABM system, failed to garner enough votes. Amendments to prevent ABM from being funded were defeated 50–50 and 49–51, but the Senate—and the Armed Services Committee in particular—never again reacted so uncritically to major weapons requests by the Pentagon (Clymer 1999). Moreover, the amendments failed principally because President Johnson promised senators that he would never deploy the ABM and wanted it only as a bargaining chip in arms control talks with the Soviets (Johnson 2006).

When the ABM issue continued past Johnson's final year into the Nixon administration, Kennedy again allied with Symington, Cooper, and Hart to work against it. With one of the ABM sites slated to be in Massachusetts, Kennedy assigned his staff to investigate both constituents' opinions and expert views on missile defense (Lippman 1976; Clymer 1999). He then wrote a public letter to Defense Secretary Laird saying that the system was too expensive and unlikely to work (Clymer 1999). One week later Laird announced a temporary halt and review of the plan (Lippman 1976). Shortly afterward President Nixon announced that the system would defend missile sites instead of population centers. Nixon's policy shift was in part a result of campaign politics. As noted earlier, he assumed that Kennedy would be his opponent in the presidential race in 1972. Nixon felt that he could not afford a possible loss to Kennedy on the ABM issue, so he voluntarily changed the locations of the ABM systems (Small 1999).

Not long after, another version of Cooper-Hart failed 51–49, but "Senate opposition forced the [Nixon] administration to change its stated rationale for the missile, thus bequeathing Nixon a pyrrhic victory that set the stage for the Strategic Arms Limitation Treaty (SALT I), which curtailed both sides' ABM systems. More important, the [Senate's] new internationalists' ability to dominate the technical aspects of the debate emboldened them to attack other weapons systems. The legislative effects of this change were dramatic: the upper chamber experienced more than 100 roll-call votes on defense appropriations bills between 1970 and 1975" (Johnson 2006, 158).

Kennedy's work on this issue, in combination with that of other entrepreneurs, thus not only shaped arms control and weapons deployment but also set the stage for the empowerment of new entrepreneurs.

Kennedy also pushed for a variety of more aggressive arms control efforts. When the Ford administration reached an agreement to place a ceiling on delivery vehicles, Kennedy worked closely with Walter Mondale (D-Minn.) and Charles Mathias (R-Md.) to endorse not just a ceiling but progress toward real reductions as well (Clymer 1999). Also in 1974, he spoke in Moscow about the mutual interests of the United States and the Soviet Union in ending the arms race. Later in Los Angeles, he advocated an agenda for renewed substantive negotiations as part of the Strategic Arms Limitation Talks (Lippman 1976). Later that year Kennedy repeated this call in a speech in Vienna and an article in *Foreign Policy* (Clymer 1999).

In 1975 Kennedy's amendment to dismantle the missile site in Grand Forks, North Dakota, was narrowly defeated (40–39) (Associated Press 1975). He also proposed an unsuccessful amendment to eliminate the Minuteman II missile. In April 1975 he outlined an eight-point arms control program to the Arms Control Association in Washington, stressing a test ban and other measures to reduce the role of nuclear weapons in superpower relations (Lippman 1976).

The following year Kennedy tried to limit arms sales, especially in the Middle East. Here too he used a multifaceted approach, combining international travel, public speeches, writing, and legislative activities. From speeches in the Senate to addresses in the Middle East to an article in *Foreign Affairs*, Kennedy pressed for a ban on arms sales to Persian Gulf states, arguing that the practice of selling arms to developing states was comparable to hooking someone on heroin (Clymer 1999). He and Senator Hubert Humphrey sponsored a bill to change arms sales procedures so as to require the administration to justify to Congress the reasons for the sales and their regional impact (*U.S. News and World Report* 1976). Shortly thereafter the Carter administration began conventional arms transfers talks to address precisely these concerns, and arms sales procedures were amended to expand the role of Congress.

A third example of Kennedy's efforts is his leadership, support, and advocacy of the nuclear freeze movement and related arms control measures. In March 1982 he and Mark Hatfield (R-Ore.) offered a freeze resolution.

The Reagan administration responded by offering its first arms control strategy, announcing its decision just two days later (Clymer 1999).[3] In letters to the *New York Times* (Kennedy et al. 1983a; Kennedy et al. 1983b), he and his colleagues defended their freeze proposal against attacks from critics. He and Hatfield also used the receipts from a book on the freeze published in 1982 to fund a forum for American and Russian scientists in December 1983 in which the perils of nuclear war and nuclear winter were discussed (Clymer 1999).

After unsuccessful nuclear freeze votes in 1983 and 1984, Kennedy found other ways to press his case on arms control. He sought and received an appointment to the Senate Observer Group to monitor arms control negotiations between the United States and the Soviet Union, which enabled him to engage in what amounted to oversight activities. When Mikhail Gorbachev signaled his willingness to renew arms control negotiations, Kennedy visited Moscow and held extensive discussions on arms control and other foreign policy issues with Gorbachev and Foreign Minister Eduard Shevardnadze.[4] On his return he wrote an op-ed piece for the *Washington Post* to urge greater activity (Kennedy 1986c). He also told administration officials that Soviet leaders had decided to "de-link" intermediate nuclear forces in Europe from the Strategic Defense Initiative (Reagan's missile defense program), a concession that proved important in the following year when the INF Treaty was completed and the Strategic Arms Reduction Talks were given new life. When the administration failed initially to capitalize on this opportunity, Kennedy chided it again, now in the *New York Times* (Kennedy 1986a). "At a time in U.S.-Soviet affairs when the governments were not talking much, Kennedy was an important channel" (Clymer 1999, 394).

Theme 3: Human rights and humanitarianism. Kennedy often focused on human rights and humanitarian issues. These concerns dominated his foreign policy agenda and produced wide-ranging efforts. In 1975 he co-sponsored amendments to the foreign assistance bill to provide United States support to the United Nations Works and Relief Agency, the United Nations Development Program, and UNICEF (*Congressional Quarterly Almanac* 1975). Two years later he pressed the State Department for open-ended entry into the United States for Soviet and East European refugees (Gwertzman 1977).

In the 1980s Kennedy tried to protect immigration opportunities in the

Immigration Reform and Control Act of 1983 and the Immigration Act of 1989. In 1984 he helped link aid to El Salvador to human rights progress there (Dale 1984a; Dale 1984b), and he proposed relief for a famine in Ethiopia (Kennedy 1990). In 1985 he and Senator Alan Simpson (R-Wyo.) used the op-ed pages of the *New York Times* to promote their criteria for a new UN High Commissioner on Refugees, in an effort to shape the debate and selection process at the UN (Simpson and Kennedy 1985). Kennedy used the Judiciary Committee as a forum for hearings in 1988 on United States policy toward refugees around the world (Committee on the Judiciary 1988). He and Simpson followed in 1989 with a report on famine in the Horn of Africa and called for the delivery of humanitarian aid. The two also wrote directly to the UN secretary general Javier Pérez de Cuéllar, urging him to appoint a special envoy to oversee relief operations in Sudan, which he did (Kennedy 1990). In 1989 he demanded a full investigation of United States aid to El Salvador after right-wing death squads murdered six Jesuit priests and two others (Cohen 1989).

This listing suggests the breadth of Kennedy's concerns; three more examples provide good illustrations of his more concerted efforts. First, Kennedy had a special interest in the effects of war on the plight of refugees and civilians in Indochina, perhaps a consequence of his chairmanship of the Judiciary Committee's subcommittee on refugees. In the process he turned a backwater subcommittee into an active panel on refugee issues, holding hearings on refugee issues in Indochina in 1969 (Lippman 1976). Determined to force recognition of this problem, Kennedy stepped up his efforts in the 1970s, even as he worked to end the war. In March 1970 he sent a list of questions on the refugee situation to Secretary of State Rogers and used Rogers's responses to focus his criticism of the war (Lippman 1976). His subcommittee also conducted an investigation and issued a report on Laotian refugees (*Congressional Quarterly Almanac* 1970), followed by an additional set of hearings on the region. The next year he held hearings on the effects of the bombing campaign in Laos and Cambodia, arguing that there was a direct link between the growth of Laotian refugees and increases in United States bombing in the area (Finney 1971).

Kennedy also took action to shape the United States policy response. In addition to more hearings in 1972, he sponsored amendments to assist war victims. He proposed to designate $2 million to Cambodia for humanitarian assistance, and $70 million in humanitarian assistance in South

Vietnam. Both measures passed the Senate but died in conference (*Congressional Quarterly Almanac* 1972). Efforts in 1973 to renew the Cambodian earmarking also failed, but his efforts to earmark aid to Laotian refugees were successful (*Congressional Quarterly Almanac* 1973). When the war ended in 1975 Kennedy's subcommittee staff study severely criticized the Ford administration's efforts and recommended a new policy approach (Binder 1975). A few years later, in the midst of the genocide by the Khmer Rouge in Cambodia and the Vietnamese intervention there, Kennedy used a speech before the Council on Foreign Relations to call for an international conference on Indochina that would arrange a ceasefire in Cambodia and assist Indochinese refugees ("Kennedy Seeks International Indochina Conference" 1979). His persistence had an impact on policy, both by shaping its content directly and by influencing the executive branch to take steps that it otherwise would not have taken (Lippman 1976). Levels of humanitarian aid were higher because of Kennedy than they would otherwise have been. According to a State Department official, "Kennedy made that subcommittee the custodian of moral values in foreign policy" (quoted in Lippman 1976, 63).

A second illustration of Kennedy's humanitarian entrepreneurship is his efforts on United States policy toward Chile during the 1970s and 1980s. After President Allende was overthrown in 1973, Kennedy sought measures to confront the military regime of Augusto Pinochet. After he held a hearing at which witnesses described mass executions and other gross violations of human rights (Clymer 1999), Kennedy unsuccessfully tried twice to bar military aid to Chile (*Congressional Quarterly Almanac* 1973). Ever persistent, in 1976 he succeeded, in part because of the increased attention to the same issues generated by his fellow entrepreneur Frank Church's investigations into the CIA's involvement in the Chilean coup d'état. Kennedy proposed, and Congress passed, an amendment prohibiting aid to Chile, overcoming both a hostile conference committee and a presidential veto (Clymer 1999).

In 1980 Kennedy denounced a plebiscite scheduled by Pinochet and called for the administration to support OAS and UN actions condemning the plebiscite ("Kennedy, 40 Congressmen Call Chile's Vote a Fraud" 1980, § A, 26). The next year the Reagan administration tried to relax the restrictions on relations with Chile, including the ban on military sales. Behind the scenes, Kennedy worked out a deal to require presidential certification of significant progress on human rights to allow military aid. In 1986, as pressure again built to relax constraints on the relationship between the United States and Chile, Kennedy visited Chile to highlight Pinochet's human rights record. A Chilean plebiscite in 1988 chose civilian over military rule, and when Pinochet stepped down in 1990 Kennedy was in Santiago for the ceremony (Clymer 1999).

A third and final illustration of Kennedy's entrepreneurship is provided by his efforts on South Africa in the 1980s. In 1984 he had lunch with Bishop Desmond Tutu, who told him that "the world will not pay attention until someone like you comes to South Africa and brings the cameras and the spotlights with you" (Clymer 1999, 363). In January 1985 Kennedy did that, after a Christmas visit to Ethiopia and the Sudan working in the refugee shelters. After seeing apartheid in person, he told South Africa's foreign minister Pik Botha to expect congressional action against South Africa. As the administration official Chet Crocker (1992, 259–60) recalled, Kennedy was "first out of the blocks" and had a powerful impact on the agenda. Almost immediately after he returned home, Kennedy and Lowell Weicker (R-Conn.) introduced their sanctions bill and held a press conference to explain and publicize the effort. Their bill prohibited the extension of credit to the South African government, the sale of computers, new investment, and the import of the South African coins known as krugerrands. Kennedy also offered a nonbinding resolution condemning apartheid, which passed 89–4. Both he and Weicker testified at hearings before the Banking and Foreign Relations committee on their bill (Clymer 1999).

As in previous efforts, Kennedy took his case directly to the public. His speech in January 1985 to the Combined Chambers of Commerce in Johannesburg calling for an end to apartheid was edited and reprinted in the *Washington Quarterly* (Kennedy 1985c). In an article in *Ebony* (Kennedy 1985b) Kennedy further pressed for sanctions. In *Africa Report* he called for a more aggressive United States policy against apartheid (Kennedy 1985a). In August, Kennedy participated in a written "debate" with others—including the assistant secretary of state for African affairs Chet Crocker—in which he pressed for sanctions (Foltz, Crocker, Kennedy, Marzullo, Foisie, and Parker 1985). He and his staff met almost weekly with various groups supporting sanctions (Clymer 1999).

Kennedy's own bill was defeated in the Foreign Relations Committee, but he worked closely with others, including his friend Christopher Dodd, to develop proposals that did pass and included many if not most of Kennedy's provisions. According to Crocker, Kennedy was one of a group of influential members that included Dodd, Weicker, and the Republican senators Richard Lugar (Ind.), chairman of the Foreign Relations Committee, and Nancy Kassebaum (Kan.) whose actions shaped the sanctions efforts (Crocker 1992, chap. 11). On the floor, Kennedy, Lugar, and others reached a deal to vote on a somewhat weakened bill, which passed 80–12. Between passage and the conference with the House, the Reagan administration attempted to preempt the legislation with an executive order incorporating many of the sanctions. When Kennedy and other sanctions supporters attempted to bring the conference report up for a vote, they failed several times and were eventually blocked by a procedural tactic. Although the year ended without congressional sanctions legislation, sanctions were enacted by executive order in an attempt to prevent just such congressional action — a clear case of (belated) "anticipated reaction" (Treverton and Varley 1992).

The pro-sanctions entrepreneurs were far from finished, however. In 1986 Kennedy, Weicker, and Representative William Gray (D-Pa.) introduced new legislation to extend sanctions. The House went further and voted for a full trade embargo, which Kennedy immediately introduced in the Senate as his own bill (Clymer 1999). While Kennedy pressed for sweeping sanctions legislation, Kassebaum arranged a meeting with President Reagan in which she warned him that he had only a few weeks before he would lose the ability to influence the actions of Congress (Crocker 1992, 304–5). Seeking to define the problem, in July Kennedy wrote an aggressive opinion piece for the *New York Times* (Kennedy 1986d), in which he criticized Reagan's defense of the minority regime. The same day he and Weicker held a forum on South Africa (Clymer 1999), and the next day Kennedy testified before the Foreign Relations Committee, stating "Congress must act to put the United States back on the right side of history and human rights" (Kennedy 1986b, 37).

Kennedy then crafted a bill that could pass both the Senate and the House. When the White House approached Lugar to solicit his assistance in countering the sanctions movement, Lugar declined, and "told the administration that it had forfeited the opportunity to lead on South Africa" (Crocker 1992, 327). Kennedy's measure received overwhelming support, and when it passed both houses President Reagan vetoed it. In response, the House voted to override the veto, and after an impassioned plea on the chamber floor by Kennedy, the Senate followed: the Comprehensive Anti-Apartheid Act of 1986 was thus enacted into law.[5] In 1990 the African National Congress leader Nelson Mandela was freed by the regime, and in 1994 South Africa elected him as president in free and fair elections.

In summary, Kennedy used all four avenues of influence. He introduced legislation (direct legislative), held hearings and issued reports (indirect legislative), traveled abroad and met with foreign leaders (direct nonlegislative), and aggressively used the media to promote his agenda (indirect nonlegislative). His policy impacts were found in helping to end the Vietnam War, linking military security assistance to El Salvador to human rights progress, shifting the ABM system from urban areas to protection of missile sites, ensuring a congressional role in approving arms transfers, passing the nuclear freeze resolution, getting increased United States support for refugees worldwide, ending United States aid to Pinochet's regime in Chile, and enacting South African sanctions.

James Wright: Taking the Lead for Peace and Prosperity

Jim Wright was born in Fort Worth in 1921. Educated in public schools in Fort Worth and Dallas, he attended Weatherford College and the University of Texas. In December 1941 Wright withdrew from the University of Texas and enlisted in the Army Air Corps, later winning the Distinguished Flying Cross for combat duty in the South Pacific. After the war he combined a business career with a political one. He served in the Texas State House of Representatives from 1947 to 1949, was mayor of Weatherford from 1950 to 1954 (and president of the League of Texas Municipalities in 1953), and was elected to the U.S. House of Representatives in 1954. In the House he rose through the Democratic Party ranks, serving as House majority leader from 1977 to 1986 and then as speaker from 1987 until his resignation in 1989 (*Congressional Biographical Directory* 2001).

As an elected leader of the House, Wright chose to respond to a variety of events. For example, the "Koreagate" scandal of 1978 involving illegal campaign contributions by South Korean interests prompted several initiatives. Wright introduced a nonbinding resolution postponing all nonmilitary aid to South Korea until its regime allowed its former ambassador to the United States to be questioned under oath. He later introduced a successful floor amendment to cut off aid to South Korea under the Food for Peace program (Russell 1978). Wright was also one of the prominent supporters of a bill making it illegal to reveal the names of intelligence operatives working abroad (Lardner 1980). Finally during a visit to Moscow in 1987, he proposed that the United States and the Soviet Union mount a joint humanitarian relief operation in Mozambique. President Gorbachev reacted positively to this proposal, but the Reagan administration rejected it (Ottaway 1987b). Wright also pushed the Soviets on human rights. On the day Gorbachev arrived in Washington for a summit conference, Wright addressed 200,000 people in Washington who were protesting the treatment of Soviet Jews (Torry and Mintz 1987). The next day Wright pressed Gorbachev on human rights and regional issues during a meeting at the Soviet Embassy (Oberdorfer and Cannon 1987). Beyond these entrepreneurial acts, Wright's personal initiatives can be grouped under two broad themes.

Theme 1: Improving Latin American lives.   Wright entered Congress in 1955 feeling that the "United States had not paid sufficient attention to the developing world" (Wright 2001). Family history turned his focus to Latin America. His grandmother ran a railroad company store on the border between the United States and Mexico and taught him to respect Latin Americans (Wright 1993). His father commanded a National Guard unit federalized to protect the border from Pancho Villa's troops but still sympathized with the goals of Mexican progressives. In 1937 Wright visited the Pan-American Exposition in Dallas, where he discovered a new set of Latin American heroes (Bolívar, San Martín, Hidalgo, Juárez, et al.). Throughout his youth he traveled to Mexico often (Wright 1993).

Once in Congress, Wright took Spanish classes at the Foreign Service Institute and successfully sought assignment to the delegation from Congress that met annually with Mexican legislators. He later went on to chair the delegation. In 1969 he went to the Mexicali valley to see firsthand the damage done by pollution flowing from the United States into the Colorado River. After that visit he and Morris Udall (D-Ariz.) met with President Nixon to press for pollution controls. These efforts led to an executive agreement in 1973 between the United States and Mexico to restrict the salinity content in the river and to the appropriation of $280 million to implement that agreement. Across his legislative career Wright made over forty trips to Latin America, visited every Central American country, and met six Mexican presidents (Wright 1993; Wright 2001).

Wright's greatest foreign policy accomplishment developed out of his personal intervention in a Central American peace plan in the 1980s. Although initially suspicious of the Sandinista movement in Nicaragua (Goshko 1978), his position regarding Nicaragua began to change. By 1983 Wright was one of Representative Boland's key supporters in the effort to stop United States support for the contras, who were trying to overthrow the Nicaraguan Sandinista regime. At that time Wright told a contra leader that the United States should not be funding the invasion of Nicaragua (Derian 1983). In a closed session he told the House Foreign Affairs Committee that covert operations in Nicaragua should be shut down (Geyelin 1983). In addition, on the House floor he advocated diplomatic alternatives to force in Central America and introduced a successful floor amendment designed to move United States policy in a different direction by instructing the president to seek diplomatic intervention in Central America by the Organization of American States (*Congressional Quarterly Almanac* 1983). As Wright characterized it, "Everyone with whom we talked believed . . . that a show of friendship by the United States would influence political developments for the better" (quoted in Rodman 1994, 242–43).

Wright's efforts to redirect United States policy took a number of forms. In 1984 he wrote directly to President Daniel Ortega of Nicaragua asking for free and fair elections there (Wright 1993). He and Senator William Roth (R-Del.) subsequently led a bipartisan United States delegation to monitor those elections (McCartney 1984). After revelations that the United States had covertly mined Nicaraguan harbors, Wright made a public statement predicting that the House would stop funding all covert operations in Nicaragua (Democrats 1984). Also in 1984, he sent a letter to the Sandinista leadership urging them to allow the contras to participate in the Nicaraguan political process ("That 'Dear Commandante' Letter" 1984).

Wright also tried to persuade President Reagan. In 1985 he wrote him a letter warning that war games near the Nicaraguan border in Honduras could lead to a military conflict between the United States and Nicaragua (*Congressional Quarterly Almanac* 1985). When the Iran-contra scandal broke, he told Reagan in a White House meeting in November 1986 that "none of us get pleasure from the embarrassment" of the United States government, but he urged the president to fully inform Congress of covert operations as the law required (Huffman 1987, § A, 1). He issued a press statement alleging that the president had ordered the director of central intelligence, William Casey, not to inform Congress of the weapons sales to Iran in contravention of federal law, and insisting: "We have got to have assurances the law is obeyed, and the president has to be told he cannot selectively comply" (Pincus and Doder 1986, § A, 1).

In 1987 Wright used a variety of tactics to keep the pressure on the White House, calling for an end to illegal covert operations in Nicaragua and a moratorium on aid to the contras. He went public to alter the climate of opinion, giving the Democratic response to the president's State of the Union address (Dewar and Walsh 1987) and making a series of public statements to the press (Dewar 1987a; Walsh 1987; Dewar 1987b). He worked within the chamber as well, testifying before the subcommittee on legislation of the House Permanent Select Committee on Intelligence to endorse changes that would make it harder for the president to avoid notifying Congress of covert operations (Ottaway 1987a).

In August Reagan asked Wright to join him in a joint diplomatic effort to find a peaceful solution for Nicaragua. Since the president made the overture, Wright's initial participation in the peace plan was not an entrepreneurial act. Yet the president and other top administration officials fully expected the talks to fail and wanted to use that failure as a justification for more aid to the contras (*Congressional Quarterly Almanac* 1987; Wright 1993). When Wright chose thereafter to continue his own efforts to help broker a Central American peace, his actions became entrepreneurial.

Wright used the power of his office to support the efforts of President Oscar Arias of Costa Rica and the four other Central American presidents to negotiate a peace in the Nicaraguan civil war.[6] He sent an aide to the Contadora talks that produced the Central American peace accord known as the Arias plan (McGrory 1987), and he made many public statements to the press supporting the Arias plan and denouncing the Reagan administration for actively opposing it (Goshko 1987c; Goshko 1987f). When President Arias came to Washington, administration officials initially declined to meet with him and objected to Wright's efforts to have Arias officially speak to a joint session of Congress. So Wright invited Arias to give an "unofficial" address to the House and Senate before it convened for the day's business. Most members of Congress attended the speech, and even some Republican supporters of the contras (like Newt Gingrich) were moved by Arias's address. After the address Wright met with Arias privately for an hour (Goshko 1987c).

Wright's efforts on behalf of the Arias peace plan continued, in newspaper op-ed pieces (Wright 1987), in an appearance on ABC television (*Congressional Quarterly Almanac* 1987), and in other press interviews and public statements (*Congressional Quarterly Almanac* 1988; Goshko 1987a). In November 1987 Wright met three times in as many days with President Ortega and Cardinal Miguel Obando y Bravo, who was acting as an intermediary between the contras and Sandinista leaders. These meetings were harshly criticized by administration officials, who had refused for two years to meet with any Sandinista representatives (*Congressional Quarterly Almanac* 1987). After the White House accused the speaker of diplomatic meddling, Wright demanded a meeting with the president and received it on 16 November (*Congressional Quarterly Almanac* 1987).

After the meeting Wright offered a public statement: "I hope the administration will understand that I am not trying to usurp its role and that I am not under any illusion that I am a diplomat, [but as speaker] if friends of mine from Central America or otherwise come and want to see me, the door's always open" (*Congressional Quarterly Almanac* 1987, 130). He concluded by saying that some officials in the Reagan administration "don't want a negotiated settlement" (*Congressional Quarterly Almanac* 1987, 130) and "are literally terrified that peace might break out" (Goshko 1987e, § A, 1). Scrambling to control the resulting public relations damage, Secretary of State Shultz sought a meeting in Wright's office to patch up their relationship. After the meeting both men told reporters they focused on areas of agreement regarding the implementation of the Arias plan (Pianin 1987). By this point administration officials were responding to Wright's agenda, not the other way round (Geyelin 1987).

According to Peter Rodman, a former official in the Reagan administration, Wright's efforts were effective. As he recalled, "The most serious effect of Wright-Reagan however, was on our Central American allies, who . . . were panicked into an immediate endorsement of the Arias Plan— exactly the opposite of the administration's intentions. . . . Over the next two years, the Central Americans hammered out details of the Arias Plan" and administration hopes of providing military aid to the contras were dashed (Rodman 1994, 432–33). Secretary Shultz (1993, 958–68) also conceded that Wright's peace efforts prompted important breakthroughs and undercut militarists on all sides, although he recalled the "meddling" with less-than-positive comments.

Pressure from Speaker Wright continued in 1988. After the administration's request for military aid to the contras was defeated, Wright wrote to Reagan and Shultz inviting their ideas for a plan for humanitarian aid to the contras, but the administration did not respond. Wright therefore introduced a floor amendment to provide humanitarian aid, spoke on its behalf, and saw it pass the House (*Congressional Quarterly Almanac* 1988). He followed the vote by meeting with contra leaders whom he warned not to resume the civil war after the temporary ceasefire. Wright again endorsed the Arias peace plan (Pichirallo 1988). He followed that meeting by holding one with the Nicaraguan vice president, repeating the same message (Goshko 1988).

Wright's personal involvement in the Central American peace process ended in September 1988. At that time he set off a controversy when in one of his daily press conferences he accused the CIA of trying to create disturbances in Nicaragua that would lead to the undermining of the Arias peace plan. The controversy centered on whether Wright violated House rules by leaking classified information (*Congressional Quarterly Almanac* 1988). At his next two press conferences, Wright stressed that his statements were based on publicly available information and showed reporters the relevant news clippings (*Congressional Quarterly Almanac* 1988). However, he stepped away from the issue at that point.

Theme 2: Promoting American economic interests.   Wright was a proponent of a strong national defense and, not surprisingly, a champion for weapons systems made in or near his district. In 1981 the Reagan administration announced that it would stop buying A-7 attack aircraft made by the LTV Aerospace Corporation in the Dallas–Fort Worth area. Wright restored funding for the last of 42 A-7s scheduled to be sold to the Air National Guard (Wilson 1981; *Congressional Quarterly Almanac* 1981). In 1982 Wright introduced a successful amendment to prohibit the United States military from becoming dependent on a single foreign source for a defense item. The issue arose when the Defense Department chose to buy a type of radio exclusively from an Israeli corporation rather than from the E-Systems Corporation, which was based in Dallas (Geyelin 1982).

In the mid-1980s the size of the United States trade deficit, and particularly the deficit with Japan, attracted Wright's attention. He created a Democratic Party Task Force on Trade in 1985 to hold hearings around the country and propose legislative initiatives to reduce the deficit. And he told the Japanese trade envoy, in the United States for an official visit, that the United States would no longer tolerate unfair trade practices (Auerbach 1985).

When 1986 ended without significant action on the trade deficit, Wright told the Democratic Leadership Council that the twin issues of the trade deficit and improving American competitiveness would be top priorities for 1987 (Taylor 1986). In January he hosted a meeting of government, industry, labor, and academic leaders to address these issues, but administration officials declined invitations to attend (Kenworthy 1987). He raised these issues again in the Democratic response to the president's State of the Union Address (Dewar and Walsh 1987). Wright then became one of the prime movers behind an amendment sponsored by Richard Gephardt (D-Mo.) calling for countries that had large trade imbalances with the United States to reduce those imbalances by 10% per year or face trade retaliation (Auerbach 1987b). Throughout the rest of the year Wright made many public statements on behalf of the Gephardt amendment (Cannon and Auerbach 1987; Auerbach 1987a; Auerbach 1987c; Auerbach 1987d).

The amendment passed the House but not the Senate. Despite Wright's meetings with the AFL-CIO Executive Council, with the chairpersons of all House committees involved in the trade bill, and with White House officials in an effort to get a favorable conference committee decision (Swoboda 1988), the conferees dropped the Gephardt amendment from the trade bill (Auerbach and Burgess 1988). However, the impact of their efforts prompted the Reagan administration to change its behavior and take action on unfair trade practices (Rowan 1988).

In summary, like Church and Kennedy, Jim Wright used all four entrepreneurial approaches. He introduced legislation (direct legislative); pressed for oversight legislation of covert actions (indirect legislative); held task force hearings, testified before House committees, and routinely corresponded with and met with administration officials including the president (direct nonlegislative); and traveled extensively abroad, met with foreign leaders both here and abroad, and aggressively used the media to promote his agenda (indirect nonlegislative).

Wright's policy impacts were notable. While early in his career he was able to help improve relations with Mexico by focusing on border water issues, late in his career he nurtured to fruition a Central American peace plan that ended a civil war in Nicaragua against the wishes of the Reagan administration. His efforts also forced the Reagan administration to "buy American" when it came to defense systems and to address the nation's trade deficit.

Forcing the end to the Vietnam War was the high point of congressional foreign policy assertiveness during the period 1968–89. Yet congressional assertiveness during this period went beyond ending the war, and congressional foreign policy entrepreneurs were heavily involved in pressing Congress to use virtually all its foreign policy powers. They made it more politically difficult for presidents to begin new wars; focused national attention on controversial covert intelligence activities and forced more congressional control of those agencies; influenced who would be appointed secretary of defense; forced important changes in the country's antiballistic missile defense system, along with increasing pressures to limit the number of United States nuclear warheads; promoted a focus on human rights and humanitarian concerns, culminating in economic sanctions on South Africa that were the tipping point in leading to the abandonment of apartheid; reversed administration policy by promoting a diplomatic end to the Nicaraguan civil war; and contravened the administration's free trade orientation by protecting United States jobs. The policy-making influence of congressional foreign policy entrepreneurs from 1968 to 1989 cannot be denied.

6

CONTENDING WITH THE THAW

ENTREPRENEURSHIP IN THE POST–COLD WAR PERIOD,
1990–2000

When President Bill Clinton muttered, "Gosh, I miss the Cold War," he was specifically referring to the relative ease with which Cold War presidents were able to mobilize public support for their foreign policy ventures. He might also, however, have had his mind on the U.S. Congress, where MCs were responding to the new post–Cold War world with increasing assertiveness and partisanship. As we have seen, congressional foreign policy entrepreneurs asserted themselves strenuously during the Cold War Dissensus, but the absence of the Soviet threat and the increasing importance of intermestic concerns made the post–Cold War period a virtual invitation for MCs to enter foreign policy debates. As the cliché states, Congress abhors a vacuum, and the opportunity to fill the vacuum left by the end of the Cold War's guideposts was compelling. For entrepreneurs, the opportunity presented by the changing problem context (or stream) was especially significant. How did entrepreneurs exploit this policy environment?

A Quantitative Overview

Just under 20% of the entrepreneurship of the period 1946–2000 came during the post–Cold War years, as table 24 shows. This volume is roughly proportional to the years of the post–World War II era occupied by the post–Cold War years. As in the Cold War years of 1946–89 (Consensus and Dissensus), most entrepreneurship occurred in the Senate. However, the

Table 24: Foreign Policy Entrepreneurship by Chamber,
Party Characteristics, and Era

	Post–Cold War, 1990–2000	Cold War, 1946–1989	Total, 1946–2000
Senate	51.8%	61.7%	59.8%
	(260)	(1,307)	(1,567)
House	48.2%	38.3 %	40.2%
	(242)	(812)	(1,054)
Member of majority party	71.1%	61.7%	63.5%
	(357)	(1,307)	(1,664)
Member of opposition party	73.1%	63.6%	65.4%
	(367)	(1,347)	(1,714)
Total	(502)	(2,119)	(2,621)

difference between House and Senate entrepreneurship narrowed from the preceding forty years to the point that entrepreneurship was almost as likely from the House as the Senate. At the same time, entrepreneurship in the post–Cold War period became increasingly tied to the majority party, continuing a trend across the Cold War years. Similarly, and significantly, entrepreneurship was increasingly partisan, coming from members of the party opposing the president. In short, entrepreneurship after the Cold War kept pace with the general politicization of foreign policy observed by others (e.g. Carter and Scott 2004; DeLaet and Scott 2006).

After the Cold War ended, the agenda of congressional foreign policy entrepreneurs shifted somewhat from the Cold War and, especially, from the post-Vietnam years. As table 25 shows, political-diplomatic and economic-developmental issues gathered increased attention from entrepreneurial MCs (about 10% more in the first category, and 25% more in the second), while attention to military-security issues fell noticeably. Still, military-security issues remained the category to which entrepreneurs devoted the most attention. Significantly, as table 25 also shows, entrepreneurs were much more likely to concern themselves with strategic issues than with structural issues (for both general foreign policy and the defense policy subset), and this emphasis was stronger after the Cold War than during it. Hence, MCs were not increasing their foreign policy engagement

Table 25: Foreign Policy Entrepreneurship by Issue Category and Era

	Post–Cold War, 1990–2000	Cold War, 1946–1989	Total, 1946–2000
Political-diplomatic	20.7% (104)	18.6% (395)	19.0% (499)
Military-security	46.8% (235)	53.8% (1,141)	52.5% (1,376)
Economic-development	31.1% (156)	25.3% (537)	26.4% (693)
Cultural-status	1.4% (7)	2.2% (46)	2.0% (53)
Total	19.2% (502)	80.8% (2,119)	100% (2,621)
Structural policy	40.4% (203)	45.4% (961)	44.4% (1,164)
Strategic policy	59.6% (299)	54.6% (1,158)	55.6% (1,457)
Defense structural policy	27.7% (57)	32.4% (275)	31.5% (332)
Defense strategic policy	72.3% (149)	67.6% (574)	68.5% (723)

Table 26: Entrepreneurship and Committee Assignments by Era

Member	Post–Cold War, 1990–2000	Cold War, 1946–1989	Total, 1946–2000
Traditional foreign policy committees	54.4% (273)	53.6% (1,136)	53.8% (1,409)
Other committees	45.6% (229)	46.4% (983)	46.2% (1,212)
Total	19.2% (502)	80.8% (2,119)	100% (2,621)

on what is typically characterized as narrow, parochial concerns (e.g. defense procurement), but on broader questions of policy and strategy.

Table 26 shows that post–Cold War entrepreneurship arising from members on the traditional foreign policy committees was consistent with the average during the Cold War years. However, the early Cold War (1946–67) saw much less use of this access point (43.3%) than later Cold War years (1968–89), during which it surged (57.5%). Hence in the post–Cold War

Table 27: Access Points and Activities Used by
Year and Era

Year	Number of Access Points Used	Number of Activities Used
1992	5	8
1994	5	8
1996	5	6
1997	6	5
1999	7	5
Average, Post–Cold War	5.6	6.4
1946	3	3
1950	5	8
1954	4	5
1958	5	4
1959	4	4
1960	3	5
1961	4	5
1962	5	8
1963	4	6
1965	6	9
1968	5	9
1970	6	8
1972	4	7
1973	5	7
1975	6	9
1979	6	7
1984	5	7
1985	6	7
1986	6	9
1987	7	10
Average, Remaining Post–World War II	5.0	6.9

years MCS continued to use the traditional foreign policy committees for a majority of their efforts. Continuing a trend started after Vietnam, the most active entrepreneurs sought out the traditional foreign policy committees and, using that platform and the expertise gained from it, challenged presidential foreign policy agendas.

Table 27 shows that MCS changed tactics to engage in their entrepreneurship. Compared to the Cold War years, MCS used more access points to pursue their entrepreneurial activity, and the range of means used to push their foreign policy agendas was nearly as varied as in the post-Vietnam era. Hence the structural changes of the post-Vietnam Congresses continued to be felt in the post–Cold War years (e.g. Rohde 2005). In particular, more subcommittees meant more access points for entrepreneurs, whether as subcommittee members or chairpersons. More subcommittee power meant that it was harder for chairpersons of standing committees to limit what entrepreneurial MCS on those subcommittees could do, which meant that more means were available to those MCS.

Table 28 further articulates this last point. During the post–Cold War years entrepreneurs relied substantially on direct legislative avenues, more so than during the Cold War, and especially more than during the Cold War Dissensus (1968–89). As in previous years, the combination of direct legislative avenues and indirect nonlegislative routes accounted for about 90% of the ways that MCS pursued their policy agendas. Indirect legislative

Table 28: Entrepreneurial Uses of Avenues of Influence by Era

	Post–Cold War, 1990–2000	Cold War, 1946–1989	Total, 1946–2000
Direct-legislative	68.7% (345)	65.1% (1,380)	65.8% (1,725)
Indirect-legislative	4.0% (20)	2.5% (52)	2.7% (72)
Direct-nonlegislative	5.0% (25)	7.0% (148)	6.6% (173)
Indirect-nonlegislative	22.3% (112)	25.4% (539)	24.8% (651)
Total	19.2% (502)	80.8% (2,119)	100% (2,621)

methods, which include resolutions, appointments, and procedural legislation, were used somewhat more than before.

Entrepreneurs in the Post–Cold War

But were they successful? No observer need look too hard to find examples of congressional policy entrepreneurs who put their stamp on United States foreign policy. In the post–Cold War years entrepreneurs grappled with the need to find direction in an environment where the familiar Cold War signposts no longer applied, which led MCs to pursue a variety of concerns. As the following examples indicate, many of their efforts has significant consequences for key issues shaping the post–Cold War world.[1]

Some MCs focused on the legacies of the Cold War and made major contributions to new foreign policy directions. For example, as the Cold War ended and the Soviet Union dissolved, it became critical to ensure the nuclear weapons of the former Soviet Union did not end up in the wrong hands. In 1991 and 1992, two entrepreneurs—Senators Sam Nunn (D-Ga.) and Richard Lugar (R-Ind.)—pushed for an innovative program eventually known as the Nunn-Lugar Cooperative Threat Reduction Program. This program authorized United States funds to support unemployed and underemployed weapons scientists in the former Soviet Union, as well as to secure and eliminate nuclear weapons. It became law in 1992, and despite some neglect from Presidents Bush, Clinton, and Bush it continues to be a critical initiative in combating the proliferation of nuclear weapons. By mid-2007 the Nunn-Lugar initiative had not only built a new factory to handle the destruction of approximately two million nerve gas artillery shells but had also "deactivated 6,982 nuclear warheads, destroyed 653 intercontinental ballistic missiles and chopped up 30 nuclear submarines" (Birch 2007, § A, 16).

Others were instrumental in redefining and redirecting United States foreign policy toward the countries of the former Soviet Union, building on the aid program established in 1989 for Eastern Europe and noted in chapter 5. In August 1991 Dick Gephardt (D-Mo.), Les Aspin (D-Wis.), Sam Nunn (D-Ga.), David Boren (D-Okla.), and Richard Lugar (R-Ind.) pressed for aggressive new policies to aid the newly independent states.[2] While the administration delayed, Dante Fascell (D-Fla.) introduced the Transition to Democracy in the Former Soviet Union Act of 1992, which proposed assistance packages of $150 million in 1992 and $350 million in 1993 (Tarnoff 2004). As Secretary of State James Baker later acknowledged (James Baker 1995), these efforts spurred the administration to offer the Freedom Support Act in April 1992. The final bill, passed and signed in the fall of 1992, was a mix of the congressional language proposed by Fascell and the administration proposal developed in the State Department (James Baker 1995; Tarnoff 2004).

During the Clinton administration, enlargement of the NATO alliance was spurred in part by the efforts of congressional foreign policy entrepreneurs. According to Goldgeier (1999, 35), early on "the most outspoken official voice in Washington in favor of enlargement . . . was Senator Lugar, who was one of the most intellectually respected members of Congress on foreign affairs." Influenced by a study on the topic by the RAND Corporation, Lugar gave a forceful speech on 24 June 1993 arguing for NATO expansion: "It is now time for a new mission and new membership" (Goldgeier 1999, 35). Just days before Lugar had urged that Poland, Hungary, and the Czech Republic be considered for immediate inclusion in NATO.

Lugar was not alone. When the Clinton administration was slow to act, in part because of bureaucratic disagreements over the idea, in early 1994 the Republicans Benjamin Gilman (N.Y.) and Henry Hyde (Ill.) introduced legislation in the House to enlarge NATO, while Paul Simon (D-Ill.) and Hank Brown (R-Colo.) did the same in the Senate. Gilman proposed the "NATO Expansion Act of 1994, a bill providing a sense of Congress that Poland, Hungary, the Czech Republic and Slovakia should enter NATO as full members by January 10, 1999" and wrote a letter to his colleagues on 22 April arguing for the initiative (Goldgeier 1999, 80). In May, Hyde introduced the NATO Revitalization Act, which called for benchmarks and a timetable for new members to join NATO. In January the Senate voted 94–3 on a resolution supporting admission of new countries, while Lugar pushed for abandonment of the "policy for postponement" and insisted that "the West must make plain to Russia that we are now discussing how to expand NATO, not whether to expand it. The best way to communicate that message is by agreeing on a schedule for associate and then full membership for the Visegrad states" (Goldgeier 1999, 81). Several weeks later Hank Brown and Paul Simon introduced a version of the NATO Participation Act, which passed the Senate overwhelmingly in July.

In the summer of 1994 Dick Armey (R-Texas) worked with Gilman and Hyde to develop NATO enlargement language in the National Security Revitalization Act, part of the Republican Party's "Contract with America." Although the administration opposed it, the House passed this bill in February 1995, after the Republican midterm election victories in 1994 (Goldgeier 1998, 82–83). All this helped to overcome resistance from the administration and led to more aggressive efforts to enlarge NATO. By 1996, with Robert Dole (R-Kan.) seeking to outflank Clinton on the issue as part of his presidential campaign, the administration finally moved more aggressively, especially after Congress overwhelmingly passed the NATO Enlargement Facilitation Act in mid-1996. By the end of the decade NATO was expanded to admit new members, and Congress, the NATO Observer Group of the Senate, and individuals such as Jesse Helms (R-N.C.), Joseph Biden (D-Del), and Lugar were important in the negotiations and endgame as well.

In 1993 Biden focused his foreign policy attention on Cold War legacies. Not only did he take the lead in defending the continuation of Radio Free Europe and Radio Liberty, he also proposed to establish Radio Free Asia to expand the operations of the network into a new arena. He was successful, and with these broadcast programs preserved, their operations became the core of continued information campaigns, which were expanded later in the wake of the September 11 attacks to form an important component of the war against terrorism.

After a scandal erupted when the intelligence analyst Aldrich Ames was unmasked as a spy, Senator John Warner (R-Va.) grew frustrated with the failure of the administration to reform the intelligence community to meet post–Cold War threats and needs. He introduced legislation and built support to establish a commission that would study the roles and capabilities of the intelligence community and recommend changes. His proposal was incorporated into the Intelligence Authorization Act of 1995; the commission completed its work in early 1996 and in its report, "Preparing for the 21st Century: An Appraisal of U.S. Intelligence," recommended reforms of the intelligence community, management of the CIA, covert action, economic intelligence, intelligence support to policy makers and military operations, space reconnaissance, "right-sizing" of intelligence agencies, and oversight of intelligence. Many of the commission's recommendations foreshadowed those of the more recent 9/11 Commission and thus laid the foundation for the intelligence reforms that reshaped the intelligence community in 2004.

A group of entrepreneurs applied substantial pressure on the Clinton administration to intervene in Haiti in support of the democratically elected government of Jean-Bertrand Aristide, which had been deposed by the military. Senators Dodd, Tom Harkin (D-Iowa), Russ Feingold (D-Wis.), Kerry, Carol Moseley Braun (D-Ill.), and Paul Wellstone (D-Minn.) introduced the Haitian Restoration of Democracy Act, which triggered sanctions and helped pave the way to intervention. In 1993 and 1995 Senators Kerry and John McCain (R-Ariz.) were the prime movers behind the recognition of Vietnam, advocating for the policy shift, introducing legislation, and providing political cover for the administration (e.g. Klein 2002, 60). That same year, the entrepreneurs Bob Dole (R-Kan.) and Joe Lieberman (D-Conn.) grew impatient with the unwillingness of the Clinton administration to act aggressively in the escalating conflict in Bosnia. Employing a range of tactics to pressure the administration, they capped their efforts by introducing legislation to lift the embargo on weapons to the Bosnian Muslims. According to the former NSC staff member Ivo Daalder and the diplomat Richard Holbrooke, this pressure galvanized the administration into action and, with the Bosnian Croatian victories on the battlefield, helped produce the Dayton Peace Accords of 1995 (Daalder 2000; Holbrooke 1998).

Some entrepreneurs sought to provide leadership in addressing the challenges of a globalizing economy. For example, Representative Jim Leach (R-Iowa) responded to the Mexican peso crisis in 1994–95 by devising a solution and then providing it to the administration without asking that his role be recognized. He initially proposed a debt relief plan in Congress, but it failed to gain the support of House Speaker Newt Gingrich (R-Ga.) and was shelved. Leach then went to Treasury Secretary Lawrence Summers with the plan, which Summers embraced and the administration implemented without going to Congress. Summers asked Leach not to reveal his role, for fear that his doing so would erode support for the idea within the administration, so Leach remained quiet while the bailout proceeded.[3] The plan stopped the run on the peso, and the bailout loans were paid back early and with interest.

Senator Chuck Hagel (R-Neb.) played a key role in 1999 in efforts to reform the use of sanctions as a foreign policy tool, limit the application of unilateral sanctions, and exempt agricultural and humanitarian items such as medicines from sanctions. Joined by the entrepreneurs Doug Bereuter (R-Neb.), Lee Hamilton (D-Ind.), and Phil Crane (R-Ill.) in the House, and Lugar and Bob Kerrey (D-Neb.) in the Senate, this effort passed, prompting the Clinton administration to preempt further congressional action by announcing a series of modifications and changes to its use of sanctions.

Entrepreneurs also took the lead in addressing emerging security problems such as the spread of weapons of mass destruction to countries like Libya and Iran. In 1996 two entrepreneurs, Alfonse D'Amato (R-N.Y.) and Ted Kennedy (D-Mass.), led the way to the Iran and Libya Sanctions Act, which imposed sanctions against foreign companies (and their home countries) that engaged in certain economic transactions with the two countries. The following year, the entrepreneurs Curt Weldon (R-Pa.) and Gilman in the House and Lieberman in the Senate followed by pushing the Iran Missile Proliferation Sanctions Act, in an effort to prevent foreign companies (chiefly Russian) from helping Iran to develop and build new ballistic missiles. The initiative passed the House and Senate overwhelmingly but was vetoed by President Clinton in 1998. Just as Congress was preparing for an override vote, which appeared likely to succeed, the administration announced punishments for the Russian firms in question, and President Yeltsin's government initiated an investigation into the activities of the suspect firms.

These examples show the variety of issues on which post–Cold War congressional foreign policy entrepreneurs had impact. Their concerted efforts spanned the avenues of influence available to MCs—from the obvious direct legislative routes to those that are indirect and nonlegislative. These entrepreneurs made important contributions to shaping United States approaches to the changing circumstances and demands of the post–Cold War world. They were critical to forging United States approaches to Russia, the newly independent states of the Soviet Union, Eastern Europe, NATO, and China. Some were aggressive in directing United States policy toward the developing world in places such as Haiti, Cuba, and Nicaragua. Entrepreneurs in Congress shaped the machinery of American foreign policy institutions, as well as relations with the UN and other international organizations. To highlight their impact, as well as the range of activities in which entrepreneurs engage, the following case studies illustrate the activities of three particularly aggressive entrepreneurs: Curt

Weldon (R-Pa.), Chris Smith (R-N.J.), and the most prolific foreign policy entrepreneur in the post–World War II period, Jesse Helms (R-N.C.).

Curt Weldon: Direct Action to Drive the Agenda

Curt Weldon was born in Marcus Hook, Pennsylvania, in 1947. After taking four years of Russian language in high school he became the first graduate of West Chester State College with an education degree and a major in Russian area studies (Weldon 2002a). After graduation he served the citizens of Marcus Hook first as a teacher and volunteer fire chief and later as mayor from 1977 to 1982. From 1981 to 1986 he was a county councilman for Delaware County. He ran unsuccessfully for the House of Representatives in 1984 but was elected in 1986 (*Congressional Biographical Directory* 2001). In the House he served on the Armed Services Committee (at one point known as the National Security Committee) and chaired its Military Research and Development Subcommittee; he also served on the Science Committee and the House Select Committee on U.S. National Security and Military/Commercial Concerns with the People's Republic of China (Weldon biography 2007). He was defeated for reelection in 2006.

Before entering Congress Weldon actively sought to learn more about the Soviet Union. He participated in a State Department exchange program, hosting a visiting delegation of young Russian leaders in 1985. Among the key contacts that he made in that first visit some went on to achieve prominent positions in Russian society, including a former first deputy prime minister, the director of the leading foreign policy think tank that advised President Putin and former Prime Minister Kasyanov, and the leader of the Russian cable television industry (Weldon 2002a). As Weldon puts it, "The Russians respect and like me. I've stayed in their homes. I understand Russian people and their history" (quoted in the *Washington Post*, 13 June 2000, § A, 8). In Congress Weldon pressed a wide array of foreign policy issues, including protecting the oceans from radioactive waste (*Congressional Quarterly Almanac* 1994), addressing the threat of encryption and satellite technology lost to China (Schmitt 1998), and creating a congressional caucus to promote trade and defense cooperation with Singapore (Hader 2002). He also traveled extensively abroad and in each case tried to formalize a relationship between Congress and the other country's legislative body. Formal relationships were created with the legislative bodies of Russia, Ukraine, Moldova, Uzbekistan, Turkey, and China (Weldon 2002a). Beyond these pursuits, Weldon's major entrepreneurial contributions can be grouped under five themes, often distinguished by his preference for direct action.

Theme 1: Shaping United States-Russian relations. Weldon entered office with a desire to improve relations with Russia (Weldon 2002a). Given some of the peculiarities of key Russian political figures (Yeltsin's health and questions of corruption; the presence of organized crime figures in the Duma, etc.), Weldon decided that "if Russia were going to succeed, the focus should be on institutions and not people" (Weldon 2002a). He believed that Congress needed to reach out to and strengthen the Duma and the Federation Council. This personal policy position, shaped in part by Weldon's educational background and travel to Russia, led him to engage in a series of creative entrepreneurial initiatives that shaped both the structures and substance of relations between the United States and Russia.

In the early 1990s Weldon helped to create a joint U.S.-Russian Energy Caucus to work at the parliamentary level on the changes in legislation that would be necessary to encourage western investment in Russia's oil and gas industry (Weldon 2002a). After the Republican capture of the House in November 1994, Weldon secured Speaker-elect Gingrich's approval to start a formal relationship with the Duma. The result was the bipartisan Duma-Congress Study Group, which Weldon co-chaired (Weldon 2002a). As a consequence of these formalized relationships, Weldon claimed that he had "been to Russia 29 times and [knew] every major leader in the Russian government." He also took "over 200 members of Congress to Russia or introduced them when Russians" came to America (Weldon 2002a).

Weldon's efforts to promote opportunities and structures for cooperation and communication did not end there. In 1997 he proposed a massive new exchange program for young Russians and Americans, but the Clinton administration opposed it. So in 2000 he established and funded an exchange program routed through the Library of Congress for implementation (Weldon 2002a). In that same year Weldon invited representatives from Unity, Vladimir Putin's Duma faction, to attend the Republican presidential nominating convention. In addition to contributing to the development of more mature political parties in Russia, Weldon's short-term goal was to improve the Republican Party's relations with Russia.

In 2001 Weldon sought the input of every think tank in the United States conducting programs in Russia that he could identify and assembled a forty-five-page plan titled *U.S.-Russian Partnership: A New Time, a New Beginning*. This document made 108 recommendations across 11 policy areas (agriculture, defense, economy, education and culture, energy, environment, health care, judicial and legal, local government, science, and space) intended to facilitate cooperation between the United States and Russia. After briefing top officials in the national security advisor's office and the Departments of State and Defense about these proposals, he sent copies of the document to both Presidents Bush and Putin (Weldon 2002a). During a trip on Air Force One in July, Weldon took advantage of the opportunity to press his recommendations to President Bush. Similarly, while he was in Russia in September, he briefed Russian leaders on his ideas as well (Pianin 2001). Shortly thereafter Weldon translated the document into Russian and put it up on three Russian websites. While in Moscow for the summit between Bush and Putin in May 2002, a top member of the Duma told Weldon that his document's proposals had formed the basis of the Russian side of the discussions with Bush at the summit (Weldon 2002a).

Theme 2: Seeking to end the Kosovo War. There is some evidence that one of the most dramatic benefits of Weldon's close relationship with Russian legislators, and the structures of contact and cooperation that his entrepreneurship established, may have been his largely unknown behind-the-scenes role in helping to end the NATO bombing of Yugoslavia in 1999. During the bombing he was invited by the Duma's deputy speaker to Belgrade to join Russian officials in an effort to convince President Slobodan Milosevic of Yugoslavia to accept western proposals to end the conflict. When Weldon informed Deputy Secretary of State Strobe Talbott of the invitation, he was told that the Clinton administration would not support the trip, since targets in Belgrade were currently being bombed. Weldon called off the visit to Belgrade, complaining that "this was not an attempt to end-run anyone . . . [but the White House] let a tremendous opportunity slip through its fingers" (Reuters 1999).

However, according to Weldon, Talbott told him that the administration would not object to a bipartisan delegation meeting with Russian officials as long as the meeting was in a neutral city (Weldon 2002a). Weldon assembled a delegation of eleven House members to go to Vienna (*Congressional Quarterly Almanac* 1999), where they met on 30 April and 1 May with Duma members and Dragomir Karic, a private Yugoslav citizen who had close ties to Milosevic.[4]

Before leaving for the meeting Weldon asked the director of central intelligence, George Tenet for background on Karic but was told that the agency knew very little about him. From the Army's Information Dominance Center, Weldon was able to acquire a detailed profile of Karic and information about his family's extensive banking business, his alleged ties to the Russian Mafia, and his connections to Milosevic, which included Milosevic's having lived in a house that Karic provided. Because of these connections, the Russians claimed that Karic essentially "owned" Milosevic and could "deliver" him (Weldon 2002a).[5]

According to Weldon (2002) the American and Russian legislators crafted their own proposal to end the Kosovo War. The proposal called on both sides to introduce measures in their legislatures calling for an end to NATO's bombing of Yugoslavia, withdrawal of Serbian forces from Kosovo, the introduction of an international peacekeeping force in Kosovo that included United States and NATO forces, and the termination of military activities by the Kosovo Liberation Army (Eilperin and Harris 1999). This was the first time that Russian officials appeared willing to accept a NATO presence in a Kosovo peacekeeping force (Weldon 2002a). At the meeting this proposal was faxed by Karic to Milosevic, who then invited Weldon's delegation to Belgrade to sign the agreement and pick up three United States POWs who would be released to their custody (Canadian Immigration and Refugee Board 2007). When Weldon called Undersecretary of State Thomas Pickering to ask for authorization to go to Belgrade, Pickering asked him not to do so, and Weldon agreed.[6] Instead Weldon had all eleven members of the delegation sign the agreement they had crafted, which they sent to every NATO parliament, the pope, the patriarch of the Eastern Orthodox Church, and Kofi Annan at the UN (Weldon 2002a).

Upon his return to the United States Weldon launched an aggressive campaign on behalf of his diplomatic initiative. He gave several press conferences promoting the agreement (*Congressional Quarterly Almanac* 1999; Dewar and Eilperin 1999), appeared on the CNN program *The Capital Gang* and the next day on John McLaughlin's PBS program *One on One* (Jackson 1999), and published an op-ed piece in the *Washington Post* defending his decision to work with the Russian legislative delegation to press for a resolution of the Kosovo conflict (Weldon 1999). He also met with Secretary of State Madeleine Albright, who criticized him and his delegation for meddling in foreign policy and usurping the role of the administration (and especially the State Department).

Weldon and his colleagues fought back. Several liberal Democrats who were part of the delegation angrily took Albright to task for her criticism of their efforts. After the meeting Weldon told the press that the group had not negotiated directly with a foreign country (as Dragomir Karic was not a Yugoslavian official or government employee) and that he had kept the Clinton administration constantly informed of all the group's activities: "This was not a shoot-from-the-hip approach. I have not done anything in a partisan way. They can't legitimately criticize what we've done" (Eilperin 1999, § A, 19).

During Weldon's interview with the authors (2002), it was clear he believed his delegation's efforts helped hasten the end of the war by routing a workable diplomatic formula to Milosevic through one of his trusted family friends. This formula contained a key Russian concession—the idea of NATO troops in the Kosovo peacekeeping force—that Milosevic had consistently rejected publicly. Further, that family friend—Dragomir Karic—shared a desire to end the war quickly, as his family's business and real estate holdings were being destroyed by the NATO bombing campaign, and he was in a personal and financial position to pressure Milosevic.

We may never know what made Slobodan Milosevic suddenly accept the diplomatic formula that ended the war. However, he counted on Russian support to keep NATO allies divided and NATO peacekeepers out of Kosovo. Thus a very important threshold was crossed when the Russian government changed its position on 6 May—just a few days after Weldon's private meetings—to accept the presence of NATO peacekeepers in Kosovo (Byman and Waxman 2000; Daalder and O'Hanlon 2000; Hosmer 2001). It is plausible that Weldon's intervention played some role in Russian acceptance of the notion of a NATO role in the peacekeeping force (*Independent* 1999).

Many sources agree that Dragomir Karic accompanied the Duma delegation that met with Weldon's delegation in Vienna (e.g. National Post 1999; Nicoll 1999; *Observer* 1999; Ridgeway 1999; Silverstein, Neubauer, and Cooper 2004). With his three brothers, Karic was part of "the largest private sector business empire in Yugoslavia" (Porteous 2000, 5). While some called the brothers "the Rockefellers of Serbia" (Lashmar 1999), others described Karic and his three brothers as "part of a 'kleptocracy,' in which business and political leaders jointly run the economy to their mutual benefit" (Fennell 1999). Reports from Canada indicate that the family's Karic Bank was created in 1989 with government assistance to help fund the war efforts in Croatia and Bosnia, the family made its fortune running the UN embargo against Yugoslavia, and the family bank laundered millions of dollars in illegal earnings through Russian banks (Fennell 1999).

Moreover, it is clear that ties between the Karic family and the Milosevic family were close. The eldest Karic brother, Bogoljub, was a minister without portfolio in Milosevic's regime and lived next door to him in a Belgrade suburb (Antic 2001). Bogoljub acted "as the Milosevic family banker, investing part of the family's money" while Milosevic was incarcerated in The Hague (Antic 2001). Milosevic's son Marko was a business partner with Goran Karic, a son of one of the Karic brothers (Lashmar 1999). When Milosevic's first grandson was born, twelve members of the Karic family arrived with the ultimate baby gift—"several kilos of gold" (Fennell 1999). After the end of the Kosovo war, Dragomir, Bogoljub, and other members of the Karic family were barred from entry into the European Union. Bogoljub was on the list of banned individuals as a government minister, and Dragomir and his other two brothers were on the list under the category of "Persons close to the regime whose activities support President Milosevic" (European Union 1999). Similarly, the Canadian government in 2007 ruled that even though Dragomir Karic had been a legal resident of Canada since 1993, he was now inadmissible to Canada since "the evidence demonstrates that Mr. Karic was well and truly an advisor to Milosevic" (Canadian Immigration and Refugee Board 2007).

Multiple sources also note the close ties that Karic had with Russia. The Karic family businesses expanded into Moscow in the early 1990s (*Economist* 1999), a time when the Russian Mafia had penetrated as many as 80% of the private enterprises in Russia, according to a later Russian government estimate (Dempsey and Lukas 1999). The family businesses made fortunes buying raw materials from the Russian government and then selling them abroad. Dragomir Karic was also reported to have "close ties with Viktor Chernomyrdin, Yeltsin's special envoy" to Milosevic during the Kosovo War (Fennell 1999).

Thus Karic was well positioned to represent Milosevic to both the Russians and Americans at the meeting in Vienna of 30 April to 1 May. In addition to Weldon, both Representatives Bernie Sanders (I-Vt.) and Roscoe G. Bartlett (R-Md.) reported that Karic made many phone calls to Milosevic during the meeting. When the meeting ended with Milosevic's acceptance of NATO involvement in an international peacekeeping force for Kosovo, Karic went immediately to Germany to confer with government officials there (Canadian Immigration and Refugee Board 2007).

The diplomatic reversal by the Russians came at the meeting of G-8 foreign ministers in Bonn only five days later. The Russians publicly accepted the presence of NATO troops among the international peacekeepers in Kosovo (*Economist* 1999), and Chernomyrdin began pressing Milosevic to accept Western terms. Given Milosevic's sudden acceptance of the western terms, it is plausible that Weldon's behind-the-scenes activity may have played an important role in helping to bring a diplomatic termination to the hostilities by conveying a tough United States and Russian position to Karic, a confidante of Milosevic who could then pressure him to take the offer before Yugoslavia suffered even greater destruction. If Weldon's account and the substantiating evidence discussed here are accurate, his role, activities, and impact clearly highlight the possibilities for a dramatic "under-the-radar" effect by committed congressional foreign policy entrepreneurs.

Theme 3: Addressing national security issues affecting the United States and Russia.   Although Weldon sought to improve relations with Russia, he long described himself as "Russia's best friend but her toughest critic" (Weldon 2002b). As the problem context shifted with the demise of the Soviet Union, Weldon's concerns also shifted. One area of concerns was the potential proliferation activities of Russian corporations or entities not always controlled by the government in Moscow. After newspapers in 1996 revealed that Russians had illegally transferred components of missile guidance systems to Iran in violation of the Missile Technology Control Regime, Weldon wrote a letter to President Clinton urging that these reports be investigated. When the former Russian general and security council secretary Alexander Lebed told Weldon that only 48 of 132 suitcase-sized nuclear bombs could be accounted for in Russian inventories (Lebed later increased the number of missing "suitcase" bombs from 84 to 100 during an appearance on *60 Minutes*), Weldon pressed the administration for action and publicly stated: "The potential for very sophisticated nuclear technology and weapons to get into the hands of Third World nations and other groups is very real and it's something I don't think the administration follows up on. The Russian Government doesn't have control" (Smith and Hoffman 1997, § A, 19; Associated Press, 6 September 1997).

Weldon's concerns about potential Russian threats did not end when Clinton left town. Shortly before President Bush's summit with President Putin in May 2002, Weldon introduced an amendment to the defense authorization bill that would permit the government to engage in the research and conceptual design work for a new class of nuclear warheads. This amendment was in response to an intelligence briefing at which MCS were informed that the Russians appeared to be preparing for a new round of nuclear weapons tests. In an effort to promote transparency in nuclear testing, the amendment would have allowed Russian scientists to visit nuclear test facilities in Nevada in return for allowing American scientists to visit test facilities in Novaya Zemlya. The amendment overwhelmingly passed the House (Shanker 2002; Associated Press 2002). Later that year, after an editorial in the *New York Times* accused Weldon of trying to gut the Nunn-Lugar program that funded the dismantling of old Russian nuclear weapons, he wrote a letter to the editor in which he said that he supported Nunn-Lugar and was only trying to put "common-sense conditions on the flow of funds" to Russia. His preferred legislation also gave the president limited authority to waive those conditions (Weldon 2002b). Finally, in 2003 Weldon led a bipartisan congressional delegation to visit the previously secret weapons-grade plutonium plant in Zheleznogorsk, in an effort to promote mutual transparency regarding weapons of mass destruction for both the United States and Russia (Baker 2003; *Fort Worth Star-Telegram*, 27 August 2003, § A, 8).

Theme 4: Promoting missile defense.   After the Cold War Weldon was convinced that the probability of a missile attack had increased. Thus he became one of the leading congressional advocates of both national and theater missile defense systems (*Congressional Quarterly Almanac* 2000). With the help of a few others, Weldon took this issue from the political periphery to the mainstream. The *Washington Post* described a "relentless, almost obsessive campaign by Weldon and his allies to undermine the [Clinton] administration's objections to the whole approach. Over the past six years, Weldon has held more than 100 hearings and briefings on the subject, hectoring administration officials, challenging CIA estimates

about the seriousness of the military threat from North Korea and pressing, successfully, for more funding to develop a missile defense program.
To some degree, observers say, Weldon and other missile defense proponents helped push the administration into a corner and forced officials to
accept the basic premise of their approach, if not their most grandiose ambitions" (Pianin 2000a, § A, 8).

Weldon used his chairmanship of the House National Security Military
Research and Development Subcommittee as a forum to push for missile
defense systems designed to protect the United States from the accidental
launch of a Russian missile or a launch from Iran, Iraq, or North Korea.
In 2000 he said: "The largest loss of American life in the last 10 years was
when 31 young Americans came back in body bags from Saudi Arabia because we couldn't defend against a low-complexity Scud missile . . . My goal
is to never let that happen again" (Pianin 2000a, § A, 8). Consequently, he
eagerly sought bipartisan allies so that his efforts could not be dismissed
by the Clinton administration as mere partisanship (Pianin 2000a).

Beginning in 1996 Weldon proposed a national missile defense system
for the United States (Landay 1996). That year he sued President Clinton
in federal court for having missed congressionally mandated deadlines for
developing theater missile defense systems. Though the suit was later dismissed, the administration was put on notice that missile defense had serious proponents in Congress (Pianin 2000a).

The next year, Weldon chaired a subcommittee hearing on the missile
defense program, wanting to know why there had been nine consecutive
test failures. Weldon was troubled by recent intelligence reports that Iran
might be no more than eighteen months from testing and deploying two
types of missiles that could threaten Israel and most United States forces
in the Persian Gulf area. After hearing the testimony of the Air Force general heading the Ballistic Missile Defense Organization (who thought that
increases in missile defense funding sought by Weldon were premature),
Weldon angrily adjourned the subcommittee meeting and in a loud voice
told the general: "I can't trust you" (Associated Press 1997b, § A, 12).

In 1998 Weldon was at the center of a congressional campaign to focus
attention on the missile threat. Frustrated by what he saw as skewed intelligence, Weldon applied pressure in hearings to change the assessments.
Weldon held a special closed session of his military research and development subcommittee to hear intelligence estimates of the missile threats

facing the United States. In his own words, he "went ballistic" when a CIA analyst stood behind an estimate that his agency had made in 1995 that there would be no missile threat to the United States before 2010 (Dobbs 2002). Stressing that unrest in Russia threatened to trigger the transfer of Russian missile technology to countries such as Iran, he accused the CIA analyst of politicizing intelligence data, presumably to please the Clinton White House (Dobbs 2002). Weldon then wrote a bill to speed deployment of defense systems focused on missiles launched from Iran or North Korea. The bill passed the House (*Congressional Quarterly Almanac* 1998). At a news conference in Jerusalem on 24 April he said: "The Iranians are 12–18 months away from completing and deploying a missile. This is absolutely unacceptable. Time is of the absolute essence. We need to close the window. We have a window of vulnerability that most affects Israel. We are going to have to have an anti-ballistic missile system" (Rodan 1998, 2).

Weldon went on to chastise the administration for not pressing Russia harder to stop Russian corporations from helping Iran's military programs, saying that Russia had violated the Missile Technology Control Regime of 1987 seven times in six years and that twenty Russian agencies and research facilities that received funds from the United States had transferred missile technology to Iran. As a result of these concerns Weldon helped to draft the Iran Missile Sanctions Act, to impose economic sanctions on any entity helping Iran's missile programs (Rodan 1998). His pressure was also instrumental in a congressional initiative to establish a new commission headed by Donald Rumsfeld to study the ballistic missile threat (Dobbs 2002). When completed, the Rumsfeld commission drew significantly more alarmist conclusions than the United States intelligence community had and prompted further action by MCs like Weldon.

Weldon then had a meeting at the White House with Vice President Al Gore about the Iran Missile Sanctions Act. Gore said that the bill was a mistake that would undermine the president. After the bill easily passed the House, Gore invited Weldon and other MCs back to the White House, imploring them to drop the matter. After the bill easily passed the Senate, Clinton vetoed it. Weldon believed he had the votes to override the veto, since the bill had garnered 398 votes in the House and 98 in the Senate. He met with Speaker Gingrich, but Gingrich would not allow an override vote to come to the House floor (Weldon 2002a).

In the face of consistent criticism by Weldon and his colleagues, and with new CIA estimates confirming the missile threats posed by Iran and North Korea, the Clinton administration reversed its earlier position the next year and announced that it would spend $6.6 billion over five years to deploy a national missile defense system. Weldon issued a public statement saying that he was encouraged by the policy change but still "skeptical" about the administration's commitment to the issue (Priest 1999, § A, 1; Dobbs 2002). His bill committing the United States to build a national missile defense system passed the House by a three-to-one margin (*Congressional Quarterly Almanac* 1999).

Weldon did not let up. In 2000 he hosted a private, weeklong conference in Philadelphia of corporations potentially involved in national or theater missile defense systems. In a press statement, Weldon called upon the various corporate vendors to become more active in lobbying the government and public on behalf of missile defense. "They have a responsibility, I think, to use their resources to at least make the case why it's important business-wise. We're not doing this because it means jobs, but the fact that it does mean jobs makes it somewhat critical for them to tell that story" (Schneider 2000b, § H, 1). Shortly thereafter, Boeing announced that it would run ads to educate the public about the need for national missile defense (Schneider 2000a, § E, 3).

Two weeks later Weldon met with Russia's deputy prime minister to promote the idea that Russia and the United States could cooperate in theater missile defense. In Weldon's words, "We should have been doing this all along" (Gordon 2000, § A, 7). In 2003 he tried taking his message to both North and South Korea. While there he issued a public statement reporting what North Korean officials had confirmed to his delegation: they were nearly through preprocessing spent nuclear fuel rods that could become bomb-quality material within months (Associated Press 2003).

Theme 5: Promoting the V-22 Osprey. One of the earliest and most visible entrepreneurial roles that Weldon played was leading the congressional effort to acquire the V-22 Osprey, a tilt-rotor aircraft designed to replace the older, less-capable Marine Corps helicopters (Jones 2002). Weldon's persistent efforts to raise the profile of this policy solution overcame the resistance of the first Bush administration and sustained the program throughout the post–Cold War period. After Defense Secretary Dick Cheney proposed a budget excluding the V-22 in 1989, Weldon wrote a letter to the *Washington Post* defending the aircraft as a less expensive alternative to the helicopter systems embraced by the administration (Weldon 1989). Weldon used his seat on the House Armed Services Committee to shift funds from the B-2 bomber account to the V-22, and then offered a floor amendment to get $157 million added to the defense budget for the V-22, which passed despite opposition from the White House (*Congressional Quarterly Almanac* 1989).

Knowing that the battle was far from over, Weldon helped form the Tilt-Rotor Caucus in 1990 to coordinate the efforts of congressional proponents, defense contractors, labor unions, and the Marine Corps to champion the V-22 (Jones 2002). In a public statement he announced that the outlook for the V-22 was good (Morgan 1990). In 1991 Weldon again led the successful effort to include funding for the V-22 in the defense budget, and added language directing the Pentagon to spend the funds previously appropriated for the V-22 (Jones 2002).

When the Bush administration made one last attempt to end the program in 1992, Weldon again prevailed. He led the effort to eliminate funding for the helicopter that the administration preferred and to add $755 million to the defense budget for continued research and development of the Osprey. In a victory statement he said: "We have gotten everything we asked for. We will build new Ospreys and move this revolutionary program forward" (*Congressional Quarterly Almanac* 1992, 599).

In 2000 the crash of a test vehicle killed nineteen Marines and generated new controversy over the V-22. As a result, Weldon resurrected the Tilt-Rotor Caucus to defend the Osprey (Copley News Service 2001) and arranged for a display of a V-22 at the temporary housing facility that he organized for House Republicans attending the Republican national convention in Philadelphia (Pianin 2000b). After another fatal crash in December 2000, Weldon again defended the aircraft, publicly stating that reported hydraulic and computer problems were important problems to fix but that the technology of the V-22 was essentially sound (Flaherty 2001). As a result of his efforts, the United States continued to develop the V-22 for the Marine Corps.

Across these issues, Weldon was an aggressive entrepreneur with a penchant for direct action, whether creating a joint caucus with Russian legislators or trying his hand at direct diplomacy to end a war. He strategically combined direct legislative tactics (introducing bills and amendments) with a variety of indirect and nonlegislative approaches, including consultations with the executive branch and signals to it, combative hearings, and creative use of foreign contacts. Arguably Weldon's greatest impact was his behind-the-scenes promotion of principles acceptable to both sides that later helped to end the NATO war over Kosovo. His assertiveness and initiative also preserved the V-22 Osprey and generated substantial momentum toward a national missile defense program.

Chris Smith: Human Rights and Population Policy

Born in Rahway, New Jersey, in 1953, Christopher H. Smith received his education at St. Mary's High School in Perth Amboy (N.J.) and Trenton State College, where he graduated in 1975 with a B.A. in business administration. The son of a teamster turned sporting-goods wholesaler (Dao 1997), Smith went to work as the executive director of New Jersey Right to Life, for which he had formed a chapter at Trenton State as an undergraduate. After one year in the New Jersey state legislature (1979) and an unsuccessful bid for the House of Representatives (1978), Smith defeated the incumbent Republican Frank Thomson Jr. in 1980 in what Smith termed "a fluke election" (Dao 1997). He has served in the House ever since, with assignments on the Veterans Affairs and International Relations committees. His position as chairman of the latter committee's International Operations and Human Rights Subcommittee has provided substantial access and opportunities for Smith's foreign policy interests. He has also been the co-chairman of the Pro-Life Caucus for two decades (*Congressional Biographical Directory* 2001).

According to Smith, "religion is the unifying force" in his policy positions, "from opposing abortion and the death penalty to supporting human rights in other nations" (Dao 1997). A devout Catholic, he is best known for his foreign policy activism and his entrepreneurship on human rights and anti-abortion issues. He has also devoted attention to a variety of additional interests, the breadth of which can be seen in his legislative agenda since 1994 (when the Republicans captured control of the House). They fall into four categories, with human rights receiving the most attention.[7]

1. Economics and development: proposals to require the return of property confiscated in the formerly communist regimes (1996, 1997, 1998);

proposals to expand and strengthen the debt relief of the Enhanced Highly Indebted Poor Country Initiative (2002, 2003).

2. Conflict and security: resolutions to pressure Turkey to end its conflict with the Kurds (1996, 1997); a resolution to demand Russian withdrawal of troops from Moldova (1996); a proposal to lift the arms embargo on Bosnia (1995); a resolution calling on NATO to take direct, coercive action against Serbia in Kosovo (1998); a proposal to forbid the provision of defense services and training to countries already prohibited from receiving funds under the International Military Education and Training program (IMET), military aid, or arms sales (1998, 1999).

3. Refugees: a proposal to protect refugee assistance funds in the State Department budget (1995); a proposal to lift limits on refugees admitted to the United States (1996); proposals to support refugees and immigrants from Central America (1999, 2001); a proposal to amend immigration laws to protect refugees fleeing from torture (2002).

4. Human rights and the promotion of democracy: a proposal to prohibit United States aid to countries that impede the delivery of humanitarian assistance (1995); proposals to implement the Convention Against Torture (1995, 1998); proposals to enact sanctions against countries failing to prohibit child labor (1996, 1998); a proposal to require a presidential report on any blocking of borders in the former Soviet Union that impedes the delivery of humanitarian assistance (1997); resolutions to support human rights and democratization in the Central Asian Republics (1999, 2000); a resolution encouraging Azerbaijan to hold elections (2000); a resolution to develop a coordinated strategy of democracy promotion in Serbia (1999); a resolution condemning human rights violations in Kazakhstan (2002); a resolution condemning Cuba for human rights violations (2001); resolutions condemning rising anti-Semitism in Europe and calling for action to counter it (2002, 2003); proposals to promote democracy in Vietnam (2001, 2002); a proposal to prohibit funding certain Cuban programs until all political prisoners are released (2001); a resolution condemning North Korea for human rights abuses and calling on the administration to offer and support a resolution of the UN Human Rights Commission doing the same (2003).

While this list indicates a broad-gauged agenda, Smith is best known for his emphasis on issues related to international family planning and abortion, which he considers human rights issues.

Theme 1: Abortion, population control, and human rights in China. From his first days in Congress, Smith devoted considerable and steady attention to condemning Chinese policy and preventing any United States support for China's population control policies. During the Reagan administration Smith sponsored successful amendments prohibiting the use of United States funds in UN programs in China aimed at population control and authorizing President Reagan to deny funds to any international organization on the basis of family planning activities (*Congressional Quarterly Almanac* 1985). In the post–Cold War era Smith worked hard to sustain this policy in the face of efforts to reverse it, and to reinstate it when it was abandoned. The chief target of Smith's attention was the UN Population Fund (known by its former acronym, the UNFPA — United Nations Fund for Population Activities); according to Smith, the fund supports a population policy in China that includes coerced abortions.

For example, when the House considered a foreign operations bill in 1990 which initially included $15 million for the UNFPA, Smith proposed an amendment stipulating that "no funds . . . shall be made available to the United Nations Population Fund unless the President of the United States certifies that the United Nations Population Fund does not provide support for, or participate in the management of a program of coercive abortion or involuntary sterilization in the People's Republic of China" (*Congressional Record*, 16 November 1989, H8826). Smith's amendment initially passed 219–203, but the House, then controlled by the Democrats, reversed itself two days later and included the funds in the bill, which President Bush vetoed.

In 1991 China was again in Smith's sights, as he sought to raise the profile of the issue in the problem stream of United States foreign policy. With Representative Frank Wolf (R-Va.), Smith traveled to China to gather information and hold a week of meetings with Chinese officials on human rights. Smith and Wolf focused on the detention of Chinese citizens after Tiananmen, the harassment and imprisonment of members of various religious groups, and "the coercive population control policies, the intrusive tactics employed by the government which includes forced abortions, involuntary sterilization, female infanticide, and mandatory insertion of

IUDS" (*Congressional Record*, 25 April 1991, H2560). Smith and Wolf condemned the policies during their meetings with the Chinese, calling them crimes against humanity. On their return, Smith took to the floor of the House to provide a lengthy accounting of his trip, along with supporting information, to frame the issue, define the problem, and persuade his colleagues to maintain pressure on the Chinese regime and withhold UNFPA funds. His efforts were important later that year, when the Democratic House again took steps to earmark funds ($20 million) for the UNFPA, an attempt that again failed and against which Smith led the charge (e.g. *Congressional Record*, 19 June 1991, H4738–39; *Congressional Record*, 30 October 1991, H8698–99).

Smith stepped up his efforts when Bill Clinton won the White House in 1992 and prepared to abandon the prohibition on United States funding of the UNFPA. First, Smith continued to frame the problem by peppering the official record of Congress with accounts of China's brutal population program (e.g. *Congressional Record*, 28 April 1993, H2061; 29 April 1993, E1093). He also worked to shape policy alternatives, leading a group of representatives to introduce legislation tying China's most-favored-nation (MFN) status (now called normal trade relations, or NTR) to human rights progress, specifically an end to abortion and involuntary sterilization (*Congressional Record*, 4 May 1993, H2201).[8] In June, Smith sought to attach an amendment to the State Department authorization bill that would deny UNFPA funds unless the president certified that China's population policy was not coercive or that the UNFPA had terminated its activities in China (*Congressional Record*, 16 June 1993, H3674).

When the Clinton administration delayed the decision on China's trade status for a year, Smith led another fact-finding mission to China to gather information for the upcoming MFN debate. When he returned he offered testimony to congressional committees, and he took the House floor to catalogue his findings for the record (e.g. *Congressional Record*, 24 February 1994, E264–66). In these statements Smith introduced supporting evidence, including a report by John Aird, former chief of the China Branch of the U.S. Census Bureau.[9] When the administration delinked China's MFN status from human rights in mid-1994, Smith denounced the decision (e.g. *Congressional Record*, 9 August 1994, H7228–30) and kept up the legislative pressure. For instance, in May and June 1995 Smith twice offered amendments to bar funding for the UNFPA without presidential

certification that it had ceased its operations in China (http://thomas.loc
.gov), both of which passed the House but were ultimately vetoed by President Clinton in April 1996.[10]

Smith's actions from 1997 to 1999 further illustrate his persistence
on the issue, and his broad efforts to inject alternatives into the policy
stream. For example, in May 1997 Smith introduced legislation to establish principles for United States corporations engaged in China and Tibet
(http://thomas.loc.gov). Although that measure died in committee, just
two months later he offered legislation to require increased monitoring of
China's prison labor and the goods produced by it, which passed the House
but died in the Senate (http://thomas.loc.gov). In both June and September he offered measures to expand international broadcasting into China
as well (http://thomas.loc.gov). In 1998 Smith sponsored the successful
H. Res. 364, urging the administration to introduce and advocate a resolution condemning China's human rights practices in the UN Commission
on Human Rights (e.g. *Congressional Record*, 17 March 1998, H1181–92,
1208–9). The next year Smith tried to attach to his own Embassy Security Act an amendment to prohibit funding of the UNFPA (*Congressional
Record*, 19 July 1999, H5801). The House rejected the amendment, voting 221–198 to retain $25 million for the UNFPA ("Not an Abortion Issue"
1999).[11]

Two more recent actions further highlight Smith's activities on this
issue. In 2002, faced with a foreign aid appropriations bill containing $34
million for the UNFPA, Smith wrote directly to President Bush and asked
him to withhold the funds ("A Test for Mr. Bush" 2002). Shortly thereafter, Smith took his case public by using another common tactic, writing
an opinion piece that condemned both the UNFPA and China's program
(Smith 2002). Bush acceded to Smith's request, first temporarily holding
the funds pending a final decision, and then, in July, making the decision
permanent. Siding with Smith, Bush rejected the conclusions of a fact-
finding team sent by his own State Department in May 2002 and withheld
the funds from the UNFPA (Kramer 2002).

Theme 2: The "Mexico City" policy.   While his efforts on China and
population policy were relatively narrow, Smith engaged more broadly on
international family planning issues from his earliest days in Congress.
In what his detractors characterized as an annual ritual, Smith regularly
sought to bar United States funding of international agencies involved in

family planning and population policy, chiefly out of concern that they might support (directly or indirectly) the practice of abortion overseas.

After the International Conference on Population in Mexico City in 1984, the Reagan administration announced the so-called Mexico City policy of withholding United States contributions to international agencies and nongovernmental organizations that performed or promoted abortion as a population control policy. Until Bill Clinton assumed the presidency, the Mexico City guidelines were followed by the executive branch, and Smith's efforts were chiefly directed toward defending the policy against those who sought its reversal in the Congress.

In 1993, however, Clinton rescinded the guidelines. From then on Smith engaged in a persistent campaign of entrepreneurship to reinstate the policy through legislation. He sponsored numerous amendments, linking them to issues such as funding for the State Department, foreign aid, foreign affairs restructuring, UN dues, and IMF contributions. He used the House floor, committees, and the public as avenues to press his preferences. Eventually he achieved modest success in fiscal year 2000, when a compromise version of the policy became law for one year. After the presidential election of 2000 his preference became policy when President George W. Bush reinstated the Mexico City policy on 22 January 2001.

An account of Smith's campaign might best pick up his activities in the fall of 1994, just before the Republican victories in the congressional midterm elections that put them in the majority in both chambers. In September 1994 the UN's International Conference on Population and Development was held in Cairo. Smith was an observer at the conference and returned to castigate the administration for its efforts to "ensure universal access to family planning and related reproductive health services, including access to safe abortions" (Smith, quoting from a cable to United States embassies, *Congressional Record*, 13 September 1994, E1840). According to Smith: "As the repeal of the Mexico City policy clearly demonstrated, this administration will continue to fund . . . organizations which seek to undermine and change the laws in countries that provide limitations on abortion. Moreover, we can expect to see the State Department and its allies involved in the international conference on women to be held in Beijing next year to achieve what it failed to get in Cairo" (*Congressional Record*, 13 September 1994, E1840). Smith took the floor again in October to criticize the administration for its stance in Cairo, and to call for efforts to counter what he characterized as the "extreme pro-abortion position" and "population control machine" run by the White House (*Congressional Record*, 7 October 1994, E237, 238).

When Smith returned to Washington from winter recess in 1995, there had been a major shift in the political stream. Smith was now a member of the majority party and he assumed chairmanship of the International Operations and Human Rights subcommittee of the House International Relations Committee. From this newly empowered platform his entrepreneurial efforts to make the Mexico City guidelines United States foreign policy took shape. In May, Smith offered an amendment to the American Overseas Interests Act that required a return to the Mexico City restrictions. The House voted 240–181 in favor of the provision (e.g. "Abortion and Foreign Aid" 1995; "House Moves to Eliminate Pro-Abortion Foreign Aid" 1995). A month later the House voted again for Smith's amendment (Eisenstadt 1995). In December the Senate passed a version of the bill that did not include Smith's provision, but House conferees, pressed by Smith (who was supported by the House leadership), insisted that it be added. The conference report, with Smith's provision, was approved in March, only to be vetoed by President Clinton on 12 April 1996. Hence Smith's first effort resulted in an impasse, as well as blocking action on other issues because of the veto that it triggered.

Smith doggedly returned to the attack in 1997. While Congress allocated funds for family planning in the fall of 1996, Smith led efforts to delay their disbursement until the following year, pending presidential certification and an additional vote (*Washington Post*, 4 February 1997, § A, 22). As the administration offered the certification necessary to release the funds, Smith took his next step. Early in the year he went public with his argument, writing publicly: "I and my pro-life colleagues in Congress want to know the extent to which organizations that receive United States foreign assistance are engaged in the performance of or active promotion of abortion overseas" (Smith 1997, § B, 7).

At the same time, Smith promised that he would try to attach anti-abortion provisions to every spending bill for fiscal 1998 (Doherty 1997). Smith then passionately defended his proposal and urged his colleagues to withhold the funds and support his bill (*Congressional Record*, 13 February 1997, H546). Ultimately the House approved disbursement of the funds (220–209), but it also passed Smith's bill (231–194) tying that disbursement to the reinstatement of the Mexico City restrictions ("House OKS Money to Aid Family Planning Overseas" 1997).

In the meantime, taking advantage of the annual policy window afforded by the budget cycle, Smith attached his initiative to both the foreign operations bill and the State Department authorization, winning the support of the House in both cases. This led to a head-on collision between Smith and his fellow entrepreneur Senator Helms, who was painstakingly working toward a deal with the administration and Senate Democrats to combine State Department funding with payment of United States arrears to the UN and Helms's highly cherished foreign affairs reorganization plan. As discussed later in this chapter, in June Helms forged a bargain with the Senate Foreign Relations Committee's ranking Democrat, Joseph Biden, and the administration, only to see it jeopardized by Smith's actions in the House, which caused Clinton to threaten a veto. On 30 July Helms and other senators urged Smith to drop the abortion provision, but Smith refused (Myers 1997).

In September the two agendas collided. In the House representatives voted 234–191 to keep Smith's amendment in the foreign aid bill, which then passed 374–49 (Associated Press 1997a). The Senate version of the bill, which contained Helms's carefully crafted compromise on UN dues and agency reorganization, did not include the Mexico City provisions. Both Gilman, chairman of the House International Relations Committee, and Speaker Gingrich promised to support Smith in the negotiations with the Senate (e.g. Myers 1997; Gray 1997). In October, as conferees tried to iron out the differences in the face of a veto threat from Clinton, Smith promised: "[I will] do everything I can to sink my own [foreign aid] bill if the Mexico City language is dropped in conference" (D'Agostino 1997b, 5).

This position drew the fight between Smith and Helms further into the public arena. According to an aide to Helms (speaking publicly), having concluded that "Mexico City can't pass this Senate" or a presidential veto, Helms decided "to sink this entire bill just to make a political point when we are on the verge of eliminating two governmental agencies doesn't make any sense." Smith responded publicly, saying that "Jesse Helms has been a let-down on this" (D'Agostino 1997b, 5). As the fight heated up and the stalemate continued, Helms's aide Marc Thiessen publicly stated that "Smith has burned all of his bridges over here. . . . Senator Helms has had it with him." When Smith commented that he was "bewildered at [Helms's] interest in rearranging foreign policy agencies at the expense of the unborn," Thiessen angrily countered: "Chris Smith said that Senator Helms has been a let-down on this? How dare he? Who is Chris Smith to say that?" (D'Agostino 1997a, 4). According to William Safire (1999, § A, 25), "an irate Helms told Smith, 'I was fighting abortion when you were still wetting your diapers,' and to attach his rider to something else." Smith would not relent.

In November the issue also became linked to an urgent request from the White House for $3.5 billion for the IMF to stabilize the Asian currency crisis (see Carter and Scott 2002; Scott and Carter 2005). Members of the administration met several times with Helms, Smith, and other congressional leaders, and the members met together separately as well. Ultimately Senator Helms, Speaker Gingrich, President Clinton, and Representative Smith all held their ground, and the whole bundle of initiatives failed. Hence, Smith's entrepreneurship scuttled UN reform, United States payment of its UN arrears, reorganization of the foreign affairs agency, emergency IMF funding, and the foreign operations bill.

Early in 1998 Smith again successfully attached his amendment to the State Department authorization bill, which the House leadership held up until the fall. He also again took his case to the public, writing in the *Washington Post* that "without the Mexico City policy, U.S. taxpayer dollars continue to enrich and empower foreign organizations that pressure developing countries to abandon their pro-life laws" (Smith 1998, § A, 21). In the House, Smith managed to get his amendment attached to the pieces of legislation funding the IMF, funding the State Department, paying UN dues, and reorganizing the foreign affairs agencies (Aizenman 1998). Clinton again promised to veto any legislation with the Mexico City restrictions attached.

The impasse persisted through the fall. Round after round of bargaining ensued under the pressure of the final spending bills. Ultimately a deal was struck (in conference, without Smith's participation) by which the issues were separated. Funds for the State Department and the IMF (with the reorganization plan) were combined in an omnibus appropriation, which passed Congress and was signed into law on 21 October 1998. The Mexico City restrictions and the UN dues continued to be linked, narrowly passing both houses of Congress and drawing the promised presidential veto on the same day that measures funding the IMF and State were signed (Stout 1998).

As might have been expected, Smith was not finished. In 1999 he successfully attached his Foreign Families Protection Amendment to the foreign operations bill, after making several concessions to allow presidential waivers of some of the Mexico City restrictions. In the Senate, Helms worked out a deal in the State Department authorization to pay the United States arrears and adjust United States contributions to the UN, brokering a compromise with Secretary of State Albright and Senator Biden ("UN Dues, Round 3" 1999).[12] When the Senate voted 98–1 in favor of the arrangement the legislation went to the House, where Smith promptly engineered a deal by which neither the UN funds nor the Mexico City restrictions were included in the House version of the bill. This action left a conference committee to work out the disagreement while Smith insisted on a "both or neither" arrangement (Pomper 1999b). At the same time, however, Smith attached his Mexico City amendment to the fiscal 2000 foreign aid bill, which passed the House 228–200 (Pomper 1999a). Another fall showdown was in the works.

As an impasse similar to that of the preceding year took shape, Smith again found himself facing off with Helms. Helms argued, "I have not changed my stand against abortion . . . I am just fed up with it being used as a ploy leading to nowhere" ("Embarrassing Deadbeat" 1999, § A, 28), while Smith continued to insist that the way to get "our money's worth from the UN" was, in part, to reinstate the Mexico City restrictions (Smith 1999, § A, 34). After another presidential veto and the hasty construction of a new foreign operations bill, a compromise was reached. Smith's amendment on the Mexico City restrictions was included with a provision for a presidential waiver, $385 million in family planning funds were allocated, and Helms's compromise on UN dues was accepted (Kettle 1999).

Almost immediately, however, the compromise was threatened. Criticism was directed at the White House for its concession to Smith (e.g. Borst 1999; Mann 1999; Mann 2000). As a consequence, Clinton exercised the waiver provision and argued for the reinstatement of family planning funds (Cleveland *Plain Dealer*, 9 January 2000, § A, 18). In July 2000 the House version of the fiscal 2001 foreign operations bill was passed, with the compromise version of Smith's provision from the preceding year. When Clinton again threatened to veto the bill, the language was stripped from the legislation in conference in the fall. At the same time, funds for international family planning were increased to $425 million, but a stipulation was also included prohibiting disbursement before 15 February 2001, which left the allocation decision to the next president. On 22 January 2001 President Bush, newly inaugurated, reinstated the Mexico City restrictions by executive order, finally giving Christopher Smith the victory for which he had long and persistently worked.

As an entrepreneur Smith relied substantially on a combination of direct and indirect legislative strategies, supplemented with strategic efforts to frame issues and build support. He relied on the legislative process to introduce many bills and amendments serving his policy preferences, and his preferred strategy was to link his initiatives to other legislation to increase his leverage and, often, threaten to obstruct others' agendas to make progress on his own. Employing this strategy, Smith's tireless promotion of the Mexico City restrictions eventually resulted in their partial restoration in 1999, setting the stage for their full embrace by George W. Bush's administration in 2001. That the UNFPA went unfunded from 1985 to 2003 may be attributed in large part to Smith. The very limited United States policies on international population issues can be traced to Smith as well. Finally, Smith's policy agenda and strategy of linking his concerns to other issues had broad policy impact, delaying IMF funds to combat the Asian financial crisis for nearly two years, United States payment of its UN dues for almost three, and reorganization of the foreign affairs agencies for over a year because of Smith's determination to pursue his priorities.

Jesse Helms: "Ratholes," Reforms, Roadblocks, and "Rogues"

Senator Jesse Helms merits considerable attention as a congressional foreign policy entrepreneur. A regular participant in foreign policy debates after his election to the Senate in 1972, he was the most active and prolific foreign policy entrepreneur in the post–World War II era. Well known for his assertive and contrarian style, Helms ascended to the chairmanship of the Senate Foreign Relations Committee in 1995, ensuring that his agenda and activities would have a powerful effect on United States foreign policy in the post–Cold War period. He also served on the Agriculture, Nutrition, and Forestry Committee and the Rules and Administration Committee ("Jesse Helms" 2002).

Helms grew up in Monroe, North Carolina, and attended Wingate Junior College and Wake Forest College (*Biographical Directory of the American Congress* 1996). After Navy service from 1942 to 1945, Helms began a career in journalism as the city editor of the *Raleigh Times*, and he later became news and program director of the Tobacco Radio Network and Radio Station WRAL in Raleigh (*Almanac of American Politics* 1998). Helms's political service began in 1951, when he became an assistant to Senator Willis Smith (D-N.C.), a position he held until 1953 (Furgurson 1986). After directing the radio and television division for the presidential campaign of Senator Richard Russell (D-Ga.) in 1952, he became an assistant to Senator Alton Lennon (D-N.C.) in 1953. At the same time, Helms maintained a high level of involvement in local affairs by serving as the executive director of the North Carolina Bankers Association from 1953 to 1960 and as a member of the Raleigh City Council from 1957 to 1961 (Congressional Biographical Directory 1996).

Helms's public reputation was furthered substantially by the broadcast of his editorial segments, "The Viewpoint," on WRAL-TV in 1960 (Friedman 1989). Broadcast on seventy radio stations, these five-minute editorials—attacking communism, the civil rights movement, and academic freedom, questioning the ability of the federal government, and calling for the revival of traditional Christian values in politics—became the springboard for his political career (Damico 2001). In 1972 Helms capitalized on his reputation as a staunch defender of traditional conservative values by announcing his candidacy for the U.S. Senate seat left open by the defeat of the Democratic incumbent Everett Jordan in the Democratic primary. After a campaign in which Helms attacked the relatively liberal positions of Nick Galifianakis, his competitor, citizens of North Carolina rewarded Helms's distinctly conservative perspective by electing him to the U.S. Senate, where he served until 2002.

From the start, Helms's foreign policy agenda was driven by anti-communism (Furgurson 1986). As a biographer once noted, there was a distinctive characteristic to Helms's foreign policy positions: "He reliably seeks out the rightmost faction in any international confrontation" (Furgurson 1986, 188). Inside the Senate Helms's tactics in support of his hard-line agenda earned him the reputation "as the Senate's most persistent obstructionist" (Furgurson 1986, 106) and the appellation of "Senator No." Helms sought to pursue his policy agenda as well as represent the parochial interests of North Carolina. This dual goal led to an interesting combination of committee assignments. He was assigned to the Senate Committee on Agriculture, Nutrition and Forestry, on which he served as chairman from 1981 through 1986 (*Biographical Directory of the American Congress* 1996), and was also a member of the Committee on Banking, Housing and Urban Affairs (1973–77). Helms's foreign policy agenda received a boost when he became a member of the Senate Foreign Relations Committee in 1979 after a two-year stint on the Armed Services Committee (*Congressional Directory* 1979). In 1995 he assumed the post of chairman of the Foreign Relations Committee, a position he maintained until 2001 when the Democrats became the majority party in the Senate (Dewar 2001).

In the quantitative database, Helms accounts for almost a hundred instances of congressional foreign policy entrepreneurship, more than any other individual in the dataset. Throughout his tenure Helms actively promoted his brand of American foreign policy, as some journalists put it, "waging skilled parliamentary guerilla warfare against what he perceived as the tendency of successive presidents to be too soft on combating communism, too willing to surrender American sovereignty to vaguely defined multilateralism and too complacent about squandering U.S. tax dollars on dubious foreign ventures" (Goshko and Williams 1994, § A, 1). Even after the end of the Cold War, these three areas of concern continued to dominate Helms's foreign policy efforts. In addressing them Helms sought to elevate their prominence in the problem context, inject his preferred alternatives into the debate, and take advantage of favorable political opportunities to see them addressed to his liking.

Theme 1: Opposition to foreign aid.   In one of his more memorable— and widely quoted—pronouncements in November 1994, Helms stated: "The foreign aid program has spent an estimated $2 trillion of the American taxpayers' money, *much of it going down foreign ratholes*, to countries that constantly oppose us in the United Nations, and many which reject concepts of freedom. . . . We must stop this stupid business of giving away the taxpayers' money willy-nilly" (from a news conference after the midterm elections of 1994, quoted in Goshko 1994, § A, 14; emphasis added). When Helms advocated cutting foreign aid to zero for targeted recipients, he was acting entrepreneurially.

One strand of Helms's assertiveness on foreign aid concerned the funding of various international development organizations by the United States. His opposition was driven by his preference for unilateralism and his conviction that these organizations—including the International Development Authority (IDA), the UN Development Program (UNDP), and even the International Monetary Fund and the World Bank—not only escaped United States control but also reflected hostile interests. Helms often sought to eliminate United States aid funneled through the organizations. For example, in 1994 Helms sponsored two floor amendments to the foreign assistance bill to delete all funds for the IDA and the UNDP. Neither amendment passed.

Helms's antipathy toward foreign aid also sprang from his dislike of the idea that American taxpayers should provide money to unaccountable foreign governments. This conviction led Helms to many actions, including a move in 1993 to deduct from any country's foreign assistance the amount that the country's diplomats in the District of Columbia owed in unpaid parking fines—at the time about $4.4 million from the top ten offenders ("No Applause for Sen. Helms" 1993). Helms used his position in the Foreign Relations Committee to attach the amendment to the foreign aid bill. Ultimately Congress included the rider on the foreign relations appropriations bill, requiring foreign governments to pay their parking fines or have the equivalent amount plus a 10% penalty deducted from their foreign aid package. In November 1993 Israel became the first country to pay its fines under the new law (Wheeler 1993).

Helms regularly proposed eliminating foreign aid to punish recipients for their policies or actions. Even after elections in Nicaragua in 1990 ousted the Sandinistas and brought Violeta Chamorro to power, Helms ordered the minority staff of the Foreign Relations Committee to conduct an investigation and release a report detailing any past property seizures, Sandinistas remaining in government, and repression of former contras. Citing the restrictions and requirements of the Hickenlooper amendment (see chapter 4), when the report was released on 31 August 1992 Helms used Senate procedures to put a hold on over $100 million in aid to Nicaragua. According to Helms, Nicaragua was "overwhelmingly controlled by terrorists, thugs, thieves, and murderers at the highest levels. . . . The Sandinistas are still in control in Nicaragua. . . . What are we supposed to do? Just sit back with our thumbs in our ears and pay no attention and send them millions of dollars? Not this Senator" (quoted in Monk 1992, § A,

26). Aid was frozen until December 1992, when the lame-duck Bush administration released about half the funds. Later, in April 1993, the new Clinton administration released the remaining half, citing progress on the issues that Helms had raised (Holmes 1993). Helms immediately took the floor of the Senate, saying, "This $50 million foreign aid giveaway is an outrageous waste of the American people's money and an insult to them" (*Congressional Record*, 2 April 1993).

Helms similarly targeted other countries, often using floor or committee amendments and speeches as vehicles for his efforts to define problems, make policy, and drive the debate. For example, in 1992 he sponsored a successful amendment to require presidential certification that Russia was not providing assistance to Iran's nuclear program before any assistance was provided to Russia, thereby jeopardizing the Bush administration's efforts to help the Russian regime's transition from communism (*Congressional Quarterly Almanac* 1992). In 1994 he introduced a successful floor amendment that barred aid to Russia without a presidential certification of Russian compliance with its chemical and biological treaty obligations (*Congressional Quarterly Almanac* 1994). The annual budget cycle provided the critical recurring policy window for these efforts. Moreover, Helms continued his efforts to restrict aid to Russia after he became chairman of the Foreign Relations Committee (e.g. Greenhouse 1994; Kelley 1995). In 1995 he took his case to the public in the pages of *USA Today*, arguing for cutting off aid to Russia because of its support for Iran (Helms 1995d).

Likewise, in 1996 Helms used the platforms of the Foreign Relations Committee and the Senate floor to make a series of public statements pressuring President Clinton to disqualify Colombia for United States assistance by "de-certifying" its efforts to cooperate with the United States on drug trafficking (*Congressional Quarterly Almanac* 1996). As the head of the Foreign Relations Committee, Helms devoted considerable attention to influencing the debate on Colombia, scheduling several hearings on the matter, characterizing United States policy as "a grave moral and geopolitical mistake" (Helms and Bennett 1995), accusing President Ernesto Samper of siding with the drug cartels (Helms 1996a), and calling on the United States to take firm steps to persuade Colombia to renew its antidrug efforts and then to support it with aid, training, intelligence, and matériel (Helms 1999).

Helms engaged in other efforts to reform foreign aid as well, including attempts to shift most aid to the Export-Import Bank and the Overseas Private Investment Corporation, which promoted trade and commerce with the United States (e.g. Goshko 1994). Additionally, Helms advocated funneling foreign aid through private organizations, thereby dramatically reducing the professional aid bureaucracy. He regularly championed this idea through speeches to such organizations as the Heritage Foundation and the American Enterprise Institute, and through the introduction of bills and amendments in the Senate. In 1996, for example, his proposal to privatize aid died in committee, but the idea remained a priority for Helms at the start of George W. Bush's administration. In a speech to the American Enterprise Institute in January 2001, he announced that he would embrace an increase in international assistance funds if all future United States aid was funneled through private charities and religious groups (Schmitt 2001). Helms outlined his idea to replace the U.S. Agency for International Development with a far smaller International Development Foundation that would distribute funds through such organizations as Catholic Relief Services. The Republicans' loss of majority standing in April 2001 and the terrorist strikes of September 2001 combined to put this proposal on the backburner.

Theme 2: "Reform" of the agencies and personnel of the foreign policy establishment.   Perhaps Helms's most concerted assault on foreign aid in the post–Cold War period was his four-year-long campaign to force the restructuring of United States foreign policy agencies. The campaign was aimed at foreign aid, the foreign aid establishment, and the wider foreign policy institutions of the executive branch, including the State Department, the U.S. Arms Control and Disarmament Agency, and the U.S. Information Agency. In 1995 Helms initiated this significant entrepreneurial campaign. As he put it: "Let's not mince words: Our foreign policy institutions are a complete mess. Over the past four decades, key foreign policy functions have been spun-off into a constellation of money-absorbing, incoherent satellites, each with its own entrenched, growing bureaucracies and its own bureaucratic interests. The result has been an incoherent mish-mash, which no one policy maker controls, and which does not— and cannot—effectively serve either the president or the national interest" (Helms 1995c, 8).

This example of entrepreneurship fits into Helms's larger effort to shape the machinery of American foreign policy to his liking. He was often assertive in his reaction to presidential nominees, seeking to ensure that the "wrong" people did not take up positions of influence.[13] As an entrepreneur, he often linked his concerns and influence over appointments to other substantive issues on which he had strong preferences. His record along these lines extends back to his first days as a senator, and presidents of both parties ran afoul of Helms's priorities and tactics on more than one occasion. Yet it was the restructuring initiative of the post–Cold War that constituted Helms's most sweeping attempt. In the campaign to overhaul the foreign policy bureaucracies, Helms combined a variety of legislative and non-legislative strategies in pursuit of several longstanding concerns: antipathy toward foreign aid, suspicion of the foreign affairs bureaucracy, and ideological interests in shaping personnel choices.

Helms first raised the restructuring initiative in 1994, demanding the abolition of the Agency for International Development, the Arms Control and Disarmament Agency, and the U.S. Information Agency. That same year he offered an unsuccessful floor amendment freezing all slots for assistant secretaries of state pending reorganization (*Congressional Quarterly Almanac* 1994). However the policy window opened wider after he became chairman of the Foreign Relations Committee in 1995.[14]

At hearings with Secretary of State Warren Christopher in February 1995, Helms asked: "Now, if the Cold War is over and if there is agreement that the U.S. government must conduct its affairs differently, then why are the same old bureaucracies spending the same amount of money on the same worn-out programs? . . . Simply said, radical reform must be made, Mr. Secretary, I tell you it is going to happen. Now is the time, not 2 or 3 or 4 years down the road. Now is the time" (Committee on Foreign Relations 1995b, 2). On 15 March 1995 Helms released his proposal, claiming that it would save an estimated $3 billion from the international affairs budget. Not only did he call for eliminating the three agencies noted above (whose functions would be merged into the State Department), but he also proposed a series of changes to the existing State Department to streamline and centralize the agency (e.g. Hook 1998; Helms 1995c). As he explained it, "With or without this consolidation, foreign aid spending will be cut this year—there is absolute unanimity in Congress on that matter. The question for those who support continued foreign aid is this: in a world of shrinking budgets, would they rather have scarce tax dollars go to support 9,000 AID bureaucrats and contractors? Or would they like to see that money spent on and for projects on the ground where it will do some good?" (Helms 1995c, 8). In typical Helms fashion, his campaign centered on a legislative proposal. As one of his staffers noted, Helms "orchestrate[d] [his strategy] based on 'what are we doing with the bill'" (Munson 2001). His committee completed its work on his Foreign Relations Revitalization Act of 1995 in May (see e.g. Committee on Foreign Relations 1995b for a series of hearings on the proposal). It was ready for the Senate floor in July 1995.

Helms's expansive reform initiative met with opposition from Clinton's White House and the foreign policy agencies themselves. Faced with this determined resistance, Helms escalated his efforts, using a variety of procedural and substantive levers. According to one observer's characterization: "As part of his campaign, the North Carolina Republican has halted business meetings of the Senate Foreign Relations Committee, frozen 400 State Department promotions and blocked more than a dozen treaties and other international agreements, including the second Strategic Arms Reduction Treaty and the Chemical Weapons Convention, so they cannot be voted on by the full Senate. As a result, 30 ambassadorial nominees and one Assistant Secretary of State are awaiting confirmation, about 15 percent of American embassies around the world have been left without new ambassadors and the day-to-day foreign policy business on Capitol Hill has ground to a halt" (Sciolino 1995, 1). Thus Helms used his procedural powers as chairman of the committee to hold appointments, treaties, and other matters hostage to his restructuring initiative.

A stalemate ensued. Lacking sixty votes to overcome a filibuster, Helms could not take his bill to the floor for a vote. The administration could not get its personnel confirmed or its international agreements ratified, because Helms would not allow them out of his committee. Months of bargaining followed. In August Helms managed to obtain a meeting with the president, an hour in which he and his staff presented their case for restructuring (Sciolino 1995). Immediately that afternoon, Helms responded to the president's gesture and released a group of nominees and a handful of minor treaties to the Senate floor, along with a statement promising "further good faith from the administration will be met with further good faith from the committee" (quoted in Sciolino 1995, 1).

With White House approval, the ranking committee Democrat, John Kerry, initiated discussions to reach a deal with Helms. Their efforts dragged on throughout the fall (e.g. Lippman 1995b; Black 1995) while the committee remained adjourned. Frustrated, Helms attached the bill to the foreign aid authorization to try to open debate, only to withdraw it when it became clear that his attachment would derail the entire bill (Sciolino 1995). Finally, in December a deal was reached according to which Helms agreed to release eighteen ambassadorial nominations, several minor tax treaties, and both the START II arms control treaty and the Chemical Weapons Convention in return for action on his restructuring initiative (Hook 1998).

In 1996 the carefully crafted deal collapsed. The so-called Helms-Kerry compromise trimmed Helms's budget cuts to $1.7 trillion and allowed the president to preserve two of the three agencies, provided that he submit a State Department reorganization plan by 1 October 1996 (Hook 1998). But this agreement was attached to the State Department authorization bill as an amendment. As the bill wound its way through Congress, the conference committee attached a series of restrictions on international affairs spending, including a measure sponsored by Chris Smith that linked payment of American UN arrears to international family planning issues (Granger 2002). President Clinton vetoed the bill in April 1996 (ironically, Helms's entrepreneurial initiative on restructuring failed in part because of Smith's entrepreneurial initiative on family planning).

After the 1996 election Helms revived the initiative, offered the Foreign Affairs Reform and Restructuring Act of 1997, and informed his colleagues and the administration that ambassadorial appointments and the Chemical Weapons Convention (cwc) would remain locked up in the Foreign Relations Committee until action on his bill was completed (Granger 2002). Helms was determined to complete the reform and to avoid the partisan stalemate that had prevented it to that point (Committee on Foreign Relations 1997).[15] Hence Helms, Biden, and the administration crafted a deal whereby Helms would release the appointments and the cwc, while the administration would support the restructuring initiative.

In April 1997 the Senate ratified the cwc and the Clinton administration released a plan supporting the restructuring of the agencies (Granger 2002). Because of the linkage between the restructuring bill, the UN payments, and the family planning issue driven chiefly by Smith, and the high priority placed on obtaining emergency funding for the International Monetary Fund (e.g. Carter and Scott 2002; Scott and Carter 2005), the

Foreign Affairs Reform and Restructuring Act was placed on the back-burner until the fall of 1998. In October of that year the final version of the legislation was signed by President Clinton. The bill eliminated the ACDA and the USIA, merging their operations into the State Department. USAID survived but was placed under the direct control of the secretary of state, and a number of its independent functions (especially the legislative and public affairs elements) were eliminated and integrated into the State Department (e.g. Lippman 1998b). On 1 April 1999 both the ACDA and USIA ceased to exist, but United States foreign aid programs continued to be administered by USAID.

Theme 3: Unilateralism and American sovereignty. Helms devoted much of his career to the embrace of unilateralism and the defense of United States sovereignty. Although he was fairly consistent in his opposition to United States involvement in multilateral agreements and organizations, the absence of Cold War imperatives and the heightened salience of multilateral institutions treaties in the post–Cold War period resulted in greater opportunity for entrepreneurial action by Helms. In this context Helms's unilateralist entrepreneurship in the post–Cold War period can be regarded as having two strands: United States security policy and United States policy toward international organizations.

Much of Helms's advocacy of a unilateralist security policy hinged upon the threat of weapons proliferation by other nations and his preference for implementing new defense technology. When Helms thought that a bilateral or multilateral security agreement hindered the advancement of United States defense technology, he consistently advocated discarding the agreement. This was most evident in his opposition to the Anti-Ballistic Missile (ABM) treaty and his corresponding advocacy of national missile defense. Helms argued, "The bottom line is that the ABM treaty is prohibiting important tests of our most promising systems and impairing our ability to have a rudimentary missile defense ready by 2004—when the threats posed by some rogue states are expected to mature" (Helms 2001a, § B, 11). The military capabilities of these "rogue states" were also of great concern. Helms believed that there had been ample opportunity for these states to develop nuclear weapons and ballistic missiles while the United States disregarded military and security advancements and remained defenseless (Helms 2001a).

In 1996 Helms used the ABM treaty as a political tool, proposing a bill that would terminate the treaty in order to prompt the Clinton administration on the issue of national missile defense (Lippman and Graham 1996). This political maneuvering was an attempt not only to prod the Clinton administration toward a specific action but also to force a public debate of the issue. Helms followed with two letters to the administration. The first demanded that the president obtain Senate approval of any modification to the ABM treaty occurring in the course of negotiations with Russia. The second urged the president to deploy a national missile defense system. In 1999 Helms pushed the issue further by threatening to attach similar legislation to any other treaty brought before the Foreign Relations Committee. His rider would have delayed the ratification or enactment of the treaty to which it was attached, until the administration submitted to the Senate the negotiated amendments to the ABM treaty. As one journalist noted, "By moving treaties through, but attaching the limiting language on implementation, he shifts the burden to the White House" (Lippman 1999, § A, 5).[16]

Helms's second strand of unilateralist entrepreneurship was directed at international organizations, where Helms felt that American sovereignty was lost and that United States resources and energies were squandered by expansive and unaccountable bureaucracies. Helms illustrated his concern in the preface to *Empire for Liberty* (Thiessen ed. 2001, xxi): "Multilateralism is becoming the prevailing current in international affairs today. Our European allies (who should know better) are running headlong into the multilateralist camp, ceding more and more of their sovereignty to the European Union, the United Nations, and other emerging supranational institutions. . . . But America is different. Americans know full well that in order to conduct a foreign policy guided by the virtues on which our democracy was founded . . . we must be willing to make many sacrifices, in treasure and, in some cases, lives. But there is one thing we Americans must never, ever, sacrifice: our sovereignty."

Helms's pursuit of unilateralism was shown in his response to the idea that the United States would take part in the International Criminal Court. While opposing United States participation in the court was not in itself an entrepreneurial act, Helms's sponsorship of the American Service Members Protection Act was entrepreneurial. The bill purported to preempt any United States participation in the Court and to protect any United States military personnel from its prosecution (Carter and Jackson 2002).

A similar entrepreneurial unilateralism was focused upon United States involvement in the United Nations. In the post–Cold War period Helms's resistance to it was grounded upon two basic arguments: the growing expense of the United Nations, its activities, and bureaucracy, and the alleged violation of the rights of sovereign states to pursue national interests. Helms sought to shape the debate and "soften up" the context for his policy agenda. For example, in the well-known journal *Foreign Affairs*, Helms (1996b, 2) wrote: "With the steady growth in the size and scope of its activities, the United Nations is being transformed from an institution of sovereign nations into a quasi-sovereign entity in itself. That transformation represents an obvious threat to United States national interests. Worst of all, it is a transformation that is being funded principally by American taxpayers." These criticisms by Helms were supplemented by his practice of injecting resolutions, amendments, and letters into the policy stream, thus expressing his criticism of un procedures and his demand for reforms and respect for states' sovereignty. For example, in 1996 Helms proposed legislation to cut payments to the United Nations if the un levied a tax on the United States—the bill passed the Congress, only to be vetoed by President Clinton. In 1997 Helms presented a proposal requiring the United Nations to reduce the United States share of all un dues from 25% to 20% and to accept a reduced amount of arrears owed by the United States. This resolution included with it stipulations of management reform within the United Nations. The bill passed both houses of Congress, but Smith's provision restricting the use of United States funds for abortion was attached to it, prompting a presidential veto (Helms 1998).

Helms's attack on the United Nations resulted in several small victories. In 1997, with United States support, Kofi Annan succeeded Boutros Boutros-Ghali as secretary general of the United Nations and made reform a key item on the un agenda. In 1999 and 2000 Congress again delayed the payment of dues, and the Senate Foreign Relations Committee refused to confirm ambassadors. As it became clearer that a truce was needed between the United Nations and the Senate Foreign Relations Committee, the un made exceptional efforts to build a cooperative relationship. Helms was invited as the first United States senator to speak before the un Security Council, where he delivered a pointed address discussing the role of the un and the rights of the state (Helms 2000b). In an unprecedented act, in March 2000 the Security Council met with the Foreign Relations Committee in Washington. The appearance before the Security Council and the meeting were due in large measure to Helms's aggressive actions. As one diplomat explained, "The fact is, there has been an estrangement between the United States and the UN. What is important is getting back together" (Crossette 2000, § A, 6). In the late fall of 2000, a deal was reached linking UN reform, reduction of United States dues, and payment of United States arrears. Helms's fingerprints were all over it.

Theme 4: Targeting anti-American regimes. During the Cold War Helms's hard-line anti-communism led him to support virtually any regime or faction that took a similar stance. Thus he supported Anastasio Somoza and then the contras against the Sandinistas in Nicaragua, P. W. Botha and the white minority regime against the African National Congress in South Africa, Jonas Savimbi and the UNITA rebels against the leftist regime in Angola, Roberto D'Aubuisson and the right-wing ARENA party against both the moderate Christian Democrats and the leftist rebels in El Salvador, and so on. After 1990 Helms continued to give special attention to what he characterized as anti-American regimes, especially those he considered leftist holdovers from the Cold War. Targets of his entrepreneurship included Iran, Iraq, Indonesia, Libya, Yugoslavia, Colombia, and India. Considerable entrepreneurial efforts were directed toward North Korea, Russia, China, and Cuba in particular.

When Helms targeted a country, he employed a range of approaches to affect policy, including resolutions, amendments, and legislative proposals. In 1990 he tried by introducing an amendment to require that diplomatic recognition be extended to Lithuania (*Congressional Quarterly Almanac* 1990). According to some, including President George H. W. Bush, this pressure not only shaped the administration's policies but prompted an anticipated reaction later when the administration was considering a response to similar events in Ukraine (Bush and Scowcroft 1998; Beschloss and Talbott 1993).

In 1994 Helms offered a successful Senate floor resolution linking MFN status for China to its progress on human rights and support for nuclear nonproliferation (*Congressional Quarterly Almanac* 1994), but his attempt in 1994 to require suspension of all aid programs to any country guilty of expropriating property from American citizens failed (*Congressional Quarterly Almanac* 1994). In 1998 Helms was a principal sponsor of the International Religious Freedom Act, a bill aimed chiefly at China for its alleged persecution of Christians (*Congressional Quarterly Almanac* 1998). In 1999 he offered, but then withdrew, an amendment to establish strict rules and procedures for export licenses for trade with China (*Congressional Quarterly Almanac* 1999). In terms of legislative proposals, key examples (in addition to the restructuring proposal discussed earlier) include the Helms-Burton Act in 1995–96 to extend and strengthen sanctions against Castro's Cuba, as well as countries and companies doing business with Cuba, a proposal in the Foreign Relations Committee in 1999 to provide both covert and overt aid to democratic forces in Serbia seeking to overthrow Slobodan Milosevic (which failed in committee), the successful Serbian Democratization Act of 1999, imposing an array of sanctions to topple Milosevic's regime, and the introduction in 1999 of the Taiwan Security Enhancement Act to provide more political, economic, and military assistance to Taiwan (*Congressional Quarterly Almanac* 1995; *Congressional Quarterly Almanac* 1996; *Congressional Quarterly Almanac* 1999).

However, as is clear from the preceding pages, entrepreneurship rarely ceased with formal legislative efforts, and Helms was no exception. For example, Helms supplemented his legislative approach with efforts to extract information by requiring and requesting reports and by holding hearings. Examples of the first approach include his successful floor amendment in 1990 requiring a presidential report on Soviet compliance with the INF Treaty, which he planned to use to begin a campaign to prevent further arms negotiations (*Congressional Quarterly Almanac* 1990). In 1992 and 1994 he succeeded in requiring presidential certification before aid was released to Russia, to ensure first that Russia was not aiding Iran's nuclear program and later that Russia was complying with its treaty obligations on chemical and biological weapons (*Congressional Quarterly Almanac* 1992; *Congressional Quarterly Almanac* 1994). Finally, in 1999 Helms offered legislation in the Foreign Relations Committee to require a report on the treatment of religious and political prisoners in China, legislation which was withdrawn from consideration before a vote was taken (*Congressional Quarterly Almanac* 1999).

Helms relied heavily on hearings as well. When he was the ranking minority member of Foreign Relations, he used committee staff to conduct investigations in preparation for further action (e.g. the minority staff report on Nicaragua in 1992 that led to an aid freeze), and he was aggressive in calling witnesses, asking questions, and inserting information into hearings that supported his agenda. Later as committee chairman, he used his agenda-setting powers to direct the committee toward issues of his preference, which gave him considerable opportunity to define the problem, affect the agenda, and promote his preferred alternatives. For example, from 1995 to 2000 Helms scheduled twenty-two hearings on issues related to China policy, twelve on Iraq, eleven on Russia, five each on North Korea and Iran, and four on Cuba (Committee on Foreign Relations 1997; Committee on Foreign Relations 1999a; Committee on Foreign Relations 2001b).[17] These hearings constituted almost 30% of the total hearings of the committee (209) during this period and were linked to many of the entrepreneurial resolutions, amendments, and legislative proposals described above.

Helms also contacted executive branch officials directly. As noted earlier, he consulted and negotiated with the Clinton White House on the restructuring proposals on several occasions. He also used letters to policy makers to press his case. For example, in 1990 he sent a letter directly to President George H. W. Bush laying out his opposition to arms control negotiations with the Soviet Union (*Congressional Quarterly Almanac* 1990). In 1997 he sent letters to President Clinton and Secretary of State Albright challenging what he regarded as lax enforcement of the Helms-Burton Act and calling for greater accountability to Congress (*Congressional Quarterly Almanac* 1997). Such actions inserted his positions into both policy debates and policy implementation.

Finally, Helms devoted considerable effort to conditioning the policy-making climate. Frequent forays into the committee room and onto the Senate floor to offer comments, and frequent authorship of opinion pieces and articles for publication in mainstream outlets, were designed to affect the debate both inside the Beltway and in the broader public. Helms frequently used these opportunities to frame issues according to his preferences, to goad an administration to action, or to build support for his legislative proposals.

Few countries attracted as much attention from Helms as Cuba. In the mid-1990s it was the target of a major example of his entrepreneurship, as he sought to extend and strengthen sanctions against Castro. The Helms-Burton Act, or the Cuban Liberty and Democratic Solidarity Act (LIBERTAD), was Helms's response to concerns that not only was Clinton not doing enough to pressure the Castro regime, the administration was even considering easing up on Cuba. In early 1995 Helms had his aide Dan Fisk draft the legislation, which was unveiled in February (Haney and Vanderbush 2002). The act would have allowed lawsuits by United States citizens against foreign companies benefiting from expropriated property in Cuba, as well as barring executives from these companies' entry into the United States. Helms held hearings on the act in May and June 1995 (Committee on Foreign Relations 1995a), fighting for the initiative against the wishes of the administration. Helms also went public. In an opinion piece in the *Washington Post* in May, Helms (1995b, § A, 21) defended sanctions against Cuba, arguing that "ending the embargo would play right into Castro's hands." He also advocated a "final push" to terminate the Castro regime: "the goal of S.381 is to protect the rights of American citizens, cut off Castro's lifeline of hard currency, and send this clear and unmistakable message to foreign businessmen: if you want to do business in the Cuban and American economies, you have to make a choice." Elsewhere, Helms argued that "the embargo is working. My bill will tighten it and deny Castro the two things he most desperately wants: international legitimacy and U.S. hard currency. . . . The Libertad Act will cut off Castro's lifeline of hard currency and increase his pariah status within the international community. It makes clear that only a democratically elected Cuban government will receive the benefits of American trade and recognition" (Helms 1995a).[18]

Helms-Burton passed the House of Representatives largely intact, but opposition from the executive branch caused the Senate to delete its more controversial provisions (Haney and Vanderbush 2002). The differences between the two versions stalled the bill in conference. However, after the Cuban air force downed an unarmed plane piloted by four Cuban-Americans from the "Brothers to the Rescue" organization, the political context shifted dramatically. The stronger provisions of the original bill were restored and the Clinton administration managed only to obtain a provision allowing the president to waive certain parts of the bill for six-month periods if national interests so required. On 12 March 1996 President Clinton signed the bill.

After weaving together his successful legislative and nonlegislative strategy, Helms did not rest. Eager to see the sanctions strictly applied (and more than a little frustrated with Clinton's decision to waive the provision allowing lawsuits against foreign companies), Helms held hearings on its implementation in July 1996 (Committee on Foreign Relations 1996). As noted earlier, he sent letters in 1997 to both Clinton and Albright challenging them on their failure to enforce the act (*Congressional Quarterly Almanac* 1997). In 1998 Helms led a group of twenty-one colleagues to introduce legislation establishing a four-year program to provide $100 million in humanitarian assistance to Cuba, to be channeled through the Catholic Church and independent nongovernmental organizations, a measure that he believed would drive a wedge between the Cuban people and Castro's regime (e.g. Lippman 1998a). Then, in 2000, as arguments resurfaced for using trade and engagement to liberalize Cuba (as was being done in China), Helms again took to the public arena to defend his act, arguing: "Cuba is not China. . . . Cuba has undertaken none of the market reforms that China has in recent years; there is no private property, and there are no entrepreneurs with whom to do business. . . . American investment cannot and will not change any of this" (Helms 2000c, § A, 15). As a result of these efforts, Helms's entrepreneurship—proposing an initiative, campaigning for it, seeing it enacted, and defending it—drove the United States approach to Cuba in the post–Cold War period. Indeed Madeleine Albright, Clinton's ambassador to the UN and secretary of state, acknowledged that the administration had been forced to react to Helms, and was maneuvered by Helms on the issue all along (Albright 2003, esp. 331, 701).

Across these themes and concerns, Helms relied on every avenue of influence and a wide range of activities and access points to engage in his entrepreneurship. Like other entrepreneurs, he organized his efforts principally around bills and amendments, using the floor of the chamber and his committee assignments—and especially his chairmanship of the Foreign Relations Committee—as a platform for his efforts. Helms was prepared to offer amendments and legislation on the issues that concerned him most. Many seemed to have little chance of passage, but successful passage was not always the point. As one of Helms's biographers has noted: "Each of his amendments . . . was drawn to make a point, not to win on a roll-call vote, not even primarily to delay or weaken bills whose passage was imminent. They were aimed beyond the Senate chamber and the strict purposes of legislation. He was reaching out to a national constituency, to frustrated Americans among whom his hard-line tactics stood for courage and leadership rather than obstruction and obfuscation" (Furgurson 1986, 106).

When chairman of the Foreign Relations Committee, Helms used his agenda-setting powers to direct attention to issues of his choice, relying on his committee to design legislative initiatives, hold hearings to gather information and send signals, and establish roadblocks that he controlled. As described, he was willing to shut down the operations of the Foreign Relations Committee or hold international treaties and diplomatic appointments hostage to achieve his goals. One of Helms's colleagues noted: "He'll do anything to gain his way. The processes here are based on two hundred years of ways to resolve differences. . . . He has no compunction about what he'll do . . . He does things that are technically allowed, but in spirit they abuse the rules" (quoted in Furgurson 1986, 23–34). Finally, Helms also used private letters and consultations and was actively engaged in the public debate through the print and electronic media.

His efforts had a powerful impact on United States foreign policy. The efforts we have discussed shaped the structures and resources of the foreign affairs bureaucracy into the twenty-first century. They also shaped Washington's posture toward Cuba, locking in a confrontational policy of sanctions and closing out other options and policies that might have brought about greater engagement. Helms's unilateralist approach conditioned a substantial portion of United States policy toward the UN, culminating in changes within the UN and in its relationship with the United States. It is inconceivable that the reduction of United States dues, the reduction of United States arrears, and the internal reforms initiated in the last two years would have occurred without Helms's policy leadership.

While the frequency of entrepreneurial acts in the post–Cold War period could not match the heights reached after the downturn in Vietnam (the Cold War Dissensus period), in other ways congressional foreign policy entrepreneurship intensified. During these years more individual entrepreneurs engaged in foreign policy making than ever before, and they widened their activities and points of access into the policy process. Their efforts were increasingly partisan, and increasingly aimed at broader strategic policy rather than structural policy. During the post–Cold War period entrepreneurs were active in direct legislative avenues of influence, but they were also broadly engaged in a linked set of activities across a variety of indirect and nonlegislative approaches. If Presidents Bush and Clinton indeed came to "miss the Cold War," the aggressive efforts of congressional foreign policy entrepreneurs are almost certainly partially responsible.

Presidents now face a policy-making setting in which entrepreneurial challenges are almost as likely to come from MCs in the House as in the Senate. The types of issues generating entrepreneurial challenges are not only military-security but increasingly political-diplomatic, economic-developmental, and even cultural-status matters. About the only thing presidents can predict with any assurance is that entrepreneurial challenges in foreign policy will come from members of the opposition party on committees with some jurisdiction over foreign policy, and that likelihood increases when they are in the chamber majority. To paraphrase President George W. Bush, never has the "chief decider" faced so many challengers on Capitol Hill.

From broad-gauged efforts across a variety of issues to focused attention on a particular narrow slice of foreign policy, post–Cold War congressional foreign policy entrepreneurs defined problems, promoted policy alternatives and heavily influenced the foreign policy agenda in Congress and the administration. As Frans Bax (1977) once noted, important congressional initiatives often come down to the actions of a few key individuals in the institution. By using an array of means and access points, and both direct and indirect policy making routes, these entrepreneurs have seized the opportunity presented by the dramatic changes of the end of the Cold War. They have sought to fill the vacuums generated by the need to identify new guideposts for foreign policy in the post–Cold War environment. Washington's response to the post–Cold War world clearly bore their imprint. Entrepreneurs such as Curt Weldon, Chris Smith, and Jesse Helms, among others of this period, affected the agendas, alternatives, policy choices, and policy behavior in ways that cannot be ignored.

7

AFTER 9/11

ENTREPRENEURS INTO THE TWENTY-FIRST CENTURY

As George W. Bush's administration responded to the terrorist attacks of September 11 with major military operations in Afghanistan and Iraq and a broad-gauged "global war on terror," it appeared that the pendulum of foreign policy power had swung dramatically toward the president. At a recent academic conference, a member of the audience addressed foreign policy after September 11 and asked "Where are all the entrepreneurs now?" Reflecting the sense that foreign policy in the wake of the terrorist attacks has been dominated by the White House, this question highlights a broader issue as well. What expectations do the evidence and insights from the post–World War II era generate for our understanding of current and future foreign policy? What patterns emerge from the past fifty years or so that provide insights into future behavior?

The preceding four chapters demonstrate that congressional foreign policy entrepreneurs are significant parts of the post–World War II foreign policy landscape. Across a wide array of issues—some minor and relatively obscure, others major and high-profile—entrepreneurs played key roles in shaping the goals and strategies of the United States in the world, the means and capabilities available to pursue those goals, and the processes by which foreign policy decisions are made. Moreover, the presence and activities of these entrepreneurs are not episodic phenomena but a systematic and sustained force in foreign policy making whose characteristics and activities are patterned and regular. This chapter outlines the major patterns of the post–World War II era and the expectations they provide for current and future behavior. Then, the chapter turns to a sample of evidence from the post-9/11 period as a test of these expectations against the current record.

Post–World War II Entrepreneurs: A Synthesis

Based on the quantitative and qualitative results of this examination, a number of findings stand out for the period 1946–2000. Consider the following trends:

1. Foreign policy entrepreneurship is growing over time in each chamber, especially as measured by the increasing number of members per year engaging in entrepreneurship.
2. Individual entrepreneurs are becoming more active, from more access points and generally in more varied ways, on foreign policy issues over time.
3. While entrepreneurship is more common in the Senate, interchamber differences dramatically narrowed by the post–Cold War period. By the 1990s only 52% of entrepreneurship occurred in the Senate.
4. In both chambers the greatest number of foreign policy entrepreneurs are in the majority party, and that pattern is particularly strong in the House. In both chambers these activists rely on the committees and subcommittees to which they belong or which they control to advance their preferred foreign policy innovations. This finding holds for the Cold War Dissensus (1968–89) and post–Cold War (1990–2000) periods but not for the Cold War Consensus years (1946–67). As the name indicates, during these years the MCs on the foreign affairs and defense-related committees subscribe to the basic anticommunist consensus of administration officials, and thus policy innovation necessarily originates with other structural locales in Congress. After the demise of the Cold War anticommunist consensus, the standing committees and subcommittees dealing with defense and foreign affairs become magnets for congressional foreign policy entrepreneurs (e.g. Johnson 2006). Consequently, which party controls Congress makes a significant difference in the foreign policy process.
5. From 1946 to 2000 the impact of partisanship grows significantly. Partisanship matters as much in foreign policy as in domestic politics, and it has done so since at least the beginning of Richard Nixon's

presidency. During the 1990s almost three-fourths of all entrepreneur-ship was the work of members of the opposition party, the vast ma-jority of that occurring when the opposition party was also in the chamber majority.

These longitudinal trends might be expected to continue, with one ex-ception. The crisis-like nature of United States foreign policy after the attacks on the World Trade Center and the Pentagon should produce a "rally-event" in which entrepreneurship declines and most MCs line up in support of the president's foreign policy initiatives, at least for a short while. However, once presidential policies begin to appear less successful, congressional foreign policy entrepreneurship should rebound. In particu-lar, a recognition by Congress that the occupation of Iraq was not as easy or as cheap as administration officials predicted might be expected to trigger a spike in entrepreneurial behavior.

Congressional foreign policy activism can come from multiple access points, as more and more standing committees and subcommittees, as well as rank-and-file MCs, become active on foreign policy issues (see Hersman 2000; Lindsay 1994a; McCormick 1993; Ripley and Lindsay 1993; and Sinclair 1993). But because of its sustained nature, foreign policy entrepre-neurship requires more commitment than activism does. Consequently, it is no surprise that since the beginning of the Cold War Dissensus, the most important access points for congressional foreign policy entrepre-neurs have been the foreign affairs and defense-related standing commit-tees and subcommittees. The importance of these committee locations is also seen in the steady rise of activities falling into the indirect legislative avenue. These committees are the ones most likely to handle nonbind-ing resolutions, confirmations of appointments, and procedural legisla-tion, and they are typically the "home court" for the activities denoted by the "new institutionalism" concept (see Lindsay 1994b). In the post-9/11 period this trend should continue, as the congressional "experts" on the foreign affairs and defense-related committees vie to offer new policies to meet new threats.

In terms of entrepreneurial acts, these MCs raise and frame new issues in their attempt to get them on the government's agenda. By doing so, they either help to create new policy windows or take advantage of exist-ing ones. Once their issues are on the agenda, they develop policy options to advance them, and they seek to build and mobilize support for their positions, both inside and outside Congress. In the short term success can be measured by achieving the entrepreneur's immediate goal. That might be raising the profile of an issue by holding hearings, giving speeches, or writing letters to national newspapers. It might be getting the ear of the president or other well-placed administration officials. It might be issuing a report. However, long-term success comes with policy innovation—when a new policy course is charted by Congress, or an existing administration policy perceived as harmful is corrected. Policy changes may come directly through congressional action, or indirectly when the administration anticipates congressional reactions and incorporates entrepreneurial preferences and proposals into its policies.

The avenues used by entrepreneurs to change policy span the gamut of possibilities. At the heart of most congressional foreign policy entrepreneurship is a focus on direct legislative action in the form of issue-specific legislation, appropriations, and other such activity. Most entrepreneurs generally seek to enact their preferences through this direct route. Examples of entrepreneurs who relied heavily on direct legislative approaches include Senator McCarran, Senator Helms, and Representative Smith. McCarran used direct legislative means to change United States policy toward Spain, codify internal security measures, and limit immigration. As we have seen, Helms's standard approach to all foreign policy issues was to introduce the issue in bill form first and then try to generate support for it. For his part, Smith attached anti-abortion amendments to seemingly anything and everything coming through the chamber.

Direct nonlegislative approaches are also relied on heavily. Senators Fulbright and Kennedy, as well as Representative Wright, used these approaches to good effect. Fulbright was a pioneer in using televised committee hearings to shape public attitudes, as he did with the Vietnam War. Kennedy used his subcommittee on refugees as a forum to highlight the plight of many refugee groups. For his part, Wright frequently contacted administration officials, often behind the scenes but sometimes with much fanfare, in an effort to change their policy stances. These were his preferred means of trying to change Reagan's Central America policies.

Entrepreneurs have relied on indirect legislative avenues as well. For example, Helms held up a number of ambassadorial appointments to force the Clinton administration to act on his preferred issues, such as the reorganization of the State Department. Senator Church relied on procedural legislation to try to improve congressional control of the intelligence community through the creation of the intelligence committees. Moreover, Senators Javits, Cooper, and Case used congressional control of procedures to try to institutionalize a congressional role in warmaking decisions with the War Powers Resolution.

Finally, all the entrepreneurs examined relied on indirect nonlegislative means such as issue framing and agenda setting. The importance of these activities should not be minimized. While senators have long used their access to the media to frame foreign policy issues in ways helpful to their policy agendas, now entrepreneurs from the House increasingly rely on them as well. Representatives Wright and Weldon are good examples of entrepreneurs who used their contacts with foreign officials to pressure the administration to change its policies. Wright used his contacts with President Arias of Costa Rica to promote a Central American peace plan, and Weldon used his contacts in the Russian Duma to promote both peace in Kosovo and better relations between the United States and Russia overall.

Contrary to expectations, it is military-security issues—not economic-developmental issues—that appear to motivate entrepreneurs most. Economic-developmental issues were the second-most likely area of entrepreneurial activity. With the continuing challenges of a global "war on terror" and the mixed impacts of globalization, we would expect these priorities to continue, with military-security issues ranking first in entrepreneurial attention and economic-developmental ones second. However, more in line with expectations, Senate foreign policy entrepreneurs gravitate more to political-diplomatic and strategic foreign policy issues than their House counterparts do, and House entrepreneurs gravitate toward economic-developmental and structural issues more than Senate entrepreneurs do. There is no obvious reason on the horizon why this pattern of emphasis should soon change in either chamber.

Thus the patterns and trends of 1946–2000 suggest that we should expect to see the following in the post-9/11 period:

—The emergence of more congressional foreign policy entrepreneurs in each chamber, as measured by the average number of individual entrepreneurs per year
—A short-term decrease in entrepreneurship after 9/11, followed by rebounding entrepreneurship totals

—continued growth of entrepreneurship in the House

—more entrepreneurship from the majority party in the chamber

—more entrepreneurship from the nonpresidential party

—continued use of more access points

—more entrepreneurship from standing committees and subcommittees with authority over foreign affairs and defense

—military-security issues ranking first in entrepreneurial activity and economic-developmental issues ranking second

—more entrepreneurship in the Senate on strategic and political-diplomatic issues and more in the House on structural and economic-developmental issues.

Entrepreneurship in the Post-9/11 Period

To examine the contours of entrepreneurship in the years following the terrorist strikes of September 11 on New York and Washington, two years from the period 2002–6 were randomly selected and the data collection procedures described in detail in chapter 3 were duplicated.[1] In the two years constituting the post-9/11 sample, 67 MCs engaged in 172 acts of entrepreneurship.[2]

The patterns of post–World War II entrepreneurship suggest several contradictory trends. First, the trends across the preceding periods suggest that more members should choose to be entrepreneurs. However, post–World War II trends also indicate that times of high threat and consensus dampen entrepreneurship considerably. Moreover, members of the majority party and of the party opposite the president are most likely to engage in entrepreneurship; those factors work against each other in the post-9/11 period (when members of the majority in Congress shared party affiliation with the president) and should therefore have a modest braking effect on entrepreneurship.

Post-9/11 results nicely fit these expectations. As table 29 shows, the number of MCs choosing to act entrepreneurially continued to increase, as post–World War II trends predicted. The post-9/11 years show an average of 33.5 MCs choosing to act entrepreneurially per year, a marked increase from the post–Cold War years (26.2) and in line with increases across the periods. At the same time, acts of entrepreneurship declined from post–Cold War annual averages, falling from an average of 106 (1990–2000) to

Table 29: Entrepreneurship Characteristics
in the Post-9/11 Period

	Overall	2003	2005
Entrepreneurs	33.5	33	34
Entrepreneurship	86	73	99

an average of 86 (2001–6). Specifically, entrepreneurship dipped in 2003 to just seventy-three acts, only slightly above Cold War Consensus figures. However, entrepreneurship then rebounded in 2005 to ninety-nine acts, just under the post–Cold War average. Hence after 2005 it appears likely that post-9/11 entrepreneurship acts rebounded back approximately to prior levels.

This pattern is quite consistent with the post-9/11 threat-and-consensus effect described earlier. Indeed, if expectations are accurate, a sample from 2002 would probably show even less entrepreneurship, while the surge of 2005 should continue in 2006 (with increasing controversy over foreign policy, especially Iraq) and 2007 (increasing controversy *and* a shift to a Democratic majority in Congress). In any event, there appears to be no decline in the entrepreneur phenomenon beyond that which this analysis would predict.

When examining the post–World War II era, one sees that Senate entre-preneurs were considerably more active than their House counterparts during the Cold War Consensus and Cold War Dissensus. In the post–Cold War period that gap narrowed dramatically, to 52% (Senate) versus 48% (House). As table 30 shows, this more even distribution continued largely unchanged into the post-9/11 period: 53% of entrepreneurship occurred in

Table 30: Entrepreneurship by Chamber

	Cold War Consensus	Cold War Dissensus	Post–Cold War	Post-9/11
House	41.4% (292)	36.8% (520)	48.2% (242)	47.1% (81)
Senate	58.6% (414)	63.2% (893)	51.8% (260)	52.9% (91)

the Senate, while 47% occurred in the House. Hence the increase in House entrepreneurship after 1990 continued.

Post–World War II patterns predict an increase in the share of entrepreneurship by members of the majority party and members of the opposition party. In the sample years of the post-9/11 period, these party features counter each other: opposition Democrats were the minority party while majority Republicans shared party affiliation with the president. Moreover, the higher threat-consensus context further complicates the situation in the short term at the least, exerting a further dampening force on entrepreneurship.

The evidence from the post-9/11 period exemplifies these contradictory trends, as seen in table 31. First, overall post-9/11 entrepreneurship is evenly divided between majority and minority party members (50%). However, in 2003 only 31.4% of entrepreneurship came from members of the majority (also the same party of the president), while in 2005, 68.6% did so. At the same time, in the post-9/11 period the partisan gap dramatically declined, with only 50.6% of entrepreneurship coming from members of the opposition party (down from over 73% in the post–Cold War era). In 2003 most entrepreneurship (64.4%) came from members of the opposition party, but in 2005, 59.6% came from members of the same party as the president!

This last finding attests to the controversial nature of administration foreign policy in this period. In combination with the frequencies, this result is entirely in line with our expectations. During the consensus-threat dip (2003), most entrepreneurship was from the opposition party, but since that party was in the minority and did not control as many levers of power in each chamber, fewer acts of entrepreneurship occurred. In 2005, with the controversy over Iraq and other foreign policy issues flar-

Table 31: Post-9/11 Foreign Policy Entrepreneurship by Party Characteristics

Member	Overall	2003	2005
Majority party	50%	31.4%	68.6%
	(86)	(27)	(59)
Opposition party	50.6%	64.4%	40.4%
	(87)	(47)	(40)

Table 32: Post-9/11 Foreign Policy Entrepreneurship
by Party Characteristics and Chamber

Member	House	Senate
Majority party	55.6%	44%
	(45)	(40)
Opposition party	44.5%	56%
	(36)	(51)

ing, entrepreneurship from the opposition remained about the same in absolute terms, but entrepreneurship from the majority party more than doubled, as members of the president's own party became increasingly unhappy with his controversial policies.

There are chamber differences on these party characteristics, however (table 32). In the Senate 44% of entrepreneurship efforts were made by Republicans, the party of the president and the majority party, while 56% were made by the Democratic opposition, despite its minority status. In the House, by contrast, 55.6% were made by the majority Republicans, despite being of the same party as the president, while 44.5% were made by Democrats and Independents in the opposition (and minority). The House is, of course, more rule-driven and structured, and members of the majority have an even greater advantage when it comes to acting entrepreneurially.

Post-9/11 results are again congruent with expectations when activities and access points are examined. As table 33 shows, overall 68.6% of entrepreneurship was direct legislative, with the remainder occurring through nonlegislative or indirect avenues. There were no substantial differences between the chambers. Specifically, in the post-9/11 period entrepreneurs used an average of 5.5 access points and engaged in an average of six activi-

Table 33: Post-9/11 Entrepreneurship and
Policy Avenues of Influence

Policy Avenue of Influence		
Direct-legislative	68.6%	(118)
Indirect-legislative	2.9%	(5)
Direct-nonlegislative	0.6%	(1)
Indirect-nonlegislative	27.9%	(48)
Total	100%	(172)

Table 34: Post-9/11 Instances of Congressional Foreign Policy
Entrepreneurship and Committees, House vs. Senate

Entrepreneur Committee Connection	Overall	House	Senate
Member of foreign policy–related committee	62.8%	51.9 %	72.5%
	(108)	(42)	(66)
Member of appropriations committee	28.5%	37%	20.9%
	(49)	(30)	(19)

ties per year. This finding represents continuity with Cold War Dissensus and Post–Cold War periods on access points, and only a modest decline in the range of activities engaged in by entrepreneurs.

Furthermore, as seen in table 34, the reliance of entrepreneurs on the traditional foreign policy committees deepened. In the post-9/11 years 62.8% of entrepreneurship was attributable to members of the traditional foreign policy committees. *This is the highest level of entrepreneurship from those committees in the entire post–World War II era.* Members of the appropriations committees engaged in 28.5% of the entrepreneurship in the post-9/11 sample as well, which is an increase over the levels of the previous periods. As in earlier years, entrepreneurship in the post-9/11 period was significantly more likely to emerge from the traditional foreign policy committees in the Senate (72.5%) than the House (51.9%). Moreover, entrepreneurship from members of the House Appropriations committee substantially increased (from about 15% to over 37%) compared to previous years, while the Senate remained roughly consistent.

The issue agenda of post-9/11 entrepreneurs clearly reflected the problem environment, as shown in table 35. As predicted, issues related to the use of force and war powers dominated the agenda (23.3%), while arms control (6.4%) and defense spending (4.1%) were also important concerns. Economic assistance, foreign trade, and the general structure of foreign aid followed. Indeed, the combination of these three economic matters accounted for over 31% of the period's entrepreneurship. Interestingly, cultural exchanges and the global environment garnered 6.4% and 4.1% of entrepreneur efforts, the first time either of these issues reached such levels of importance in any period.

When the issues are collapsed, expectations are further supported (see table 36). Over 45% of entrepreneurship in the post-9/11 period

Table 35: The Post-9/11 Entrepreneur Issue Agenda

Foreign Policy Issue	Frequency	Percent
Military operations, war powers	40	23.3
Economic assistance	27	15.7
General foreign assistance	14	8.14
Foreign trade	13	7.5
Nuclear weapons, weapons of mass destruction	11	6.4
Cultural exchange	11	6.4
Intelligence, paramilitary activities	10	5.8
Global environment	10	5.8
Defense procurement, spending	7	4.1
Diplomacy	6	3.5

was in the military-security category, while 42.4% related to economic-developmental concerns, just as predicted. Again, there are chamber differences that conform to expectations as well, with entrepreneurs in the Senate most concerned with military-security issues and entrepreneurs in the House most concerned with economic-developmental issues.

As expected (see table 37), regardless of chamber, entrepreneurship in the post-9/11 years was more about strategic policy issues (51.2%) than structural issues (48.8%). However, as in previous years, the Senate focused on strategic policy more frequently (59.3%) while the House focused on structural policy more frequently (58%). In the narrower defense policy

Table 36: Foreign Policy Entrepreneurship by Policy Category
and Chamber

	Overall	House	Senate
Political-diplomatic	7%	11.1%	3.3%
	(12)	(9)	(3)
Military-security	45.9%	38.3%	52.75%
	(79)	(31)	(48)
Economic-developmental	40.7%	39.5%	41.75%
	(70)	(32)	(38)
Cultural-status	6.4%	11.1%	2.2%
	(11)	(9)	(2)
Total	100%	100%	100%
	(172)	(81)	(91)

Table 37: Foreign Policy Entrepreneurship
by Issue Category and Chamber

	Overall	House	Senate
Structural	48.8%	58%	40.7%
	(84)	(47)	(37)
Strategic	51.2%	42%	59.3%
	(88)	(34)	(54)
Total	100%	100%	100%
	(172)	(81)	(91)
Defense structural	12.3%	16%	10%
	(8)	(4)	(4)
Defense strategic	87.7%	84%	90%
	(57)	(21)	(36)
Total	100%	100%	100%
	(65)	(25)	(40)

arena (table 37), while both chambers were substantially more likely to focus on strategic defense policy, the House was somewhat more likely to focus on structural defense policy than the Senate. Overall, though, attention to structural defense policy continued to decline, gathering only 12% of entrepreneur attention in the post-9/11 period. Thus entrepreneurial MCs were addressing more questions about *what* the United States should be doing than about *how* it should be done.

The picture that emerges in the post-9/11 period is largely consistent with the patterns observed in previous periods. The greatest exception is the degree to which entrepreneurship in 2005 was engaged in by members of the president's party, a telling indicator of how controversial foreign and security policy have become. In hindsight, it appears that by 2005 entrepreneurs from both parties were beginning to see major flaws in the foreign and national security policy of the White House.

Post-9/11 Entrepreneurs: Illustrative Sketches

As in earlier periods, in the post-9/11 period entrepreneurial MCs responded in rational ways to the events and issues of the times. Three sketches highlight the continuity between the pre-9/11 and post-9/11 periods and provide insight into the persistence of several interesting aspects of entrepreneurship.

First, as the American use of force in Iraq proved more costly and complicated than the Bush administration had predicted, MCs became increasingly uncomfortable with the policy. Opposition grew, as did proposals to chart a new course. One example of this growing concern and this growing challenge nicely illustrates one of the patterns seen in previous situations. In early 2007 Senators Richard Lugar (R-Ind.) and John Warner (R-Va.) met privately with President Bush in the White House to express their unease about the rising costs and policy failures in Iraq, urging the president to change direction (DeYoung and Murray 2007, § A, 1). When the administration did not respond to their concerns, the two senators began to offer muted public criticism, hoping to signal the need for a change. These too were ignored.

Lugar and Warner were among the key senators insisting on the inclusion of political and military benchmarks in the supplemental funding package approved by Congress in June. They also worked to establish a special commission of retired military officers to assess progress in Iraq, and requested from the Government Accountability Office an independent assessment of progress toward the benchmarks they had helped to establish (DeYoung and Murray 2007, § A, 1). By midsummer their patience had expired. Lugar took the floor of the Senate in late June and gave a speech calling on Bush to begin reducing forces in Iraq right away. He asserted: "We don't owe the President our unquestioning agreement" (DeYoung and Murray 2007, § A, 1). Less than two months later Warner made a similar public appeal (Reuters 2007). Both senators warned the president to take the lead in changing strategy before it was too late. As Lugar put it, "The President has an opportunity now to bring about a bipartisan foreign policy. I don't think he'll have that option for very long" (Associated Press 2007). In effect, these senators ratcheted up their efforts from private to public warnings to a president of their own party, and appeared poised to take the next step of more formal efforts to initiate a policy change.

Second, some entrepreneurs took action to produce policy correction. After the revelations of the torture of detainees at Abu Ghraib, Senator John McCain (R-Ariz.) expressed shock at both the events and the administration's hiding of the story, stating that "Congress should have been notified of this situation a long time ago" (Dionne 2004, § A, 33). When administration officials learned that influential Senate Republicans were considering legislation limiting the use of torture, Vice President Cheney met privately with Senators McCain, Warner, and Lindsey Graham (S.C.)— all members of the Armed Services Committee—to try to head them off (White and Smith 2005). The administration's effort failed. McCain was successful in getting the Senate to pass his amendment, by a 90–9 vote, limiting what military personnel could do to those held in custody. The legislation called for "uniform standards" of behavior by military inter- rogators to prevent any "cruel, inhuman, or degrading" treatment of de- tainees (Babington and Murray 2005, § A, 1). Reacting to the Senate vote, a month later the Defense Department announced a new eight-page direc- tive that required military interrogators to treat detainees in a "humane" way and banned "acts of physical or mental torture" (White 2005, § A, 25). According to the columnist David Broder (2005), Graham and others like him felt that it was time for Congress to be more assertive and to take more institutional responsibility for national security policy.

Third, in other instances entrepreneurial MCs were motivated by policy vacuums. In the years since the September 11 attacks, increasing attention has been devoted to global warming. For the first time in our evidence, this issue garnered substantial attention from congressional foreign policy entrepreneurs, owing in part to the administration's fierce resistance to efforts to curb global warming. According to the Pew Center on Global Cli- mate Change, the failure of the administration to act generated increasing congressional activity. In 1997–98 (105th Congress), the center reported only seven pieces of legislation (bills and amendments) concerning global warming. That number increased to twenty-five in the 106th Congress, eighty in the 107th, ninety-six in the 108th, and 106 in the 109th. In just the first nine months of the 110th Congress, 125 bills and amendments were offered.[3] Key entrepreneurs also led the effort to address global warming through hearings designed to raise awareness and generate momentum for their legislative efforts as well.

Many congressional entrepreneurs engaged on this issue, and several examples illustrate their efforts. Senator Jeff Bingaman (D-N.M.), who had a long-standing interest in this issue, built on his previous efforts to persuade the Senate to adopt a resolution in 2005 that for the first time put Congress on the record as expressing its acceptance of scientific find- ings that global warming was a significant problem with human causes, and calling for a national policy to slow, stop, and reverse the emission of greenhouse gases. Bingaman's amendment passed 53–44. According to the *New York Times*:

> despite ferocious White House opposition, the Senate went on record as favoring a program of mandatory controls of emissions of the gases that contribute to global warming. . . . The resolution was anything but meaningless. It represents a major turnaround in attitudes, especially among prominent Republicans who only a few years ago doubted a problem even existed. It is something to build on: Pete Domenici, the most influential Senate Republican on energy matters and a recent convert to the global warming cause, has already scheduled hearings to see what sort of legislation can be devised down the road. And it terrifies the White House because it is further proof that the administration's efforts to minimize the warming threat have failed and that President Bush's voluntary approach to the problem is no longer taken seriously. ("Climate Shock" 2005, § A, 14)

Additional congressional pressure followed. After the Democrats won a majority of seats in both chambers in 2006, the new House speaker, Nancy Pelosi (Calif.), established a new Select Committee on Energy Independence and Global Warming. Representative Ed Markey (D-Mass.), another active entrepreneur on this issue, was named chairman of the new committee, which immediately scheduled a series of high-profile hearings, including a "mountaintop summit" in the White Mountains of New Hampshire to highlight the impact of climate change.[4]

Under pressure, in May 2007 the Bush administration finally took some action, calling for additional talks and setting "aspirational goals," but these initiatives were widely regarded as insufficient. As Markey put it, "It is vitally important for America and this president to reengage internationally on this issue and agree to targets for reducing heat-trapping pollution. . . . Instead, all President Bush is willing to do is engage in fruitless discussions until the very end of his administration" (Fletcher and Eilperin 2007, § A, 1).

Dissatisfied by the tepid efforts, congressional entrepreneurs took additional action rather than wait for leadership from the administration. Bingaman joined with Senator Arlen Specter (R-Pa.) to introduce the Low Carbon Economy Bill in July 2007 (e.g. Broder 2007). Not long after, Senator Joseph Lieberman (I-Conn.), another entrepreneur with long-standing interests on this issue, joined with Senator Warner to introduce the American Climate Security Act of 2007, a comprehensive measure to combat global warming. Warner's comments on the legislation represent a good example of the framing efforts to which entrepreneurs resort to gain traction on their issues: "In my 28 years in the Senate, I have focused above all on issues of national security, and I see the problem of global climate change as fitting squarely within that focus. . . . In hearings before the Environment and Public Works Committee, and in meetings with the private sector, I have come to appreciate the challenges our nation faces in addressing this complex issue. In going through this process, I have also come to believe that the time for the Legislative Branch to act is now."[5] These entrepreneurs were setting the stage for more aggressive efforts to address an increasingly salient problem.

The crisis-like conditions that followed the 9/11 attacks led Congress to "rally 'round the president," at least initially. This rally event led to the perception that entrepreneurs had largely disappeared in the face of a global war on terror and an aggressive administration bent on reasserting presidential dominance. Yet the rumors of the entrepreneurs' demise have been exaggerated. As expected, in the post-9/11 period entrepreneurs responded in predictable ways to issues that matter. The patterns of entrepreneurship established between the end of the Second World War and 2000 continue to be seen in the sample from the most recent period. Moreover, the average number of MCs per year who choose to become entrepreneurs in foreign policy continues to climb, increasing from eighteen during the Cold War Consensus to twenty-five during the Cold War Dissensus to twenty-six in the post–Cold War period to over thirty-three in the post-9/11 period. Given this pattern, it seems likely that the surge in congressional foreign policy entrepreneurship should continue after the election of 2006, and early anecdotal evidence from the news media seems to suggest that it will. Far from disappearing, congressional entrepreneurs continue to be significant players in the foreign policy game.

8

PART OF THE LANDSCAPE

CONCLUSIONS ON THE ENTREPRENEUR EFFECT

As the preceding pages illustrate, the existence and importance of congressional foreign policy entrepreneurs cannot be denied. Across the entire period since World War II, a number of assertive MCs have chosen to lead the way on the foreign policy issues they care about without waiting for the administration to take action. Significant foreign policy innovation has been the result—new policies where previously there were none, policy redirection where course corrections were deemed necessary, and rejected policies where the old ones were found wanting. Examples such as policy innovation can be found in each post–World War II decade. From the coldest days of the Cold War, to the political turmoil after Vietnam and Watergate, to the new world after the demise of the Soviet Union, and to the changed circumstances after 9/11, important congressional initiatives attributable to a few key individuals can be found. American foreign policy changed as a result.

That such entrepreneurs can be found consistently over time indicates that they are no aberration, but instead are a *standard feature* of the United States foreign policy–making process. While *reactive* congressional foreign policy assertiveness is certainly generated by key external events and perceived critical issues (see Henehan 2000), the evidence presented here demonstrates that *proactive* congressional foreign policy assertiveness is always present. Moreover, the number of congressional foreign policy entrepreneurs is expanding over time. Thus claims of a "resurgent" Congress after Vietnam or a "rise and decline" in the congressional foreign policy–making role do a disservice to those MCs who are busy acting on their foreign policy agendas all the time. By failing to recognize the policy importance of these entrepreneurs acting in the name of Congress, observers underestimate the importance of Congress in foreign policy making. To use the analogy of Hersman (2000), these people help to create the ocean of foreign policy making, and the ocean matters at least as much as the waves.

In this book the policy actions of congressional foreign policy entrepreneurs have been shown to be significant in shaping United States foreign policy, even as they have gone largely unnoticed by foreign policy researchers. A few have applied the concept of policy entrepreneurs to legislators in the domestic policy arena (see e.g. Wawro 2000), and several studies implicitly suggest their importance (see Hersman 2000; Mayhew 2000; Mayhew 2005; Trubowitz 1998). However, no in-depth, systematic examination of the activities, impact, and importance of legislative policy entrepreneurs in the foreign policy arena has been conducted until now. Understanding who congressional foreign policy entrepreneurs are and what they do helps us to better understand congressional assertiveness, thereby providing a more realistic and nuanced understanding of the United States foreign policy–making process.

Further, the presence of congressional foreign policy entrepreneurs, combined with their tendency to fly under the radar of other observers, provides an answer to the puzzle noted in chapter 1: Why do presidents see an assertive Congress when academic observers largely do not? Presidents are enmeshed daily in the policy-making context inside the Beltway and these assertive MCs are an important part of that reality, a fact well documented in presidential memoirs and administration histories. In 1985 Representative Dick Cheney (R-Wyo.) offered an exaggerated but telling reflection of this perception when he complained bitterly that the president must "put up with every member of Congress with a Xerox machine and a credit card running around the world cutting deals with heads of state" (quoted in Lindsay 1994a, 53).

The actions of entrepreneurs are important. From the perspective of the White House, control of foreign policy making is becoming more difficult as congressional foreign policy entrepreneurs pursue their own policy opportunities and create obstacles for the administration to accomplish its goals in its desired ways. Presidents, their top advisors, and other foreign policy makers in the executive branch must spend increasing amounts of their time anticipating how these MCS will react to administration initiatives and how administration initiatives can be shaped to offset, outmaneuver, or co-opt the individual foreign policy agendas of entrepreneurial MCS. This was true even during the Cold War Consensus, as the former secretary of state Dean Rusk lamented (1990, 539): "I devoted about one-third of my time as secretary of state to congressional relations. . . . It was a major part of the job. Sometimes Congress's demands are excessive."

Yet from the perspective of Capitol Hill, foreign policy making is becoming more representative of the will of the people. Whether motivated by public opinion broadly defined or more narrowly by their own political affiliation, constituencies, or idiosyncrasies, the ideas that move MCS also move some elements of the public (Trubowitz 1998). As long as MCS perceive their greater involvement in foreign policy making as a public service virtue, with the political rewards outweighing the political risks, they will continue to increase their foreign policy engagement. Foreign policy embarrassments by an administration, such as the Bush administration's failure to find weapons of mass destruction in Iraq after making their presence a centerpiece of its case for going to war in 2003, will only encourage more congressional foreign policy entrepreneurship from members, especially those of the opposition party. Over time, and particularly in cases such as those noted above, opportunities for assertive congressional foreign policy involvement will expand, as will the foreign policy obstacles faced by presidential administrations.

In this concluding chapter, the preceding evidence is examined and synthesized. The chapter begins with a reflection on the theoretical framework and hypotheses of chapter 2. It then turns to a discussion of the patterns of leadership demonstrated by the entrepreneurs of the study, followed by an assessment of the policy impact of entrepreneurs.

Understanding and Explaining Entrepreneurship

Chapter 1 introduced a theoretical framework to guide the examination of these consequential foreign policy players. This framework directed attention to a number of factors that define the entrepreneurs and shape their behavior and impact. In the following pages, the framework with which the book began is reexamined, first by weighing the evidence of the preceding chapters against the hypotheses about entrepreneurs derived from the framework, and then by highlighting several aspects of the framework on which the evidence provides additional insights.

Hypotheses on Entrepreneurs and Entrepreneurship

This book proposed eighteen initial hypotheses derived from the theoretical framework guiding this study. In general, the propositions received broad support from the evidence. Fifteen of the eighteen original hypotheses received at least some support, and only two appear to be contradicted by the quantitative or case study evidence.

First, the evidence in chapters 3–6 provides strong support for six of the initial hypotheses introduced in chapter 2.

> *Hypothesis 2: Entrepreneurs are most likely members of the nonpresidential party.* Both the quantitative and case study evidence strongly supports this hypothesis. While entrepreneurs of the same party as the president are not uncommon, the data from the post–World War II era show an increasing trend toward partisan entrepreneurship, with more and more entrepreneurial actions arising from the party opposite the president. Our cases suggest that dedicated entrepreneurs will act regardless of the party affiliation of the president. Major entrepreneurs such as William Fulbright, Jesse Helms, Frank Church, and others we have discussed took action with Republican and Democratic presidents. However, beyond leading entrepreneurs such as these, more entrepreneurs join the game when the other party controls the White House.

> *Hypothesis 5: Members of the Senate are most likely to be entrepreneurs.* Both the quantitative and the case study evidence support this hypothesis. While the gap between House and Senate entrepreneurship has narrowed dramatically in recent years, the Senate retains the advantage. Five of the nine case studies are from the Senate, but more important, in the quantitative data twenty-one of the twenty-five most active entrepreneurs of the

post–World War II era are from the Senate. These individuals, fewer than 5% of all entrepreneurs, are responsible for over 25% of the entrepreneurship of the period.

Hypothesis 6.1: Entrepreneurs are most likely to be members of the foreign policy committees. Our quantitative data support this hypothesis, showing that entrepreneurship increasingly emerged from the foreign policy committees over time. It is also instructive that nine of the top ten, and eighteen of the top twenty-five, most active congressional foreign policy entrepreneurs of 1946–2000 held seats on the foreign policy, armed services, or intelligence committees. In the post-9/11 period eight of twelve most active entrepreneurs held seats on at least one of these committees as well. Our case studies suggest that entrepreneurs seek out those assignments to improve their ability to pursue their policy interests.

Hypothesis 7: Members of the majority party are most likely to be entrepreneurs. Both the quantitative and case study evidence strongly support this hypothesis. Two-thirds of the entrepreneurship in our sample was attributable to the majority party, while the case studies provide ample evidence of the institutional advantages enjoyed by majority party members.

Hypothesis 10: More members choose to be entrepreneurs over time. Evidence from the quantitative data strongly supports this hypothesis. During the Cold War Consensus about nineteen members per year engaged in entrepreneurship. By the post-9/11 period, that number was about thirty-three members per year.

Hypothesis 15: House entrepreneurs focus on structural issues, while Senate entrepreneurs emphasize strategic issues. As our evidence shows, there is a persistent gap between the two chambers, with Senate entrepreneurship involving strategic issues more often than House entrepreneurship. However, entrepreneurs from *both* chambers emphasize strategic over structural issues, and strategic issues are increasingly the focus of attention over the years of the study.

Second, the evidence from the data and the case studies provides some support, albeit weaker, for four other hypotheses.

Hypothesis 1: Constituency pressure increases entrepreneurship.
The quantitative evidence of this study does not include data directly relevant to this hypothesis. However, the case studies in chapters 4–6 suggest that constituency groups can be a significant motivating factor behind a decision to act entrepreneurially. For example, Jacob Javits was undoubtedly motivated in part by his constituency in championing Israel in the U.S. Senate, and while Representative Jim Wright's interest in relations with Mexico had its origins in his family history, it was also generated in part by the concerns of his constituency. Finally, Representative Curt Weldon's spirited and persistent advocacy for the V-22 Osprey aircraft stemmed in part from the economic interests of his constituency. However, the rest of the evidence suggests that entrepreneurs engage on issues of significance to them (and to the times) and seek to shape rather than merely respond to constituency opinion. Additionally, one congressional staff member suggested that it was the general *lack* of constituency interest in foreign policy that freed MCs to be entrepreneurs (Johnstone 2001). The evidence we have reviewed here is not thorough or systematic enough for confident conclusions about this hypothesis.

Hypothesis 11: Entrepreneurs use a greater variety of access points over time. The quantitative data suggest that entrepreneurs' use of access points broadened after the Cold War Consensus, increasing from around four access points to almost six. The evidence from the cases also suggests that entrepreneurs since the mid-1960s have relied on a wider range of access points to pursue their policy preferences; this is especially true of the most active entrepreneurs.

Hypothesis 12: Entrepreneurs use a greater variety of activities over time. Both the quantitative data and the case study evidence again provide some support for this hypothesis. The quantitative data show a modest increase in activities from the Cold War Consensus to the Cold War Dissensus; there was a subsequent dip in the post–Cold War and post-9/11 periods, but activities still remained higher than during the Cold War Consensus. The case study evidence also suggests that entrepreneurs—especially the most active—became increasingly varied in their efforts after the mid-1960s. Later entrepreneurs such as Jesse Helms and Jim Wright were able to take advantage of changes in the institution and the media to attack their issues across a broader front.

Hypothesis 14: Entrepreneurs in the Senate are more engaged on political-diplomatic issues. The quantitative data suggest that political-diplomatic issues are more often addressed by entrepreneurs in the Senate than by entrepreneurs in the House. However, the case study evidence presents a more mixed pattern, with numerous examples of political-diplomatic entrepreneurship by members of the House, including, most obviously, the attempts by Jim Wright to redirect policy toward Nicaragua and Central America and by Curt Weldon to negotiate an end to the Kosovo War.

For five of the original hypotheses, the evidence from chapters 3–6 provides anecdotal, but not definitive or systematic, support.

Hypothesis 3: Entrepreneurship increases as media attention to a particular policy issue increases. Although this hypothesis is logical and well supported by other scholarship, the evidence reviewed in this analysis presents only anecdotal and unsystematic support for it. The case studies present a number of instances where media attention appears to be associated with increasing entrepreneurship. For example, media reports of possible CIA involvement in the military coup of 1973 in Chile drove Senator Frank Church's efforts to investigate the intelligence community and to propose reforms in its operations. Senator Edward Kennedy was led to the issue of South African sanctions by media attention and a personal appeal from Bishop Desmond Tutu. Media attention regarding questionable activities by the contras also prompted Speaker Jim Wright to get involved in the Nicaraguan civil war. However, the case studies also suggest that entrepreneurs themselves are often responsible for driving up the amount of attention that the media devote to a given issue. Every entrepreneur profiled in these case studies used the media to promote the issues about which he cared, from Senator Pat McCarran's many speaking engagements and public addresses focusing on the domestic communist threat, to Fulbright's televised hearings on Vietnam, to Frank Church's skillful media campaign to keep attention on the need for intelligence reform, to Curt Weldon's full-court press for a national missile defense system. As our framework suggests, this constitutes active and aggressive shaping of the political and problem streams to open, or keep open, policy windows.

Hypothesis 6.2: Entrepreneurs who route issues through their committees are more successful. Although the quantitative data do not address this issue directly, the case study examples of William Fulbright, Frank Church, Edward Kennedy, Curt Weldon, and Jesse Helms provide some support for this hypothesis. It is hard to imagine Fulbright having been successful without the advantage he enjoyed as chairman of the Foreign Relations Committee, just as it is difficult to envision Jesse Helms's ability to link numerous (often unrelated) issues to his preferred policy initiatives without his seat on the Foreign Relations Committee. It is also instructive, as noted earlier, that the great majority of the most active entrepreneurs had seats on the foreign policy, armed services, and intelligence committees.

Hypothesis 6.3: Entrepreneurship from committee chairpersons and ranking minority members is more likely to be successful. As Jesse Helms's assistant Lester Munson (2001) told us, "sometimes you can rely on your position as the ranking minority Republican or as the chairman. . . . So [the] position helps. A guy like [Senator Richard] Lugar, who isn't in that position, has to play a different game." Again, while the quantitative data are silent, key examples from Pat McCarran, William Fulbright, Frank Church, and Jesse Helms tend to provide some limited support for this hypothesis, although the support is not definitive or systematic.

Hypothesis 8: Congressional foreign policy entrepreneurs who serve as elected party leaders are more likely to be successful in achieving their aims. Both Jim Wright and Robert Dole are among the twenty-five most active entrepreneurs according to data from the post–World War II era. Moreover, Wright, Dole, and Tip O'Neill, three key elected party leaders, appear in our case studies and provide limited anecdotal evidence on this point. All three were in stronger positions to act on their issues (respectively Central American peace, Bosnia, and fundraising for arms for Northern Ireland) as a result of being Senate Majority Leader (Dole) or House Speaker (Wright and O'Neill). Further, a study on reform of the International Monetary Fund in the 1990s indicates the key entrepreneurial roles played by Senate Majority Leader Trent Lott (R-Miss.) and House Majority Leader Dick Armey (R-Texas) (see Scott and Carter 2005). While this evidence is limited it does provide anecdotal support that warrants further analysis.

Hypothesis 9.1: Congressional foreign policy entrepreneurs who are more senior are more likely to be successful in achieving their aims. Of the nine entrepreneurs profiled in the case studies, six appeared to be more successful on significant issues later in their careers than earlier. Successes include those of Pat McCarran (on Spanish bases, internal security, and limiting immigration), William Fulbright (on the Vietnam War), Frank Church (on intelligence reform), Edward Kennedy (on South African sanctions, and perhaps on arms control), Jim Wright (on the Central American peace plan), and Jesse Helms (on State Department reorganization and various issues involving protection of United States sovereignty).

At least two hypotheses are confronted with evidence to the contrary.

Hypothesis 4: As a member's staff attention increases, entrepreneurship by that member increases. The quantitative evidence of this analysis contains no data on this matter, but the case study material includes evidence that would seem contrary to the hypothesis. In fact, numerous examples from the cases suggest that it is the entrepreneurs who direct staff attention to issues of their interest, rather than vice versa. For example, Ken Meyer (2001), a staff aide to Richard Lugar, described "these sessions that I call 'around the world with Dick in thirty minutes' in which . . . he just sits down with us and something's got him. He read something and started thinking about something and we start talking about the issues right now . . . we're contributing to his thought process but he's starting it."

Hypothesis 13: Entrepreneurship on economic-developmental issues is most frequent. Both the quantitative and case study evidence strongly contradict this expectation. Entrepreneurs are simply not more likely to focus on these issues. While electoral and constituency-driven models of congressional behavior tend to stress them, entrepreneurs are apparently driven by a different calculus and issue agenda. This special subset of congressional activism and assertiveness is particularly concerned with military-security and political-diplomatic issues, and with strategic more than structural issues.

Finally, one of our hypotheses is not addressed directly by our evidence. Neither our quantitative nor our case study evidence provides any consistent insights on *hypothesis 9.2* (the declining impact of seniority). Examples of relatively junior entrepreneurs who were successful in earlier years can be found, such as Brien McMahon (creation of the Atomic Energy Agency) and Henry Reuss (creation of the Peace Corps). This hypothesis remains plausible and logical based on the increasing fragmentation of the modern Congress and its openness to individual action, but further study is required to see if entrepreneurs like McMahon and Reuss are atypical when it comes to congressional seniority. Perhaps their commitment to policy innovation leads them to see their lower levels of seniority as just another obstacle to overcome.

The Entrepreneur Framework

Several aspects of the theoretical framework warrant additional attention as well. First, although the original framework accommodates the role of entrepreneurs in shaping the problem, policy, and political streams, the evidence in the preceding chapters suggests that the link between the entrepreneur's decision to take the lead and these policy streams is even stronger. Indeed, most troublesome to advocates of a preeminent presidency are those congressional foreign policy entrepreneurs who can generate or contribute to the problem and policy streams, thereby influencing the political stream that can force open a policy window. McCarran's championship of a closer military relationship with Franco's regime in Spain is a classic example of a committed entrepreneur reversing a long-held administration policy position. Both Presidents Roosevelt and Truman abhorred cooperation with what they viewed as a fascist regime in Madrid that "tilted" toward the Axis powers in World War II. McCarran was able to take advantage of the problem stream (how will the United States deal with the global communist threat?) by providing a solution in the policy stream (emphasizing Franco's anticommunist roots). He was able to affect the political stream by generating pressures on Truman from within the administration (by stressing the obvious advantages of Spanish air and naval bases to military audiences, so that the anti-Spain position of Secretary of State Dean Acheson was countered by the pro-Spain position of Pentagon officials). The loans that he initiated to Spain created the policy window by forcing the administration to deal with the Spanish government. Thus over several years, McCarran was almost single-handedly able to reverse an important national security policy stance during the Cold War.

Likewise, Henry Reuss used public addresses and writings to contribute to the problem stream (how can we offset Soviet aid advantages, actually improve the lives of the masses in developing countries, and in the process present a kinder American face to the world?) and the policy stream (look at the good works done by civilian private volunteers!), while taking advantage of the political stream (Democratic Party leadership in the Congress and a new Democratic presidential administration in 1961). As a result, he helped created a policy window (let's fund a study!) that resulted in the co-opting of his initiative by the new president (in many ways, a kind of anticipated reaction).

Additional examples could be drawn from our case studies, including those involving William Fulbright, Frank Church, Edward Kennedy, Chris Smith, Jesse Helms, and others discussed in less detail. Not all instances of congressional foreign policy entrepreneurship are successful, but examples such as these illustrate how congressional foreign policy entrepreneurs can help create the circumstances that enable policy innovation, particularly if they are willing to devote the necessary time to "softening up." As a House staffer once noted, winning in Washington often comes down to who is stubborn longer, and entrepreneurs have the commitment to be stubborn for a long time. The stubbornness prize probably goes to William Prox-mire, who gave 3,211 speeches on behalf of the genocide convention, rising virtually every day that Congress was in session for almost twenty years to advocate for the treaty before it was finally ratified in 1986.

The model's feedback loop from issue framing to policy windows also deserves additional mention. As Baumgartner and Jones (1993) note, long-standing policies can be swiftly changed when new issue frames create new definitions of problems. McCarran was able to offset more than a decade's worth of administrative reluctance to deal with Spain by changing the issue frame from "Franco's a fascist like Hitler" to "Who's more anticommunist than a fascist like Franco?" After Reagan's Mexico City policy on abortion was dropped by the Clinton administration, Chris Smith's continual efforts to highlight the need to go back to Reagan's policy helped create the setting where it was quickly embraced by a new Republican president, George W. Bush (who said he looked to the Reagan administration as a model to follow). Smith was prodding Bush by essentially saying, "If you want to be like Reagan, change this policy now."

This feedback highlights another aspect of entrepreneurship that emerges from our evidence: the identification of a policy problem. As we have noted and discuss in more detail below, entrepreneurs respond to both policy vacuums (their identification of problems not being addressed) and policy corrections (their identification of problems being inappropriately addressed). The latter situation in particular highlights the significance of the feedback loop in prompting entrepreneurs to respond to previous policy actions by initiating entrepreneurial campaigns of their own.

Together these observations suggest a minor amendment of the theoretical framework that places greater emphasis on the problem, policy, and political streams, and entrepreneurs' efforts to shape them and open subsequent policy windows that enable their policy innovations. In effect, rather than a secondary avenue, this may be a primary route (or the primary route) for congressional foreign policy entrepreneurship. Figure 5 modifies the original theoretical framework to accommodate this insight.

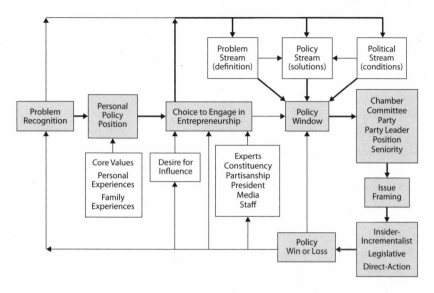

Figure 5: A Revised Theory of Congressional Foreign Policy
Entrepreneurship

Patterns of Leadership

While the combination of quantitative and case study evidence presented
in the preceding pages clearly indicates that congressional foreign policy
entrepreneurship has substantial scope and impact, there are also several
patterns of leadership revealed. Together they help shape a more subtle,
nuanced understanding of the phenomenon. Among the most significant
of these patterns are the varying *strategies of entrepreneurship* employed
by those members who choose to lead in this fashion, and varying *categories of entrepreneurs* into which these members fit. The first pattern
emerges principally from the activities and avenues used by the entrepreneurs, and the second from the issues to which entrepreneurs typically devote their attention.

Strategies of Entrepreneurship

We have argued that congressional foreign policy entrepreneurs have
a wide array of activities and access points on which to rely when they

choose to take the lead on a given foreign policy issue. The evidence presented in these pages catalogues those activities and access points and demonstrates both the range and frequency of nonlegislative and indirect efforts. In spite of the variety and complexity of entrepreneur activities, at least three distinct strategies of entrepreneurship can be identified from the case studies.

The insider-incrementalist strategy. In many ways this strategy constitutes the ideal type underlying our initial theoretical conceptualization discussed in chapter 2. It is perhaps best illustrated by William Fulbright, in his own words:

> A Senator who wishes to influence foreign policy must consider the probable results of communicating privately with the Executive, or alternatively, of speaking out publicly . . . For my own part, I have used both methods, with results varying according to circumstance. Other things being equal—which they seldom are—I find it more agreeable to communicate privately with Democratic Presidents and publicly with Republican Presidents.
>
> Since 1961, when the Democrats came back to power, I have made recommendations to the President on a number of occasions through confidential memorandums. In April, 1965, I sent President Johnson a note containing certain recommendations on the war in Vietnam, recommendations which I reiterated thereafter in private conversations with high Administration officials. When it became very clear that the Administration did not find my ideas persuasive, I began to make my views known publicly in the hope, if not of bringing about a change in Administration policy, then at least of opening up a debate on that policy. (Fulbright 1966b, 105)

What Fulbright characterizes is a sequential pattern to entrepreneurship that begins with an approach to the administration and private, behind-the-scenes consultation and advice. In effect the entrepreneur provides *private* signals to the administration about preferred policy characteristics. These signals may take the form of conversations, memoranda, letters, and the like. Should the administration respond positively by addressing the entrepreneur's concern in its policy (in a kind of anticipated reaction), further entrepreneurship is unnecessary (and the entrepreneur's impact is likely to be missed—as with Representative Jim Leach and the peso devaluation of 1995).

However, insider-incrementalists move into the public realm when the administration fails to heed the signals. These entrepreneurs incrementally escalate their efforts to bring the problem and, most probably, the proposed solution into the public arena. According to Representative Charlie Wilson (2008), an entrepreneur might initially use the threat to go public to persuade an administration to act. Should that fail, a shift to public action might take the form of hearings, statements in committee or on the chamber floor, or public appearances in the media to bring attention to the issue. The entrepreneurs thus amplify the volume of the signal to gain the attention of the administration, and to "soften up" the policy environment for further action. An entrepreneur's efforts could end at this point with suitable administration action—as with Reuss and the Peace Corps.

Should the administration continue to stall or ignore the signals, the insider-incrementalist then moves to more formal efforts, generally involving legislative action. Having been rebuffed to this point, the entrepreneur might: (1) introduce legislation on their preferred policy action or (2) use legislative and procedural tools to obstruct action on other issues or policies to link them to action on his or her own concerns. If successful, entrepreneurs see the legislation passed, or see action on the issue so that they will end the obstruction on the linked issue—as Senator Kennedy did on the issue of South African sanctions.

The legislative strategy. When an entrepreneur pursues a legislative strategy, the typical approach involves the introduction of a policy initiative, around which the entrepreneur then orchestrates a campaign designed to see it enacted. Referring to one entrepreneur who regularly adopted this approach, a staffer told us that the legislation is "also like the leader. You orchestrate your policy based on 'what are we doing with the bill.' [You plan your efforts] all with the mind of what is the timing for the bill. . . . That kind of orchestrates all of your maneuvering" (Anonymous 2001a). Legislative campaigns involve public activities to frame the issue and advocate for the proposal, informal activities to build support among colleagues in Congress and perhaps within the administration, and other activities such as hearings to press the policy process. Entrepreneurs typically following this strategy include Helms, Smith, and McCarran; Helms's campaigns on foreign affairs restructuring and tightened sanctions on Cuba described in chapter 6 are among the best examples of the strategy in action.

The direct-action strategy. In this approach, the entrepreneur de-emphasizes legislative efforts and focuses on activities to shape agendas and policy at the level of implementation. These activities frequently involve direct ties to foreign leaders or individuals, participation in negotiations, and the like. One variant is to use direct action to affect the problem, policy, and political streams, and force open a window of opportunity into which additional policy-making efforts such as legislative proposals can be directed. A second variant relies on direct action to generate policy pressure or momentum simply by affecting international events.

Examples of entrepreneurs' efforts employing the direct-action strategy include those of Wright in Central American and Weldon in Yugoslavia. Another good illustration is provided by the efforts of Charles Wilson (D-Texas) with respect to Afghanistan:

> At a time when the Contras could not get a dime from Congress, Charlie Wilson had managed to turn the CIA's cautious bleeding campaign in Afghanistan into a half-billion-dollars-a-year operation that dwarfed any prior Agency effort. For all practical purposes Wilson had hijacked a U.S. foreign policy and was busy transforming it into the first direct winner-take-all contest with the Soviet Union. . . . He was now engaged in the kind of sensitive diplomacy that is technically illegal for anyone other than the White House to conduct: cutting arms deals with the defense minister of Egypt; commissioning Israel to design weapons for the CIA; negotiating all manner of extraordinarily controversial matters with the all-important U.S. ally General Zia. There was even a moment when Wilson would find himself outside of a hotel in London introducing two delegations of the highest-level representatives of Israel and Pakistan. It was Charlie's very own peace initiative that would result in the creation of a back channel between the two ostensibly enemy nations. (Crile 2003, 374–75)

In figure 5 the highlighted box in the lower right-hand corner reflects a modification to the original framework to reflect these three basic strategies instead of the single strategy with which the study began. To be sure, entrepreneurs adopt different strategies depending upon the situation, and they may rely on multiple strategies on a given issue, and different strategies for different issues and situations. Among the key variables shaping choice of strategy, three categories seem particularly important. First, entrepreneurs would appear to adopt different strategies when they share party affiliation with the president. In particular, they are considerably more likely to rely on consultation and advice-giving approaches (i.e. the insider-incrementalist strategy). Second, whether entrepreneurs are members of the majority in their chamber of Congress is also critical. Members in the majority enjoy greater range of access and opportunity than members of the minority, who may have to resort to "blocking" and "hostage-taking" approaches. Choice of strategy will also be conditioned by the entrepreneur's committee membership and leadership roles. Those in leadership positions on the Senate Foreign Relations Committee obviously benefit as a result, as Fulbright, Church, and Helms did. Entrepreneurs who chair a policy-relevant subcommittee benefit as well, as Kennedy and Weldon did. Wright and O'Neill benefited from their positions as House speakers. Finally, choice of strategy will be conditioned by the policy context. Policy vacuums appear most likely to stimulate legislative strategies, while policy corrections seem most likely to result in insider-incrementalist or direct action strategies (depending on whether the entrepreneurs are in the president's party or the opposition party).

Categories of Entrepreneurs

In addition to varying strategies, the evidence suggests that there are different types of entrepreneurs. While there may be several approaches to categorization, an issue-based approach can be used. The range of issues or problems to which entrepreneurs devote their attention can be categorized along two dimensions.

First, there is a *problem dimension* that differentiates issues along a continuum ranging from particular, issue-specific concerns to broad strategies of engagement, principles, norms of interaction, rules, or guidelines. For example, the issue-specific end may be a set of narrow, particularistic problems in dealing with a specific regime (such as policy toward China or El Salvador), while the broad strategy may encompass broad problems

Figure 6: A Typology of Congressional Foreign Policy Entrepreneurs

such as how the United States should engage the rest of the world or what norms, rules, or guidelines should govern United States behavior (such as linking foreign aid decisions to human rights).

Second, there is a *focus dimension* that differentiates issues depending on whether the policy focus is external, policy-based, and concerned with the actions taken (e.g. using force in Iraq) or internal, process-based, and concerned with how the decision is made (e.g. the role of Congress in deciding to use force). In effect, focus can be external and based on substantive policy ("what do we do about Haiti?") or it can be internal to the country and based on process ("how do we choose to allocate foreign aid?"). The result is another continuum, a policy versus process focus.

The combination of these two dimensions results in a fourfold typology of entrepreneurs as depicted in figure 6. MCs found in the upper left quadrant care about specific issues and external policy behavior. Thus they can be typed as policy specialists. They care about how the United States should respond to problems in Haiti or South Africa or specific issues like religious persecution in China. The upper right quadrant represents process specialists. These MCs care about the process of how a specific issue is handled, like how Mexico's or Colombia's drug certification process should be conducted or how human rights certifications should be determined for states like El Salvador. MCs in the lower left quadrant care about broader questions of strategy concerning external policy behavior. Thus they can be seen as policy strategists. Examples include whether unilateral or multilateral approaches are best for military interventions or whether development issues are better addressed by technical assistance programs like the Peace Corps or economic aid programs that give recipients more discretion in the use of the money. Finally, in the lower right quadrant are MCs who focus on the appropriate processes by which categories of policy are made. Such process strategists might be concerned with how war powers questions are resolved or who gets to make the rules governing foreign military sales.

Recognizing the different entrepreneurial strategies and types improves our understanding of the roles that individual members may play when they choose to lead. Not only does this more comprehensive examination result in a more realistic picture of congressional leadership behavior in foreign policy making, but it also points the way to recognizing the full impact that congressional entrepreneurs have on foreign policy.

More Than Meets the Eye:
The Foreign Policy Impact of Congressional Entrepreneurs

The bottom line of this examination of congressional foreign policy entrepreneurs is that they significantly shape United States foreign policy in ways that many fail to recognize or appreciate. There is virtually no arena of policy in which their mark cannot be found, from the trivial (e.g. parking fines for foreign diplomats) to the profound (e.g. ending wars). This is true regardless of the policy area: political-diplomatic, military-security, economic-developmental, and cultural-status areas have all received the attention of entrepreneurs and bear the stamp of their policy making. Furthermore, whether policy is structural or strategic does not limit the efforts of entrepreneurs. In fact, where most observers find structural policy initiatives most common among MCs, we find that entrepreneurs are most active in the strategic policy arena, an area often thought to be the preserve of the White House.

As expected in chapter 1, we find that congressional foreign policy entrepreneurs seek to (1) frame policy discussions and mobilize public and interest groups; (2) direct congressional agendas to require attention to specific foreign policy issues; (3) structure and influence the formulation of foreign policies by the executive branch; (4) revise, refocus, reformulate, or replace foreign policies; and (5) fill policy vacuums with their preferred foreign policies.

Every case study in the preceding pages has numerous examples of how entrepreneurs have an impact on problem definition and issue framing. From McCarran's defining of Franco's Fascist regime as the best possible anticommunist ally to Warner's framing of global warming as a national security issue, entrepreneurs wade into the ocean of foreign policy and create conditions that may lead to waves. Examples from the case studies on Reuss, Church, and Fulbright, among others, suggest that part of an entrepreneur's impact is to "soften up" the environment to make it more conducive for future efforts, whether by that entrepreneur or by others. There is a wide array of venues in which entrepreneurs can engage in such efforts, from committee rooms to the floors of legislative chambers to the studios of the electronic news media to the pages of the nation's newspapers. As our evidence demonstrates, entrepreneurs can be aggressive in using all of them to shape the ways policy problems are understood.

Likewise, the evidence here reveals the impact of entrepreneurs in setting the foreign policy agenda, an area of policy making typically attributed to executive actors. How do they direct agendas? They skillfully use direct, indirect, legislative, and nonlegislative means to secure attention to their preferred issues. As we have seen, for example, entrepreneurs may use committee hearings, the introduction of legislation, consultations with the executive branch, and other public appearances to generate interest in and momentum behind their public issues. If they occupy strategic positions, they can also hold the administration's agenda hostage to progress on their agenda items.

Entrepreneurs also affect foreign policy by serving as cue givers to other less interested or less expert MCs. According to the former secretary of state Dean Rusk, Senator Richard Russell (D-Ga.), an entrepreneur and powerful chairman of the Armed Services Committee, "had 18 or 20 votes in his back pocket . . . that he could deliver on any vote" (Rusk 1990, 588). More recently, especially in the 1980s and 1990s, Richard Lugar had that kind of impact. As one of Lugar's staffers told us, "Sam Nunn always had that great line, and he still uses it to this day, he says, 'I've always questioned whether it was a smart idea for me to team up with Dick Lugar.' And the crowd always goes, 'What do you mean?' And he goes 'You know, before I teamed up with Dick Lugar, I used to offer a lot of amendments and a lot of bills and I would win 51–49, 52–48 and I'd be on the front page of the newspaper. I team up with Dick Lugar, and we win votes 98–2, 99–1, 96–4 and they don't care about any of that'" (Meyer 2001). Nunn's comments illustrate an entrepreneur's cue-giving power. Lugar's staffer continued in this vein, "I've worked for the Senator for six years, and in those six years at least a dozen times I've been approached by another United States senator and asked, 'How is Dick going to vote on this?' 'Well senator, he's going to support it,' 'he's going to oppose it.' And I get ready to explain the reason why and they go 'No, no, no, Dick wouldn't do anything stupid.' They just follow his lead on that kind of thing" (Meyer 2001).

According to other congressional aides, this is an important source of influence in several ways. For one, it indicates that the entrepreneur's investment of time and development of expertise are rewarded by other MCs, who look to the entrepreneur for leadership. Additionally, because the entrepreneur is a cue giver to other members, the administration has to worry about the entrepreneur's leadership on a policy issue (Anonymous 2003d), which also increases leverage and impact. Finally, the role as cue giver and the underlying expertise on which it rests means that MCs will seek out the entrepreneur's views on related issues (i.e. those "owned" by the entrepreneur), providing a kind of "force multiplier effect" leading to additional opportunity for influence. With respect to Lugar, for example, a staff aide said that other members simply "can't deal with nuclear nonproliferation without seeking his input or support. If you don't do this, people will ask you 'Where's Lugar on this?' and it will end up back with Lugar anyway" (Anonymous 2003c). In short, as Kingdon (1989) pointed out long ago, cue giving is an important component of the congressional decision-making process, and foreign policy entrepreneurs play a pivotal role in this regard with their less interested colleagues.

The cues given extend to the executive branch as well. Entrepreneurs often signal the administration as to their intentions, and in many instances the administration will co-opt those ideas they come to like, or adopt the entrepreneurs' positions to avoid a conflict with Congress (see e.g. Howell and Pevehouse 2007). Such anticipated reactions are well documented by other literature, but we find that entrepreneurs play an extremely significant role in this regard. For example, Reuss's idea of the Peace Corps was co-opted by President Kennedy in an executive order. Similar entrepreneurial pressures led the Reagan administration to order limited economic sanctions against South Africa in 1985 to try to preclude more restrictive congressional measures. An aide to Helms put it simply: "If there's the will in Congress, the president will do it anyway. He'll see the writing on the wall and he'll take action" (Munson 2001).

One interesting angle on this impact involves the role of the entrepreneur as the provider of political cover or legitimacy to the administration for subsequent anticipated reactions on controversial policy decisions. A congressional aide pointed to the normalization of relations with Vietnam as a good example. According to the aide (Anonymous 2003d): "Senators John Kerry (D-Mass.) and John McCain (R-Ariz.) pushed the Clinton Administration to recognize Vietnam in the mid-1990s. Kerry had started even earlier by creating a Fulbright program with Vietnam in the early 1990s; it was run out of Harvard and did economics training, and it was our first real official outreach (aside from the POW/MIA issue) with Vietnam. McCain certainly gave Clinton political cover in calling for recognition." Numerous additional examples across all four periods examined illustrate the degree to which administrations try to anticipate and react to congressional foreign policy entrepreneurs.

Another important way entrepreneurs shape foreign policy is by serving as part of the larger feedback loop to offer correctives when policy goes astray. As previously noted concerning the quantitative and qualitative evidence presented here, entrepreneurs often act aggressively toward what they regard as flawed or insufficient administration efforts to contend with a policy challenge. In such cases, entrepreneurs play a key role in filling the policy stream with alternatives to the administration's course of action. They seek to mobilize support for their policy alternatives and force them on the administration. Committed entrepreneurs have regular opportunities generated by the annual budget cycle and the power of the purse. For instance, our evidence shows numerous instances in which entrepreneurs use authorization and appropriations bills as vehicles for their initiatives. Similarly, hearings can be opportunities to expose weaknesses in existing policy and to offer and generate support for other policy alternatives.

Conversely, entrepreneurs also play a major role in identifying policy vacuums and offering solutions to fill them. The policy innovations often ride on entrepreneurial campaigns to frame an issue and highlight a preferred solution. When members engage in this practice, they first seek to raise awareness of the problem and its salience, using all possible means.

These range from the expected—like press conferences—to the unexpected—like landing a V-22 Osprey on Capitol Hill. Where policy correction usually begins by exposing the flaws of administration efforts, filling policy vacuums typically involves exposing the perils of doing nothing.

So what conditions are most conducive to entrepreneurial success? The evidence presented here suggests that entrepreneurial success is not contingent on any one issue area or policy category. As the preceding chapters clearly demonstrate, whether the issue is military-security, political-diplomatic, economic-developmental, or cultural-status, entrepreneurs have been successful in shaping United States foreign policy. Nor is entrepreneurial success dependent on whether the issue is strategic or structural in nature.

Three contexts lend themselves to entrepreneurial success: the structural, the political, and the policy context. The structural context refers to where entrepreneurs find themselves in Congress. We have demonstrated that being in the majority party opens more doors to policy impact, as entrepreneurs gain access to more levers of influence. They have potentially more votes to attract to their position on partisan grounds. Moreover, if they occupy key positions on policy-making committees or subcommittees, their chances of success increase markedly. Occupying such a position multiplies the formal and informal, legislative and nonlegislative ways that entrepreneurs can pursue their own agenda. While being in the nonpresidential party can increase one's likelihood of engaging in entrepreneurship, being in the majority party in the chamber increases one's likelihood of success.

Second, aspects of the political context also affect the chances of entrepreneurial success. Regardless of the reason (e.g. scandal, unpopular policies, etc.), a weakened president invites congressional challenge (Mann 1990). As the popularity of presidents such as Truman, Johnson, Nixon, Carter, and most recently George W. Bush declined, entrepreneurship became more prevalent. This is true even within the president's party, as the post-9/11 data indicate. Similarly, presidents committed to unpopular policies invite confrontations on those policies in particular. Even a president as popular as Ronald Reagan invited considerable entrepreneurship with his unpopular Central America policies.

Another aspect of the political context is the degree of attention paid to an issue by those seen by the MC as important stakeholders. These stakeholders might include key constituency groups, interest groups important to the MC regardless of whether they are well represented back home, and at times even staff members in the MC's office. As Kingdon (1989) notes, when more stakeholders important to the MC press for something, MCs are more likely to respond. That dynamic holds true for entrepreneurs as well as other MCs uninterested in foreign policy. Greater interest from stakeholders contributes to increased persistence on the part of the entrepreneur and expands the network of pressures that can be brought to bear on the policy issue, both of which should contribute to policy success.

Finally, elements of the policy context condition the outcomes of entrepreneurship. Two features seem especially important. First, we can distinguish between discrete and continuous impact. Entrepreneurs can have one-time success. Policy and process specialists focus on specific instances such as Mexico's drug certification or China's human rights, and their impact is thus specific to those instances. On the other hand, policy and process strategists have a more continuous impact by establishing procedures and principles that may affect policy for years. For example, entrepreneurs responsible for intelligence reform and oversight have changed the way the intelligence community operates for the last thirty years, while entrepreneurs who link foreign aid to human rights principles have had a similar long-term impact.

Second, the policy context is also marked by a distinction between policy corrections and policy vacuums. Entrepreneurs may seek policy corrections to deal with the consequences of current policy or to challenge the goals and means by which policy is pursued. When working in the realm of policy corrections, entrepreneurs face a number of involved actors with some stake in the existing policy. As a result, policy success is more difficult. To be successful, entrepreneurs need to overcome the inertia of existing policy, as has been well pointed out by Hinckley (1994). Not only may they have to persuade the president to change course, they must overcome the resistance from bureaucrats with stakes in prior compromises (e.g. Lindblom 1959; Allison and Zelikow 1999; Clapp, Halperin, and Kanter 2007). Again, to say that doing so is difficult does not mean that persistent entrepreneurs cannot succeed. They may just have to work longer.

Policy vacuums, on the other hand, present entrepreneurs with opportunities to act in contexts less dominated by other stakeholders. Entrepreneurs may face fewer obstacles from the executive branch when they seek to fill policy vacuums rather than make policy corrections. It is easier to be successful when they do not have to overcome the inertia of prior policy. These situations are more conducive to policy innovations, like the creation of the Peace Corps or the arming of the Afghan mujahhedin. Hence we would expect entrepreneurs to have more success in these situations.

Our documentation of the foreign policy entrepreneurship phenomenon in Congress indicates that entrepreneurs are players too important to be ignored. While presidents are typically foreign policy leaders, congressional foreign policy entrepreneurs who choose to lead frequently influence policy and occasionally rival the president. Still, other directions for future research can be readily identified. For example, more can be learned about the motivations that drive entrepreneurs. How do their personal policy positions arise? What experiences and characteristics make members more likely to engage in entrepreneurship? How can the effects of constituency groups, experts, staff, and other colleagues be sorted through? What motivating factors are most important or influential in entrepreneurs' choices? How do their choices of strategies link to outcomes? Finally, under what circumstances do they have the greatest policy impact? These and other puzzles warrant further attention as we seek a more accurate understanding of United States foreign policy making.

In the end, however, the results of our study raise important questions about the premise of presidential preeminence in United States foreign policy making. Because individual members of Congress choose to lead in the ways and on the kinds of issues discussed in the preceding chapters, presidential preeminence is too narrow a lens with which to view policy making. In the words of President Lyndon Johnson, presidential preeminence in foreign policy "ain't exactly as it was advertised" (quoted in Cronin 1979, 381).

NOTES

1. Although we have honored requests to protect the anonymity of the staff aides and their positions in Congress, we have of course kept extensive, carefully detailed records of each interview, along with a transcript (for those who allowed us to tape the interview) or detailed interview notes (for those who did not). Our use of this evidence reflects those materials, attributed when possible, and credited to "anonymous" when necessary.

Chapter 2: From Problem to Policy

1. Others use the terms "political entrepreneurs" (Schneider and Teske 1992), "strategic entrepreneurs" (Riker 1980), "public entrepreneurs" (Polsby 1984; Walker 1981), and even "policy champions" (DeGregorio 1997; Roberts 1992) to describe the same phenomenon.

2. See also Jeon and Haider-Markel (2001), Kingdon (1995), Baumgartner and Jones (1993), Roberts (1992), Polsby (1984), Cobb and Elder (1983), Walker (1981), Price (1971), and Schumpeter (1939).

3. Burden (2007) lists personal expertise as a separate factor, which we include here as part of one's personal experience.

4. See also Hibbing (2003).

5. In particular, see table 2 in Carter (1986, 335).

6. As Howell and Pevehouse (2007, 36) put it in their discussion of Congress and the use of force, members of the president's party are more likely to support presidential decisions because their worldviews match, they defer to the president's presumed information advantage, they have shared electoral fortunes, and they seek to curry presidential favor.

7. However, as numerous studies suggest, the media's coverage reflects government sources and may "index" the tone and direction of the policy debates and criticisms in the government. In particular, the media are substantially more likely

to offer critical views of the White House when policy actors in the government, and particularly the Congress, have already done so (e.g. Arnold 2004; Bennet 1990; Howell and Pevehouse 2007; Bermin 1999). This suggests that entrepreneurs may influence media attention and framing as much as they are influenced by it.

8. According to some congressional staffers (Anonymous 2003c), going public is especially important to members of the minority party, as they do not have access to the levers afforded to majority party members as the chairs of key committees.

9. While Lugar's actions on the chemical weapons convention were not strictly entrepreneurial by the definition adopted in this study, the illustration of the tactic is still relevant.

Chapter 3: Surveying the Landscape

1. A random sequence generator produced a Cold War Consensus subsample consisting of the years 1946, 1950, 1954, 1958, 1959, 1960, 1961, 1962, 1963, and 1965; a Cold War Dissensus subsample consisting of the years 1968, 1970, 1972, 1973, 1975, 1979, 1984, 1985, 1986, and 1987; and a post-Cold War subsample consisting of the years 1992, 1994, 1996, 1997, and 1999. The random sequence generator was found at http://www.random.org.

2. Author 1 coded eleven years (1946, 1950, 1954, 1958, 1959, 1960, 1961, 1962, 1975, 1987, 1997); author 2 coded twelve years (1963, 1965, 1970, 1973, 1979, 1984, 1985, 1986, 1992, 1994, 1996, 1999); and both coded 1972 and 1968 as intercoder reliability test years.

3. Note that such incremental changes may represent instances of congressional assertiveness. However, such assertiveness is not the same as the concept of entrepreneurship that guides this study.

4. Note that cutting aid to zero is not considered an incremental change. We define deleting all aid to an intended recipient as a fundamental redefinition of a foreign policy issue, and thus an entrepreneurial act.

5. The issues and coding are as follows: nuclear arms and weapons of mass destruction strategy or control (STRATEGIC); other arms control and disarmament (STRATEGIC); defense procurement and spending (STRUCTURAL); defense policy and process (STRATEGIC); military operations and war powers (STRATEGIC); economic aid (STRUCTURAL); military aid (STRUCTURAL); general foreign aid (STRUCTURAL); foreign trade (STRUCTURAL); general international economic policy (STRATEGIC); intelligence and paramilitary (STRATEGIC); diplomacy and State Department policy (STRATEGIC); State Department spending (STRUCTURAL); personnel (STRUCTURAL); human rights and democracy promotion (STRATEGIC); global environmental policy (STRATEGIC); immigration (STRUCTURAL); populations and refugees (STRUCTURAL); drug trafficking (STRATEGIC); cultural exchanges (STRUCTURAL); internal security and counterintelligence (STRATEGIC); IGO reform and

accountability (STRUCTURAL); transnational economic cooperation and infrastructure (STRATEGIC); terrorism (STRATEGIC); and general oversight (STRUCTURAL). For the narrower defense policy coding we included only nuclear arms and weapons of mass destruction (STRATEGIC); other arms control and disarmament (STRATEGIC); defense procurement and spending (STRUCTURAL); defense policy and process (STRATEGIC); military operations and war powers (STRATEGIC); and military aid (STRUCTURAL).

6. According to Scott (1997), direct legislative avenues include issue-specific legislation, treaties, the war power, appropriation, and trade; indirect legislative avenues include resolutions, appointments, and procedural legislation; direct nonlegislative avenues include informal advice, letters, consultations, oversight and hearings, and the use of courts; and indirect nonlegislative avenues include framing opinion and foreign contacts.

7. Intercoder reliability was measured with the widely used Scott's pi, which as Holsti (1969, 140) shows, is computed as:

$$pi = \% \text{ observed agreement} - \% \text{ expected agreement} / 1 - \% \text{ expected agreement.}$$

Intercoder reliability needed to be determined for the identification of entrepreneurial cases from the year selected and for three key variables in each case: the issue category, the activity used, and the access point used. To be considered reliable the value of Scott's pi needed to be .70 or higher (McManus and Dorfman 2002). The initial test year coded by both authors was 1968. The value for Scott's pi for the identification of entrepreneurial cases was unacceptable (−.27). After conferring, both authors coded the cases from 1972. That produced a better but still unacceptable value (−.07). After further consultation between the two coders, a second try for 1972 produced an acceptable value of Scott's pi (.77). From that point on, any time either coder had doubts about whether a case represented entrepreneurship rather than just congressional assertiveness, that coder contacted the other to resolve the matter of case identification. Thus for the entire dataset, the value of .77 is a conservative one, as any ambiguities or questions were continually resolved between the two coders. Intercoder reliability measures for the other variables clearly exceeded the .70 threshold for 1968. Those measures were .88 for the Brecher et al. issue categorization, .91 for the activity employed, and 1.00 for the access point used.

8. The sums for the overall period and the three periods by chamber are different, because there are members who serve in both chambers at different times within and between periods, and therefore are counted for each period and for each chamber. When either period or chamber, or both, are not disaggregated, the members are counted only once.

9. The *Congressional Quarterly* emphasizes direct legislative activity, so this conclusion is tentative. As the case studies in the ensuing chapters show, nonlegislative efforts are a common and important area of entrepreneur activity.

Chapter 4: The Rising Tide

1. Admittedly, the Cold War Consensus years represent 40% of the universe under study, so finding 27% of the entrepreneurial behavior in that period makes entrepreneurship appear underrepresented in mathematical terms. But that only holds if one expects entrepreneurship to be evenly distributed across the fifty-five years of the universe. No one who studies presidential-congressional foreign policy interactions would expect such an even distribution. The literature suggests that congressional assertiveness (of which entrepreneurship is an extreme form) took off with the downturn in Vietnam—hence around 1968. Finding 27% of the entrepreneurial activity in an era characterized as dominated by the executive will seem surprisingly high to many observers.

2. Many entrepreneurs besides McCarran and McCarthy sought to publicize communist subversion from the late 1940s through the mid-1950s. MCs typically relied on direct, nonlegislative means. Investigations by the House Un-American Activities Committee were a focus of activity by entrepreneurs like Richard Nixon (R-Calif.), Karl Mundt (R-S.D.), Parnell Thomas (R-N.J.), and John Wood (D-Ga.). Senate investigations by both the Judiciary Committee's Internal Security Subcommittee and the Government Operations Committee's Permanent Subcommittee on Investigations featured prominent roles by senators like Joseph McCarthy (R-Wis.), Homer Ferguson (R-Mich.), Alexander Wiley (R-Wis.), Herbert O'Conor (D-Md.), and John Stennis (D-Miss.) (*Congressional Quarterly Almanacs* 1948, 1952). Ultimately no evidence of widespread communist subversion was found.

3. Michael Ybarra (2004, 286) described McCarran as "a casual anti-Semite. Words like *kike* fell easily from his lips, but his prejudices were largely of his time and place." However, Ybarra's effort to downplay McCarran's anti-Semitism is negated by the many examples of it that he provides and the fact that McCarran saw Judaism as communism's "evil twin" (Ybarra 2004, 496).

4. McCarran was not opposed to all immigrants. As a former sheep rancher, he introduced bills to allow Basque sheepherders to enter the country (Ybarra 2004).

5. Recently available transcripts of LBJ's private phone conversations with aides, friends, advisers, and members of Congress, among others, show a variety of signals and warnings, especially from Richard Russell and William Fulbright, which Johnson mostly ignored. However, it is clear that his choices reflected his sense of congressional concerns and his desire to keep key members on board. See for example Beschloss ed. (2001).

6. Fulbright, along with Mansfield, Russell, Morse, and Gruening, is especially identified by Johnson advisers such as Ball (1982), McNamara (1995), Rusk (1990), Califano (2000), and Clifford (1991), and by LBJ (1971) himself, as a vigorous opponent of escalation and an advocate of a different approach. After 1965 Fulbright broke with Johnson and, as discussed, attempted to chart a new course. But see Ely (1993) for a more skeptical view of Fulbright's role.

Chapter 5: Players in the Game

1. For a detailed discussion of Central America policy and the role of members of Congress in the 1980s and 1990s see Arnson, *Crossroads: Congress, the President, and Central America, 1976–1993* (Pennsylvania State University Press, 1993).

2. Space does not allow for a full telling of this story, but it is well told in great detail by Loch Johnson (1985).

3. As he had done on the ABM issue fifteen years earlier, Kennedy used his staff and experts to improve his knowledge and access to information on nuclear issues at this time as well. In one example, a member of his staff carried out a series of trips to the Soviet Union to discuss arms control with Soviet leaders, reporting back to both Kennedy and Jack Matlock of the National Security Staff (Clymer 1999, 332).

4. Kennedy met with Reagan and members of the NSC staff before the trip, reviewing arms control issues in preparation for Kennedy's conversations (Clymer 1999, 390).

5. In 1987 President Reagan submitted a report to Congress on the sanctions, stating that sanctions were not the best way to bring freedom to South Africa. Kennedy responded with an opinion piece in the *Washington Post* (Kennedy 1987c), stating that "instead of using the first anniversary of that historic legislation to renew his opposition to the sanctions, President Reagan should be making a greater effort to persuade our friends and allies to join us in new initiatives against apartheid."

6. Wright was not alone in such efforts. In 1987 much of Dodd's effort was spent on personal diplomacy. He went to Costa Rica for the summit conference of the Contadora presidents to promote the peace process (*Washington Post*, 17 February, 1987, § A, 10). Later he met with President Daniel Ortega of Nicaragua in support of the Central American peace process (*Washington Post*, 20 September, 1987, § A, 26). Back in Washington he made a series of public statements endorsing the Central American peace process and condemning Reagan's opposition to it as counterproductive (*Washington Post*, 8 October 1987, § A, 1; 11 November 1987, § A, 1). At year's end he met with Ortega again to seek a ceasefire (*Washington Post*, 7 December 1987, § A, 34). In 1988 Dodd went to Managua and urged Sandinista officials to cooperate with the peace process. He also met with President Arias in Costa Rica, encouraging him to continue his efforts (*Washington Post*, 15 January 1987, § A, 23). When he returned from the trip Dodd wrote an op-ed piece in the *Washington Post* endorsing the Central American peace process and condemning Washington's support for the contras (*Washington Post*, 3 February 1988, § A, 19).

Chapter 6: Contending with the Thaw

1. Unless otherwise noted, these examples draw from the database of entrepreneurship described in chapter 3.

2. For example, Gephardt proposed $3 billion in credits and technical assistance to the USSR in return for economic reform, while Aspin suggested reprogramming $1 billion from the defense budget to aid the newly independent states. Nunn and Aspin together proposed $1 billion of aid to the USSR. Throughout the fall of 1991 Aspin, Nunn, Lugar, and Boren pressed for aggressive aid packages, but the administration remained silent. Pell and Biden eventually approached the American ambassador to the USSR, Robert Strauss, and informed him that Congress would support a large aid package if the administration would request it (Tarnoff 2004).

3. Representative Leach related this account to the authors in a personal interview on 10 September 2001.

4. According to the delegation member Maurice Hinchey (D-N.Y.), the Russian representatives at the meeting included Vladimir Lyshkov (chairman of the Our Home Is Russia Party), Vladimir Lukin (chairman of the Apple Party and a former ambassador to the United States), Alex Shapanov (chairman of the Communist Party), and Sergei Konovalenko (who was identified as a Duma deputy) (Canadian Immigration and Refugee Board 2007).

5. According to Weldon (2002a), the director of central intelligence, George Tenet, indicated puzzlement at why Karic, a private citizen, was being brought to the meeting by the Russians, thus making him some form of "player" in these discussions. This anecdote is troubling. If Tenet was telling the truth, Karic was not on the CIA's radar screen, indicating very little CIA knowledge of what was going on inside Yugoslavia (like who were the important people surrounding Milosevic) at a time when the United States and NATO were busy bombing it. This is a likely possibility, as apparently CIA maps did not show that a building used several years before to house a Yugoslavian government office—thus making it a bombing target—was now the Chinese Embassy! Again, if Tenet was telling the truth, it is troubling that the Pentagon knew much that the CIA did not, in what is yet another example of government bureaucracies not sharing information. (This episode happened in 1999. The position of director of national intelligence was created after the September 11 terrorist attacks, in part to facilitate the sharing of intelligence information. Only those with security clearances know whether such information sharing has become any more routine since then.) On the other hand, Tenet might have known more about Karic than he was willing to tell Weldon. If so, why would he want to hide what he knew from a member of Congress who was on the Armed Services Committee (then known as the National Security Committee) and chaired one of its important subcommittees? Did he fear that Weldon would leak this information, and if so, to whom? Weldon's best contacts were with the Russians, and they already knew who Karic was. Perhaps the military felt that it had to share its information with Weldon because of the subcommittee he chaired, but since Weldon was not a member of the Intelligence Committee, Tenet may not have felt any need to brief Weldon on Karic. Whichever way this situation is sliced, it is troubling.

6. The three POWs were then released to the Reverend Jesse Jackson, who had traveled to Belgrade (*Congressional Quarterly Almanac* 1999).

7. All of the following examples were obtained by searching THOMAS: Legislative Information on the Internet (http://thomas.loc.gov) for bills for which Christopher Smith was the principal sponsor from 1995 to 2003.

8. This measure failed, as did other congressional efforts to condition China's most-favored nation status on human rights improvement. The Clinton administration argued for a one-year extension of the conditions to give China more time to make progress.

9. Smith made additional floor statements on the topic; see e.g. *Congressional Record*, 9 March 1994, E393–94; 24 May 1994, H3891–92. He also cosponsored a failed "Sense of the Congress" resolution that Taiwan be represented at the UN (*Congressional Quarterly Almanac*, 1994).

10. These measures were in the same bills as the reinstatement of the Mexico City restrictions discussed below.

11. In 1999 and 2000 Smith was also a vocal opponent of normal trade relations with China, and of China's accession to the World Trade Organization.

12. The compromise arrangement provided $819 million in back dues and forgave $107 million in UN debt to the United States. In return, the United States share of the UN budget was to be reduced from 20% to 15%, and its share of the peacekeeping costs to 25% from 31% (D'Agostino 1999).

13. To cite just two post–Cold War examples, in 1994 Helms blocked the nomination of Robert Pastor (a former National Security Council staffer in the Carter administration) as ambassador to Panama because of Pastor's role in the Panama Canal treaties, and in 1997 he blocked the nomination of William Weld (the former Republican governor of Massachusetts) as ambassador to Mexico, putatively because of Weld's record as governor (specifically his positions on the punishment of drug crimes).

14. Good accounts of the restructuring battle include Granger (2002) and Hook (1998). It should be noted that Helms was building on ideas incorporated in earlier studies, including *State 2000: A New Model for Managing Foreign Affairs* (Washington: U.S. Department of State, 1992).

15. Helms also noted: "Candor requires that I make clear that if I had my way we would abolish AID entirely and start over again, but I also recognize that this bill is the first step in a long process of inventing and reinventing our foreign affairs apparatus" (Committee on Foreign Relations 1997, 266).

16. While not entrepreneurship, Helms's opposition to multilateral security treaties such as the Chemical Weapons Convention (ratified in 1997) and the Comprehensive Test Ban Treaty (rejected in 1999) are related aspects of his preference for unilateralism in American security policy.

17. In 1999 alone these hearings included the following topics: (1) on Russia, anti-Semitism, corruption, the war in Chechnya (twice), Russian intelligence activities against America, the Russian presidential election, religious freedom in

Russia, and Russian aid to Iranian weapons programs; (2) on China, American interests, Taiwan's relations with Washington, the Taiwan Security Enhancement Act, challenges from China, East Asia in 2000, China in the WTO, China and permanent MFN status, religious freedom in China, developments in Tibet, PNTR in China, Taiwan, and the WTO; (3) on Cuba, human rights violations, Castro's crackdowns; (4) on Iraq, United States policy, sanctions and oil for food, mobilizing the Iraqi opposition, maintaining pressure on Iraq, sanctions and the international community, progress toward liberating Iraq; (5) on North Korea, East Asia in 2000, progress in North Korea; (6) on Iran, limits to rapprochement, Iranian weapons programs.

18. See also Helms (1995e) and Helms (1996d) for published articles advocating for the Helms-Burton Act.

Chapter 7: After 9/11

1. A random sequence generator (at http://www.random.org) produced a two-year sample comprising 2003 and 2005.

2. These data exclude twenty-six first-time entrepreneurs who engaged in only one act of entrepreneurship in the two-year sample. More than two-thirds of these entrepreneurs were new to Congress after 2000 and had not had a chance to establish themselves as entrepreneurs before that. Nevertheless, to be consistent with previous data collection and coding, we do not include them. Note however that their inclusion would have raised entrepreneurship in 2003 to 87 acts and entrepreneurship in 2005 to 111 acts, which would further strengthen our argument and analysis, not weaken it.

3. This information is detailed at the Pew Center for Global Climate Change at http://www.pewclimate.org/ and http://www.pewclimate.org/what_s_being_done/in_the_congress/.

4. On the committee's formation and activities see its web site at http://global-warming.house.gov/.

5. Warner's remarks are quoted in a press release at http://lieberman.senate.gov/newsroom/release.cfm?id=280310.

BIBLIOGRAPHY

"Abortion and Foreign Aid." 1995. *San Francisco Chronicle*, 29 May, § A, 18.

Aizenman, Nurith C. 1998. "Bad Ban." *New Republic*, 15 June, 6–41.

Albertson, Maurice L., Andrew E. Rice, and Pauline E. Birky. 1961. *New Frontiers for American Youth: Perspective on the Peace Corps*. Washington: Public Affairs.

Albright, Madeleine. 2003. *Madam Secretary*. New York: Miramax.

Allison, Graham T., and Philip Zelikow. 1999. *The Essence of Decision: Explaining the Cuban Missile Crisis*. 2nd edn. New York: Longman.

Anderson, William D., Janet M. Box-Steffensmeier, and Valeria Sinclair-Chapman. 2003. "The Keys to Legislative Success in the U.S. House of Representatives." *Legislative Studies Quarterly* 28, 357–86.

Anonymous. 2001a. Personal interview with a congressional staff member, Washington, 10 September.

———. 2001b. Personal interview with a congressional staff member, Washington, 10 September.

———. 2001c. Personal interview with a congressional staff member, Washington, 10 September.

———. 2001d. Personal interview with a congressional staff member, Washington, 10 September.

———. 2001e. Personal interview with a congressional staff member, Washington, 10 September.

———. 2003a. Telephone interview with a Senate staff member, Washington, 28 May.

———. 2003b. Personal interview with a congressional staff member, Washington, 19 May.

———. 2003c. Personal interview with congressional staff members, Washington, 19 May.

———. 2003d. Personal interview with congressional staff members. Washington, 19 May.

Antic, Miroslav. 2001. "Rich Serb Tried to Buy a Life in Canada." *National Post*

(Canada), 20 December, online at http://www.nationalpost.com/search/story
.html?f=/stories/20011219/911157.html.

Arnold, R. Douglas. 1990. *The Logic of Congressional Action*. New Haven: Yale
University Press.

———. 2004. *Congress, the Press, and Political Accountability*. Princeton: Princeton University Press.

Asher, Herbert B., and Herbert F. Weisberg. 1978. "Voting Change in Congress:
Some Dynamic Perspectives on an Evolutionary Process." *American Journal of
Political Science* 22, no. 2, 391–425.

Associated Press. 1965a. "European Economic Woes Seen." *Dallas Morning News*,
23 December, § B, 8.

———. 1965b. "House OK's Measure to Free Gold." *Dallas Morning News*, 10 February, § A, 6.

———. 1965c. "LBJ Said Preparing to Ask Congress to Free Fed Gold." *Dallas
Morning News*, 8 January, § A, 8.

———. 1975. "Senate Wrangle over Missiles Stalls Decision on Defense Bill." *New
York Times*, 15 November, 13.

———. 1997a. "House Targets Abortion in Foreign Aid Bill." *St. Louis Post-
Dispatch*, 5 September, § A, 12.

———. 1997b. "Rep. Weldon Angrily Ends Hearing on Missile Defense; Lawmaker
Tells General, 'I Can't Trust You.'" *Washington Post*, 6 November, § A, 12.

———. 2002. "House Approves U.S.-Russian Nuclear Exchange Visits." *Washington Post*, 12 May, § A, 8.

———. 2003. "N. Korea's Threats; Says It Has Nukes, Demands U.S. Meeting."
Newsday (New York), 3 June, § A, 16.

———. 2007. "GOP Shows Fissures on Iraq." 26 June, http://www.msnbc.msn
.com/id/19442715/.

"A Test for Mr. Bush." 2002. *Washington Post*, 15 January, § A, 18.

Auerbach, Stuart. 1985. "Democrats Politicize Trade Issue." *Washington Post*,
5 April, § C, 9.

———. 1987a. "House Easily Approves Bill Mandating Trade Retaliation." *Washington Post*, 1 May, § A, 1.

———. 1987b. "Reagan Asks Freedom in World Trade: Stage Set for House Fight
on Gephardt Retaliation Amendment." *Washington Post*, 26 April, § A, 1.

———. 1987c. "Trade Deficit Hits $17 Million in October: Dollar, Stocks Fall."
Washington Post, 11 December, § A, 1.

———. 1987d. "U.S. Merchandise Trade Deficit Narrows: March Performance
Helped by Biggest Jump in Overseas Sales in Six Years." *Washington Post*, 15
May, § F, 1.

Auerbach, Stuart, and John Burgess. 1988. "Conferees Reach Agreement on Land-
mark Trade Bill." *Washington Post*, 1 April, § A, 1.

Avery, William P., and David P. Forsythe. 1979. "Human Rights, National Security,
and the U.S. Senate." *International Studies Quarterly* 23, 303–20.

Babington, Charles, and Shailagh Murray. 2005. "Senate Supports Interrogation Limits: 90–9 Vote on the Treatment of Detainees Is a Bipartisan Rebuff of the White House." *Washington Post*, 6 October, § A, 1.

Baker, James A. 1995. *The Politics of Diplomacy*. New York: Putnam.

Baker, Peter. 2003. "Russia Turns from Old Allies to U.S.; N. Korea Urged to Cooperate in Talks." *Washington Post*, 27 August, § A, 19.

Baker, Ross K. 1995. *House and Senate*. New York: W. W. Norton.

———. 2000. *House and Senate*. 2nd edn. New York: W. W. Norton.

Ball, George. 1982. *The Past Has Another Pattern*. New York: W. W. Norton.

Barilleaux, Ryan. 1985. *The President and Foreign Affairs: Evaluation, Performance, and Power*. New York: Praeger.

Barrett, David M. 1993. *Uncertain Warriors: Lyndon Johnson and his Vietnam Advisers*. Lawrence: University of Kansas Press.

Bass, Warren. 2003. *Support Any Friend: Kennedy's Middle East and the Making of the US-Israeli Alliance*. New York: Oxford University Press.

Baumgartner, Frank R., and Bryan D. Jones. 1993. *Agendas and Instability in American Politics*. Chicago: University of Chicago Press.

Bax, Frans R. 1977. "The Legislative-Executive Relationship in Foreign Policy: New Partnership or New Competition? *Orbis* 20, 881–904.

Bennett, W. Lance. 1990. "Toward a Theory of Press-State Relations in the United States." *Journal of Communication* 40, 103–25.

Bermin, Jonathan. 1999. *Debating War and Peace: Media Coverage of U.S. Intervention in the Post-Vietnam Era*. Princeton: Princeton University Press.

Bernstein, Robert A., and William W. Anthony. 1974. "The ABM Issue in the Senate, 1968–1970: The Importance of Ideology." *American Political Science Review* 68, 1198–1206.

Beschloss, Michael, ed. 2001. *Reaching for Glory: Lyndon Johnson's Secret White House Tapes, 1964–1965*. New York: Simon and Schuster.

Beschloss, Michael R., and Strobe Talbott. 1993. *At the Highest Levels: The Inside Story of the End of the Cold War*. Boston: Little, Brown.

Binder, David. 1975. "Kennedy Assails Refugee Program." *New York Times*, 9 June, 1.

Biographical Directory of the American Congress, 1774–1996. 1996. Washington: CQ Press.

Birch, Douglas. 2007. "Factory to Destroy Soviet Weapons." *Fort Worth Star-Telegram*, 31 August, § A, 16.

Black, Chris. 1995. "Helms, Kerry Return to Impasse." *Boston Globe*, 24 November, 15.

Blechman, Barry M. 1990. *The Politics of National Security: Congress and U.S. Defense Policy*. New York: Oxford University Press.

Borst, Barbara. 1999. "Abortion-Rights Backers Blast UN Deal. *Boston Globe*, 17 November, § A, 19.

Box-Steffensmeier, Janet M., and J. Tobin Grant. 1999. "All in a Day's Work: The

Financial Rewards of Legislative Effectiveness." *Legislative Studies Quarterly* 24, 511–23.

Brecher, Michael, Blema Steinberg, and Janice Gross Stein. 1969. "A Framework for Research on Foreign Policy Behavior." *Journal of Conflict Resolution* 13, no. 1, 75–101.

Broder, David S. 2005. "Finally, Congress Stands Up." *Washington Post*, 4 December, § B, 7.

Broder, David S., with Maralee Schwartz. 1983. "New Potential for Dividing Democrats." *Washington Post*, 8 May, § A, 1.

Broder, John. 2007. "Compromise Measure Aims to Limit Global Warming." *New York Times*, 11 July, § A, 14.

Bundy, William P. 1998. *A Tangled Web: The Making of Foreign Policy in the Nixon Presidency*. New York: Hill and Wang.

Burden, Barry C. 2007. *Personal Roots of Representation*. Princeton: Princeton University Press.

Burgin, Eileen. 1993. "Congress and Foreign Policy: The Misperceptions." *Congress Reconsidered*, 5th edn, ed. Lawrence C. Dodd and Bruce I. Oppenheimer. Washington: CQ Press.

———. 1997. "Assessing Congress' Role in the Making of Foreign Policy." *Congress Reconsidered*, 6th edn, ed. Lawrence C. Dodd and Bruce I. Oppenheimer. Washington: CQ Press.

Burner, David, and Thomas R. West. 1984. *The Torch Is Passed: The Kennedy Brothers and American Liberalism*. New York: Atheneum.

Burns, James M. 1963. *The Deadlock of Democracy*. Englewood Cliffs, N.J.: Prentice-Hall.

———. 1990. *Cobblestone Leadership: Majority Rule, Minority Power*. Norman: University of Oklahoma Press.

Bush, George H. W., and Brent Scowcroft. 1998. *A World Transformed*. New York: Alfred A. Knopf.

Byman, Daniel L., and Matthew C. Waxman. 2000. "Kosovo and the Great Air Power Debate." *International Security* 24, no. 4, 5–38.

Campbell, Andrea C., Gary W. Cox, and Mathew D. McCubbins. 2002. "Agenda Power in the U.S. Senate, 1877–1986." *Party, Process, and Political Change in Congress: New Perspectives on the History of Congress*, ed. David W. Brady and Mathew D. McCubbins. Stanford: Stanford University Press.

Canadian Immigration and Refugee Board. 2007. *Admissibility Hearing: Reasons and Decision between Minister of Citizenship and Immigration and Karic, Dragomir*. 9 February.

Cannon, Lou, and Stuart Auerbach. 1987. "Stop 'Hemming and Hawing' on Trade, Reagan Bids Japan, Also Warning Hill." *Washington Post*, 28 April, § A, 4.

Carter, Ralph G. 1986. "Congressional Foreign Policy Behavior: Persistent Patterns of the Postwar Period." *Presidential Studies Quarterly* 16, no. 2, 329–59.

———. 1989. "Senate Defense Budgeting, 1981–1988: The Impacts of Ideology,

Party, and Constituency Benefit on the Decision to Support the President."
American Politics Quarterly 17, no. 3, 332–47.

———. 1994. "Budgeting for Defense." *The President, the Congress, and the Making of Foreign Policy*, ed. Paul E. Peterson. Norman: University of Oklahoma Press.

———. 1998. "Congress and Post-Cold War U.S. Foreign Policy." *After the End: Making U.S. Foreign Policy in the Post-Cold War World*, ed. James M. Scott. Durham: Duke University Press.

Carter, Ralph G., and Donald W. Jackson. 2002. "The International Criminal Court: Present at the Creation?" *Contemporary Cases in U.S. Foreign Policy: From Terrorism to Trade*, ed. Ralph G. Carter. Washington: CQ Press.

Carter, Ralph G., and James M. Scott. 2002. "Funding the IMF: Congress versus the White House." *Contemporary Cases in U.S. Foreign Policy: From Terrorism to Trade*, ed. Ralph G. Carter. Washington: CQ Press.

———. 2004. "Taking the Lead: Congressional Foreign Policy Entrepreneurs in U.S. Foreign Policy." *Politics & Policy* 32, no. 1, 34–70.

———. 2006. "Reining In the Imperial Presidency: Congressional Foreign Policy Entrepreneurship in the Wake of Vietnam." Paper presented at the International Studies Association, Midwest Annual Conference, St. Louis, 3–5 November.

Carter, Ralph G., James M. Scott, and Charles M. Rowling. 2004. "Setting a Course: Congressional Foreign Policy Entrepreneurs in Post-World War II U.S. Foreign Policy." *International Studies Perspectives* 5, 278–99.

Chapman, William. 1982. "Senators Propose to Tighten Control of Covert Operations." *Washington Post*, 13 March, § A, 14.

Church, F. Forrester. 1985. *Father and Son: A Personal Biography of Senator Frank Church of Idaho by His Son*. New York: Harper and Row.

Church, Frank F. 1969a. Speech on the Senate floor, 20 June 1969. Reprinted in *Congressional Digest*, vol. 48 (August–September), nos. 8–9, 216, 218, 220, 222.

———. 1969b. Speech on the Senate floor, 8 October 1969. Reprinted in *Vital Speeches of the Day*, vol. 36, no. 2 (1 November), 34–39.

———. 1970a. Speech on the Senate floor, 30 April, *Congressional Record*, 13563–66.

———. 1970b. Speech delivered at the Thomas C. Hennings Lecture, Washington University, St. Louis, 3 December. Reprinted in *Vital Speeches of the Day* 37, no. 6 (1 January 1971), 170–73.

———. 1976. "Covert Action: Swampland of American Foreign Policy." *Bulletin of the Atomic Scientists* 32, no. 2, 7–11.

Clapp, Priscilla, Morton Halperin, and Arnold Kanter. 2007. *Bureaucratic Politics and Foreign Policy*. 2nd edn. Washington: Brookings Institution Press.

Clausen, Aage R., and Carl E. Van Horn. 1977. "The Congressional Response to a Decade of Change: 1963–1972." *Journal of Politics* 39, 624–66.

Clifford, Clark. 1991. *Counsel to the President*. New York: Random House.

"Climate Shock." 2005. *New York Times*, 27 June, § A, 14.

Clymer, Adam. 1999. *Edward M. Kennedy: A Biography*. New York: William Morrow.

Cobb, Roger W., and Charles D. Elder. 1983. *Participation in American Politics: The Dynamics of Agenda-Building*. 2nd edn. Baltimore: Johns Hopkins University Press.

Cohen, Gerald S. 1989. "Kennedy Urges Probe of Salvador Aid." *San Francisco Chronicle*, 20 December, § A, 27.

Coll, Steve. 2004. *Ghost Wars*. New York: Penguin.

Committee on Armed Services. 1990. *Naval Arms Control: Hearing before the Subcommittee on Projection Forces and Regional Defense*. Washington: U.S. Government Printing Office.

Committee on Foreign Relations, United States Senate. 1995a. *Reorganization and Revitalization of America's Foreign Affairs Institutions*. Washington: U.S. Government Printing Office.

———. 1995b. *Cuban Liberty and Democratic Solidarity Act*. Washington: U.S. Government Printing Office.

———. 1996. *The Libertad Act: Implementation and International Law*. Washington: U.S. Government Printing Office.

———. 1997. *Legislative Activities Report of the Committee on Foreign Relations*. Washington: U.S. Government Printing Office.

———. 1998. *Foreign Affairs Reform and Restructuring Act of 1997 and Fiscal Year 1998 International Affairs Budget Request*. Washington: U.S. Government Printing Office.

———. 1999a. *Legislative Activities Report of the Committee on Foreign Relations*. Washington: U.S. Government Printing Office.

———. 1999b. *United States–Taiwan Relations: the 20th Anniversary of the Taiwan Relations Act*. Washington: U.S. Government Printing Office.

———. 1999c. *The Taiwan Security Enhancement Act*. Washington: U.S. Government Printing Office.

———. 2001a. *Overview of Foreign Policy Issues and Budget*. Washington: U.S. Government Printing Office.

———. 2001b. *Legislative Activities Report of the Committee on Foreign Relations*. Washington: U.S. Government Printing Office.

Committee on the Judiciary. 1988. *Refugee Consultation: Hearing before the Senate Judiciary Committee*. Washington: U.S. Government Printing Office.

Congress and the Nation, 1945–1964. 1965. Washington: Congressional Quarterly Service.

Congressional Biographical Directory. 2001. *Biographical Directory of the United States Congress, 1774–Present*, online at http://bioguide.congress.gov/biosearch/biosearch.asp.

———. 2006. *Biographical Directory of the United States Congress, 1774–Present*, online at http://bioguide.congress.gov/biosearch/biosearch.asp.

Congressional Directory. 2002. October online revision at http://frwebgate.access
.gpo.gov.

Congressional Quarterly Almanac. Various years. Washington: CQ Press.

Congressional Record. 1984. Washington: U.S. Government Printing Office.

Conley, Richard S. 1999. "Derailing Presidential Fast-Track Authority: The Impact
of Constituency Pressures and Political Ideology on Trade Policy in Congress."
Political Research Quarterly 52, 785–99.

———. 2003. "Congress, the Presidency, Information Technology, and the Internet: Policy Entrepreneurship at Both Ends of Pennsylvania Avenue." *Congress
and the Internet*, ed. James A. Thurber and Colton C. Campbell, 135–60. Upper
Saddle River, N.J.: Prentice-Hall.

Cook, Timothy. 1989. *Making Laws and Making News: Media Strategies in the U.S.
House of Representatives.* Washington: Brookings Institution.

Cooper, Joseph, and Garry Young. 1997. "Partisanship, Bipartisanship, and Cross-
partisanship in Congress since the New Deal." *Congress Reconsidered*, 6th edn,
ed. Lawrence C. Dodd and Bruce I. Oppenheimer. Washington: CQ Press.

Copley News Service. 2001. "Osprey Backer Renews Support." *San Diego Union-
Tribune*, 11 May, § A, 7.

Corwin, Edward. 1957. *The President: Office and Powers, 1787–1957.* New York:
New York University Press.

Cox, Gary W. and Mathew D. McCubbins. 1991. "Divided Control of Fiscal Policy."
The Politics of Divided Government, ed. Gary W. Cox and Samuel Kernell. Boulder: Westview.

———. 1993. *Legislative Leviathan: Party Government in the House.* Berkeley:
University of California Press.

———. 2002. "Agenda Power in the U.S. House of Representatives, 1877–1986."
*Party, Process, and Political Change in Congress: New Perspectives on the His-
tory of Congress*, ed. David W. Brady and Mathew D. McCubbins. Stanford:
Stanford University Press.

Coyne, John. 1999. "Establishing the Peace Corps." Online at http://www
.peacecorpswriters.org/pages/1999/9911/911pchist2.html.

Crabb, Cecil V., Jr., and Pat M. Holt. 1989. *Invitation to Struggle: Congress, the
President, and Foreign Policy.* Washington: CQ Press.

———. 1992. *Invitation to Struggle: Congress, the President, and Foreign Policy.*
4th edn. Washington: CQ Press.

Crile, George. 2003. *Charlie Wilson's War: The Extraordinary Story of the Largest
Covert Operation in History.* New York: Atlantic Monthly Press.

Crocker, Chester A., 1992. *High Noon in Southern Africa: Making Peace in a Tough
Neighborhood.* New York: W. W. Norton.

Cronin, Thomas. 1979. "Presidential Power Revised and Reappraised." *Western Political Quarterly* 32, no. 4, 381–95.

Crossette, Barbara. 2000. "U.N. Members Slow to Accept an Invitation From
Helms." *New York Times*, 18 March, § A, 6.

Crovitz, Gordon, and Jeremy Rabkin, eds. 1989. *The Fettered Presidency: Legal Constraints on the Executive Branch*. Washington: American Enterprise Institute.

Daalder, Ivo H. 2000. *Getting to Dayton: The Making of America's Bosnia Policy*. Washington: Brookings Institution.

Daalder, Ivo H., and Michael E. O'Hanlon. 2000. *Winning Ugly: Nato's War to Save Kosovo*. Washington: Brookings Institution.

D'Agostino, Joseph A. 1997a. "WHO Plans to Join Other Agencies in Using U.S. Funds for Abortion in Refugee Camps." *Human Events* 53, no. 38, 5–6.

———. 1997b. "Helms and Smith Battle over Mexico City language." *Human Events* 53, no. 43, 4.

———. 1999. "Armey: No Abortion Money or No U.N. Money." *Human Events* 55, no. 25, 5.

Dale, Edwin. 1964. "A Program for America." *New York Times Book Review*, 23 February, 3.

Dale, Reginald. 1984a. "US Senate Backs $62M Arms Aid to El Salvador." *Financial Times*, 31 March, 2.

———. 1984b. "U.S. Senate Beats Off Challenge to Central American Strategy." *Financial Times*, 20 June, 4.

Dallek, Robert. 2003. *An Unfinished Life: John F. Kennedy, 1917–1963*. Boston: Little, Brown.

Dao, James. 1997. "Crusader and Pragmatist: The Two Chris Smiths." *New York Times*, 4 December, § B, 1.

Daugherty, William J. 2004. *Executive Secrets: Covert Action and the Presidency*. Lexington: University Press of Kentucky.

Deering, Christopher, and Steven Smith. 1997. *Committees in Congress*. Washington: CQ Press.

DeGregorio, Christine. 1997. *Network of Champions: Leadership, Access, and Advocacy in the U.S. House of Representatives*. Ann Arbor: University of Michigan Press.

DeLaet, C. James, and James M. Scott. 2006. "Treaty-Making and Partisan Politics: Arms Control and the U.S. Senate, 1960–2001." *Foreign Policy Analysis* 2, no. 2, 177–200.

Democrats. 1984. "Conservatives Attack Letter." *Washington Post*, 25 April, § A, 6.

Dempsey, Gary T. and Aaron Lukas. 1999. "Is Russia Controlled by ORGANIZED CRIME?" *USA Today Magazine* (Society for the Advancement of Education), May, online at http://findarticles.com/p/articles/mi_m1272/is_2648_127/ai_54680893.

Derian, Patt. 1983. "A Little Information, Please." *Washington Post*, 8 May, § B, 7.

Destler, I. M., Leslie H. Gelb, and Anthony Lake. 1984. *Our Own Worst Enemy: The Unmaking of American Foreign Policy*. New York: Simon and Schuster.

Devroy, Anne. 1989. "Bush Defends Sending Secret Mission to China." *Washington Post*, 22 December, § A, 27.

Dewar, Helen. 1987a. "Democrats May Link Contra Funding to Accounting of Past Aid." *Washington Post*, 20 February, § A, 26.

———. 1987b. "Michel Sees New Contra Aid Unlikely: House GOP Leader Urges President to Focus on Negotiations." *Washington Post*, 11 March, § A, 1.

———. 2001. "Biden to Head Panel on Foreign Relations." *Washington Post*, 30 May, § A, 17.

Dewar, Helen, and Juliet Eilperin. 1999. "Senate Divided on Kosovo Strategy; Back from Europe, House Members Urge Negotiated Settlement." *Washington Post*, 4 May, § A, 18.

Dewar, Helen, and Edward Walsh. 1987. "Lawmakers Agree President Failed to Regain Political Initiative." *Washington Post*, 28 January, § A, 12.

DeYoung, Karen, and Shailagh Murray. 2007. "GOP Skepticism on Iraq Growing." Washington Post, 27 June, § A, 1.

Dickey, Christopher. 1983. "U.S. Envoy Says Aid Is Vital." *Washington Post*, 19 January, § A, 1.

Dionne, E. J., Jr. 2004. "The System Was Lacking." *Washington Post*, 7 May, § A, 33.

Dobbs, Michael. 2002. "How Politics Helped Redefine Threat." *Washington Post*, 14 January, § A, 1.

Doherty, C. 1997. "Family Planning Measures Revive Abortion Dispute." *Congressional Quarterly Weekly Report*, 8 February.

Doig, Jameson W., and Erwin C. Hargrove. 1987. "'Leadership' and Political Analysis." *Leadership and Innovation: A Biographical Perspective on Entrepreneurs in Government*, ed. Jameson W. Doig and Erwin C. Hargrove. Baltimore: Johns Hopkins University Press.

Doyle, Robert J. 1989. "McCarran Act Becomes Law." *Historical Almanac of the U.S. Senate*, ed. Wendy Wolff and Richard A. Baker. Washington: U.S. Government Printing Office.

Drew, Elizabeth. 1979. *Senator*. New York: Simon and Schuster.

Drischler, Alvin P. 1986. "The Activist Congress and Foreign Policy." *SAIS Review* 6, 193–204.

Economist. 1999. "Bombs over Belgrade: Diplomatic as Well as Military: The Emerging Outline of an Agreement Between NATO and Russia over Kosovo May Be More of a Threat to Slobodan Milosevic Than the Alliance's Bombs." 8 May, online at http://infoweb.newsbank.com.ezproxy.tcu.edu/iw-search/InfoWeb?p_product=AWNB&.

Edwards, George C., III, Andrew Barrett, and Jeffrey Peake. 1997. "The Legislative Impact of Divided Government." *American Journal of Political Science* 41, no. 2, 545–63.

Ehrenhalt, Alan. 1991. *The United States of Ambition: Politicians, Power, and the Pursuit of Office*. New York: Times Books.

Eilperin, Juliet. 1999. "Albright Asks Lawmakers to End Balkan Effort." *Washington Post*, 13 May, § A, 19.

Eilperin, Juliet, and John F. Harris. 1999. "GI Release Does Not Halt Attacks; Russian Envoy, Clinton to Meet; GOP Urges Negotiation." *Washington Post*, 3 May, § A, 1.

Eisenstadt, David. 1995. "House OKs Abort Aid Cut-Off." *Daily News* (New York), 29 June, 30.

Ely, John Hart. 1993. *War and Responsibility*. Princeton: Princeton University Press.

"Embarrassing Deadbeat." 1999. *San Francisco Chronicle*, 3 November, § A, 28.

Entman, Robert M. 2004. *Projections of Power: Framing News, Public Opinion, and U.S. Foreign Policy*. Chicago: University of Chicago Press.

Ehrlichman, John. 1982. *Witness to Power: The Nixon Years*. New York: Simon and Schuster.

European Union. 1999. "Council Decision of 28 June 1999 amending Decision 1999/357/CFSP Implementing Common Position 1999/318/CFSP concerning Additional Restrictive Measures against the Federal Republic of Yugoslavia (1999/424/CFSP)." *Official Journal of the European Communities*, 29 June.

Evans, C. Lawrence. 2001. "Committees, Leaders, and Message Politics." *Congress Reconsidered*, 7th edn, ed. Lawrence C. Dodd and Bruce I. Oppenheimer. Washington: CQ Press.

Evans, Rowland, Jr., and Robert D. Novak. 1971. *Nixon in the White House: The Frustration of Power*. New York: Random House.

Fennell, Tom, with Rosanne Pavicic and Patricia Treble. 1999. "Ottawa Opposes Citizenship for a Milosevic Crony." *Maclean's Hunter Magazine* (Toronto), 3 May, online at http://www.balkan-archive.org.yu/kosovo_crisis/Jul_13-/13.html.

Fenno, Richard F., Jr. 1966. *The Power of the Purse*. Boston: Little, Brown.

———. 1973. *Congressmen in Committees*. Boston: Little, Brown.

Finney, John W. 1971. "McCloskey Says U.S. Hid Extent of Laos Bombing." *New York Times*, 22 April, 3.

Fisher, Louis. 1991. *Constitutional Conflicts between Congress and the President*, 3rd rev. edn. Lawrence: University of Kansas Press.

Flaherty, Mary Pat. 2001. "Osprey Crash Blamed on Leak, Software; Report Details Fatal December Accident, Calls for Redesign of Faulty Systems." *Washington Post*, 6 April, § A, 2.

Fleisher, Richard. 1985. "Economic Benefits, Ideology, and Senate Voting on the B-1 Bomber." *American Politics Quarterly* 13, 200–211.

Fleisher, Richard, Jon Bond, Glen Krutz, and Stephen Hanna. 2000. "The Demise of the Two Presidencies." *American Politics Quarterly* 28, no. 1, 3–25.

Fletcher, Michael, and Juliet Eilperin. 2007. "Bush Proposes Talks on Warming." *Washington Post*, 31 May, § A, 1.

Foltz, William, Chester Crocker, Edward M. Kennedy, Sal Marzullo, John Foisie, and Frank Parker. 1985. "South Africa: The Hard Questions." *America*, 3 August, 45–63.

Foreman, Christopher H., Jr. 1988. *Signals from the Hill: Congressional Oversight and the Challenge of Social Regulation*. New Haven: Yale University Press.

Fox, Harrison W., Jr., and Susan Webb Hammond. 1977. *Congressional Staffs: The Invisible Force in American Lawmaking*. New York: Free Press.

Foyle, Douglas C. 2005. "Public Opinion and Bosnia: Anticipating Disaster." *Contemporary Cases in U.S. Foreign Policy: From Terrorism to Trade*, 2nd edn, ed. Ralph G. Carter. Washington: CQ Press.

Franck, Thomas M., and Edward Weisband. 1979. *Foreign Policy by Congress*. New York: Oxford University Press.

Frank, Barney. 2001. Personal interview. Washington, 13 September.

Freedman, Lawrence. 2000. *Kennedy's Wars: Berlin, Cuba, Laos and Vietnam*. New York: Oxford University Press.

Friedman, Robert. 1989. "The Peculiar Politics of Jesse Helms." *St. Petersburg Times*, 5 November.

Frohlich, Norman, and Joe A. Oppenheimer. 1978. *Modern Political Economy*. Englewood Cliffs: Prentice-Hall.

Froman, Lewis A., Jr. 1963. "The Importance of Individuality in Voting in Congress." *Journal of Politics* 25, no. 2, 324–32.

Fulbright, J. William. 1946a. "The Word That Blocks Lasting Peace." *New York Times Magazine*, 8 January, 8.

———. 1946b. "Is It the Purpose of Russia to Dominate the World?" Delivered to a joint meeting of the American Academy of Arts and Letters and the National Institute of Arts, New York City, 17 May. *Fulbright of Arkansas: The Public Positions of a Private Thinker*, ed. Karl E. Meyer. Washington: Robert B. Luce, 1963.

———. 1947a. "A United States of Europe: It Is Not an Idealistic Dream." Delivered in the Senate 7 April. *Fulbright of Arkansas: The Public Positions of a Private Thinker*, ed. Karl E. Meyer. Washington: Robert B. Luce, 1963.

———. 1947b. "Commonwealth and Continent." Delivered at the University of Toronto, 8–9 December 1947. *Fulbright of Arkansas: The Public Positions of a Private Thinker*, ed. Karl E. Meyer. Washington: Robert B. Luce, 1963.

———. 1948. "A United States of Europe." *Annals of the American Academy of Political and Social Science* 257 (May), 151–56.

———. 1949. "The Benefits of Federation: It Is an Idea Which We Have Held to for 160 Years." Delivered in the Senate 31 January 1949. *Fulbright of Arkansas: The Public Positions of a Private Thinker*, ed. Karl E. Meyer. Washington: Robert B. Luce, 1963.

———. 1958a. "Mutual Deterrence: It Is Irrational Because of the Very Degree of Rationality It Requires." Delivered in the Senate 20 June. *Fulbright of Arkansas: The Public Positions of a Private Thinker*, ed. Karl E. Meyer. Washington: Robert B. Luce, 1963.

———. 1958b. "Iraq and Lebanon: One Foot over the Brink." Delivered in the Senate 6 August. *Fulbright of Arkansas: The Public Positions of a Private Thinker*, ed. Karl E. Meyer. Washington: Robert B. Luce, 1963.

———. 1959a. "As Fulbright Sees U.S. Policy Abroad." Excerpts from speeches and press conferences over the last year, *U.S. News and World Report*, 13 February, 87.

———. 1959b. "Berlin: What Can Be Negotiated." Delivered in the Senate 16 March. In *Fulbright of Arkansas: The Public Positions of a Private Thinker*, ed. Karl E. Meyer. Washington: Robert B. Luce, 1963.

———. 1959c. "Our Responsibilities in World Affairs." Delivered at Columbia University 7 May. *Vital Speeches of the Day* 25 (15 June), 527–32.

———. 1960. "The Synthesis of Both Liberty and Unity: Some Aspects of Our Foreign Policy." Delivered at the University of Wisconsin, Madison, 23 August. *Vital Speeches of the Day* 26 (1 October), 739–42.

———. 1961a. "United States Foreign Policy." Delivered in the Senate 29 June. *Vital Speeches of the Day* 27 (1 August), 616–19.

———. 1961b. "Total Victory: A Slogan Clinically Examined." Delivered in the Senate 24 July. *Fulbright of Arkansas: The Public Positions of a Private Thinker*, ed. Karl E. Meyer. Washington: Robert B. Luce, 1963.

———. 1961c. "For a Concert of Free Nations." *Foreign Affairs* 40, no. 1, 1–18.

———. 1961d. "Memorandum: Propaganda Activities of Military Personnel Directed at the Public" [personal memorandum sent to the secretary of defense in 1961; Fulbright inserted it into the *Congressional Record* on 2 August]. *Fulbright of Arkansas: The Public Positions of a Private Thinker*, ed. Karl E. Meyer. Washington: Robert B. Luce, 1963.

———. 1961e. "Who Is Really 'Soft on Communism?'" Delivered to the National War College and the Industrial College of the Armed Forces 21 August. *Fulbright of Arkansas: The Public Positions of a Private Thinker*, ed. Karl E. Meyer. Washington: Robert B. Luce, 1963.

———. 1963a. *Prospects for the West*. Cambridge: Harvard University Press.

———. 1963b. "France and the Western Alliance: Actual Cooperation Is Needed." Delivered in the Senate, 29 October. *Vital Speeches of the Day* 30 (15 November), 75–78.

———. 1964a. "Foreign Policy: Old Myths and New Realities." Delivered in the Senate, 25 March. *Vital Speeches of the Day* 30 (15 April), 388–94.

———. 1964b. *Old Myths and New Realities and Other Commentaries*. New York: Random House.

———. 1964c. "Let's Talk Sense about Cuba." *Saturday Evening Post*, 16 May, 8, 10.

———. 1965a. "Foreign Aid? Yes, but with a New Approach." *New York Times Magazine*, 21 March, 27, 102, 104–6.

———. 1965b. "Vietnam: A Holding Action." Delivered in the Senate 15 June. *Vital Speeches of the Day* 31 (1 July), 546–48.

———. 1966a. "The Two Americas." Delivered at the University of Connecticut 22

March. Printed by the University of Connecticut as the Ninth Brien McMahon Lecture.

———. 1966b. "We Must Negotiate Peace in Vietnam." *Saturday Evening Post,* 9 April, 10, 12, 14.

———. 1966c. "The Arrogance of Power." Delivered at the School of Advanced International Studies, Johns Hopkins University, Washington, 5 May, and reprinted in *U.S. News and World Report,* 23 May, 113–21.

———. 1966d. *The Arrogance of Power.* New York: Vintage.

———. 1966e. "Fatal Arrogance of Power." *New York Times Magazine,* 15 May, 28–9, 103–5.

———. 1966f. "The Patriotism of Dissent." *Redbook,* November, 44, 47, 49.

———. 1967a. "We Must Not Fight Fire with Fire." *New York Times Magazine,* 23 April, 27, 122, 124, 126–29.

———. 1967b. "The Price of Empire: Traditional Values." Delivered to the American Bar Association, Honolulu, 8 August. *Vital Speeches of the Day* 33 (1 September), 678–82.

Furgurson, Ernest B. 1986. *Hard Right: The Rise of Jesse Helms.* New York: W. W. Norton.

Galloway, John, ed. 1971. *The Kennedys and Vietnam.* New York: Facts on File.

Gartzke, Erik, and J. Mark Wrighton. 1998. "Thinking Globally or Acting Locally? Determinants of the GATT Vote in Congress." *Legislative Studies Quarterly* 23, 33–55.

Geyelin, Philip. 1982. "Protection vs. Protectionism." *Washington Post,* 28 May, § A, 31.

———. 1983. "Action It Is, but Covert It Isn't." *Washington Post,* 19 May, § A, 19.

———. 1987. "Wright and Reality." *Washington Post,* 23 November, § A, 17.

Giglio, James. 1991. *The Presidency of JFK.* Lawrence: University Press of Kansas.

Gilboa, Eytan. 2005. "The CNN Effect: The Search for a Communication Theory of International Relations." *Political Communication* 22, no. 1, 27–44.

Gilligan, Thomas W., and Keith Krehbiel. 1997. "Specialization Decisions within Committees." *Journal of Law, Economics, and Organization* 13, 366–86.

Goldgeier, James M. 1999. *Not Whether but When: The US Decision to Enlarge NATO.* Washington: Brookings Institution.

Gordon, Michael R. 2000. "Joint Exercise on Missiles Seen for U.S. and Russia." *New York Times,* 29 June, § A, 7.

Goshko, John M. 1978. "OAS Approves Compromise on Nicaragua Role." *Washington Post,* 24 September, § A, 15.

———. 1987a. "Administration Mulls Delay of Request for Contra Aid: Anticipated Recalcitrance on Hill a Factor." *Washington Post,* 29 October, § A, 35.

———. 1987b. "Arias on Hill 'Give Peace a Chance': Costa Rican Opposes Reagan Bid for Contra Aid during Talks." *Washington Post,* 23 September, § A, 1.

——. 1987c. "House Speaker Rebukes Reagan: Wright Says Central American Peace Plan Being Undermined." *Washington Post*, 16 September, § A, 28.

——. 1987d. "Ortega Proposes Cease-fire for a Month, Starting Dec. 5: Administration Denounces Wright's Role." *Washington Post*, 14 November, § A, 1.

——. 1987e. "Reagan Hits Wright on Peace Talks: Angry Speaker Vows 'An Open Door' for Efforts on Nicaragua." *Washington Post*, 17 November, § A, 1.

——. 1987f. "Reagan's Desire to Deal with Sandinistas Disputed." *Washington Post*, 18 September, § A, 22.

——. 1988. "Sandinista Not Blocking Contra Aid: Wright Meets with Vice President." *Washington Post*, 13 May, § A, 19.

——. 1994. "Foreign Aid May Be Early Test of New Hill Order." *Washington Post*, 21 November, § A, 14.

Goshko, John M., and Daniel Williams. 1994. "U.S. Policy Faces Review by Helms." *Washington Post*, 13 November, § A, 1.

Granger, Gregory P. 2002. "The Demise of the Arms Control and Disarmament Agency: Arms Control Politics." *Contemporary Cases in U.S. Foreign Policy: From Terrorism to Trade*, ed. Ralph G. Carter. Washington: CQ Press.

Gray, Jerry. 1997. "House Votes Plan to Curb International Abortion Aid." *New York Times*, 5 September, § A, 30.

Greenhouse, Steven. 1994. "Russian Aid under Siege by G.O.P." *New York Times*, 25 November, § A, 15.

Groseclose, Tim and David C. King. 2001. "Committee Theories Reconsidered." *Congress Reconsidered*, 7th edn, ed. Lawrence C. Dodd and Bruce I. Oppenheimer. Washington: CQ Press.

Gwertzman, Bernard. 1977. "State Department Seeking to Admit 10,000 Vietnamese." *New York Times*, 4 December, 1.

Hader, Leon. 2002. "S'pore Caucus Formed in US Congress—Move Seen as Symbol of Support for US-S'pore Ties." *Business Times* (Singapore), 11 October.

Hagel, Chuck. 1998. "American Foreign Policy: Leadership for a New Century." Address to the JFK School of Government, Harvard University, 29 September, 2.

Halberstam, David. 1972. *The Best and the Brightest*. New York: Random House.

Haldeman, H. R. 1994. *The Haldeman Diaries: Inside the Nixon White House*. New York: G. P. Putnam's Sons.

Halperin, Morton H. 1974. *Bureaucratic Politics and Foreign Policy*. Washington: Brookings Institution Press.

Hamilton, Lee, with Jordan Tama. 2002. *A Creative Tension: The Foreign Policy Roles of the President and Congress*. Washington: Woodrow Wilson Center Press.

Hammond, Susan Webb. 1989. "Congressional Caucuses in the Policy Process." *Congress Reconsidered*, 4th edn, ed. Lawrence C. Dodd and Bruce I. Oppenheimer. Washington: CQ Press.

——. 1998. *Congressional Caucuses in National Policy Making*. Baltimore: Johns Hopkins University Press.

———. 2003. "Life and Work on the Hill: Careers, Norms, Staff, and Informal Caucuses." *Congress Responds to the Twentieth Century*, ed. Sunil Ahuja and Robert Dewhirst. Columbus: Ohio State University Press.

Haney, Patrick J., and Walt Vanderbush. 2002. "The Helms-Burton Act: Congress and Cuba Policy." *Contemporary Cases in U.S. Foreign Policy: from Terrorism to Trade*, ed. Ralph G. Carter. Washington: CQ Press.

Helms, Jesse. 1995a. "We Must Stop Nuclear Sale." *USA Today*, 10 May, § A, 11.

———. 1995b. "For a More Effective State Department." *Freedom Review* 26, no. 3, 8.

———. 1995c. "Castro Needs a Final Push." *Washington Post*, 4 May, § A, 21.

———. 1995d. "Castro Blows a Gasket." *USA Today*, 14 June.

———. 1996a. "The Challenge to Colombia." *Wall Street Journal*, 4 March.

———. 1996b. "America vs. the World." *Pittsburgh Post Gazette*, 22 September.

———. 1996c. "Saving the U.N.: A Challenge to the Next Secretary-General." *Foreign Affairs* 75, no. 5, 2–7.

———. 1996d. "Immoral to Lift Ban." *USA Today*, 9 January, § A, 10.

———. 1998. Untitled. *New York Times*, 21 September, § A, 19.

———. 1999. "Defeat the Narco-Guerillas." *Wall Street Journal*, 27 July.

———. 2000a. "Respect the Sovereignty of the American People." *Vital Speeches of the Day* 66, no. 9 (February 2000), electronic version obtained through Academic Search Elite; pagination unavailable.

———. 2000b. "On Trade, Cuba Is Not China." *New York Times*, 24 June, § A, 15.

———. 2001a. "Compassionate Conservatism Doesn't Stop at the Water's Edge." *American Enterprise* 12, no. 3, 46.

———. 2001b. "Commentary; Bush Was Right to Abandon Treaty." *Los Angeles Times*, 17 December, § B, 11.

Helms, Jesse, and William J. Bennett. 1995. "Colombia: America's Favorite Narco-Democracy." *Wall Street Journal*, 4 April.

Hendrickson, Ryan C. 2002. *The Clinton Wars: The Constitution, Congress, and War Powers*. Nashville: Vanderbilt University Press.

———. 2005. "The United States vs. Terrorism: Clinton, Bush, and Osama Bin Laden." *Contemporary Cases in U.S. Foreign Policy: From Terrorism to Trade*, 2nd edn, ed. Ralph G. Carter. Washington: CQ Press.

Henehan, Marie T. 2000. *Foreign Policy and Congress: An International Relations Perspective*. Ann Arbor: University of Michigan Press.

———. 2001. "Congress and Critical Foreign Policy Issues: Past, Present, and Future." *Extensions: A Journal of the Carl Albert Congressional Research and Studies Center*, spring, 7–10.

Henkin, Louis. 1990. *Constitutionalism, Democracy, and Foreign Affairs*. New York: Columbia University Press.

Hersman, Rebecca K. C. 2000. *Friends and Foes: How Congress and the President Really Make Foreign Policy*. Washington: Brookings Institution Press.

Hibbing, John R. 2003. "The Changing Context of the Yeas and Nays in Congress."

Congress Responds to the Twentieth Century, ed. Sunil Ahuja and Robert Dewhirst. Columbus: Ohio State University Press.

Hill, Christopher. 1993. "Foreign Policy." *The Oxford Companion to Politics of the World*, ed. Joel Krieger. New York: Oxford University Press.

Hill, Kim Quaile, and Patricia A. Hurley. 2002. "Symbolic Speeches in the U.S. Senate and Their Representational Implications." *Journal of Politics* 64, no. 1, 219–31.

Hilsman, Roger. 1967. *To Move a Nation*. New York: Doubleday.

Hinckley, Barbara. 1994. *Less Than Meets the Eye: Congress, the President, and Foreign Policy*. Chicago: University of Chicago Press.

Hoffman, David, and Margaret Shapiro. 1985. "Reagan Flays Congress on Nicaraguan Rebel Aid." *Washington Post*, 22 May, § A, 22.

Holbrooke, Richard. 1998. *To End a War*. New York: Random House.

Holian, David B., Timothy B. Krebs, and Michael H. Walsh. 1997. "Constituency Opinion, Ross Perot, and Roll-Call Behavior in the U.S. House: The Case of NAFTA." *Legislative Studies Quarterly* 22, 367–92.

Holmes, Steven A. 1993. "Nicaragua to Get Blocked U.S. Aid." *New York Times*, 3 April, 3.

Holsti, Ole R. 1969. *Content Analysis for the Social Sciences and Humanities*. Reading, Mass.: Addison-Wesley.

Holsti, Ole R., and James M. Rosenau. 1984. *American Leadership in World Affairs: Vietnam and the Breakdown of Consensus*. Boston: Allen and Unwin.

Hook, Steven W. 1998. "The White House, Congress and the Paralysis of the U.S. State Department after the Cold War." *After the End: Making U.S. Foreign Policy in the Post-Cold War World*, ed. James M. Scott. Durham: Duke University Press.

Hosmer, Stephen T. 2001. *The Conflict over Kosovo: Why Milosevic Decided to Settle When He Did*. Santa Monica: RAND.

"House Moves to Eliminate Pro-Abortion Foreign Aid." 1995. *Human Events* 51, no. 22, 23–24.

"House OKs Money to Aid Family Planning Overseas." 1997. *St. Louis Post-Dispatch*, 14 February, § A, 17.

Howell, William G., and Jon C. Pevehouse. 2007. *While Dangers Gather: Congressional Checks on Presidential War Powers*. Princeton: Princeton University Press.

Huffman, David. 1987. "Regan 'Plan' Blamed NSC for Affair: Confusion Reigned in Wake of Iran-Contra." *Washington Post*, 2 August, § A, 1.

Hunt, Valerie F. 2002. "The Multiple and Changing Goals of Immigration Reform: A Comparison of House and Senate Activity, 1947–1993." *Policy Dynamics*, ed. Frank R. Baumgartner and Bryan D. Jones. Chicago: University of Chicago Press.

Independent (London). 1999. "US Troops Freed but NATO Is Unmoved." 3 May, on-

line at http://infoweb.newsbank.com.ezproxy.tcu.edu/iw-search/we/InfoWeb
?p_product=AWNB&.

Iyengar, Shanto. 1991. *Is Anyone Responsible? How Television Frames Political Issues*. Chicago: University of Chicago Press.

Jackson, David Vail. 1999. "TV Highlights." *Washington Post*, 8 May, § C, 7.

Jacobs, Lawrence R., and Benjamin I. Page. 2005. "Who Influences U.S. Foreign Policy?" *American Political Science Review* 99, no. 1, 107–23.

Jacoby, William G. 2000. "Issue Framing and Public Opinion on Government Spending." *American Journal of Political Science* 44, no. 4, 750–67.

Javits, Jacob K. 1967. "Last Chance for a Common Market." *Foreign Affairs* 45 (April), 449–62.

———. 1970. "The Congressional Presence in Foreign Relations." *Foreign Affairs* 48 (January), 221–34.

———. 1973. *Who Makes War: The President versus Congress*. New York: William Morrow.

Javits, Jacob K., with Rafael Steinberg. 1981. *Javits: The Autobiography of a Public Man*. Boston: Houghton Mifflin.

"Jesse Helms: Campaign Finance/Money: Contributions: Senate 2002." 2002. Online at http://www.opensecrets.org/politicians/summary.asp?cid=N00002287 &cycle=2002.

Jeon, Yongjoo, and Donald P. Haider-Markel. 2001. "Tracing Issue Definition and Policy Change: An Analysis of Disability Issue Images and Policy Response." *Policy Studies Journal* 29, no. 2, 215–31.

Johnson, Haynes, and Bernard Gwertzman. 1968. *Fulbright: The Dissenter*. Garden City: Doubleday.

Johnson, Loch K. 1985. *A Season of Inquiry: The Senate Intelligence Investigation*. Lexington: University Press of Kentucky.

Johnson, Lyndon B. 1971. *Vantage Point: Perspectives on the Presidency, 1963–1969*. New York: Holt, Rinehart and Winston.

Johnson, Robert David. 2006. *Congress and the Cold War*. New York: Cambridge University Press.

Johnstone, Bill. 2001. Personal interview, 10 September.

Jones, Christopher M. 2002. "The V-22 Osprey: Pure Pork or Cutting Edge Technology?" *Contemporary Cases in U.S. Foreign Policy: From Terrorism to Trade*, ed. Ralph G. Carter. Washington: CQ Press.

Jones, Gordon, and John Marini, eds. 1988. *The Imperial Congress: Crisis in the Separation of Powers*. Washington: Heritage Foundation.

Kahneman, Daniel, and Amos Tversky. 1984. "Choices, Values, and Frames." *American Psychologist* 39, 107–17.

Kassop, Nancy. 2003. "The War Power and Its Limits." *Presidential Studies Quarterly* 33, no. 3, 509–30.

Kedrowski, Karen M. 2001. "Media Strategies Used by Junior Members of Congress." *Journal of Political Science* 29, 27–47.

Kelley, J. 1995. "Russia Fears U.S. Will Back Down on Aid." *USA Today*, 2 February, § A, 6.

Kelman, Steven. 1987. *Making Public Policy: A Hopeful View of American Government*. New York: Basic Books.

Kennedy, Edward M. 1984. "Support the Peace Effort of Nicaragua's Indians." *New York Times*, 27 November, § A, 31.

———. 1985a. "A Call for Justice." *Africa Report*. May–June, 10–13.

———. 1985b. "The Case Against." *Ebony*. May, 132–40.

———. 1985c. "Edward Kennedy on South Africa." *Washington Quarterly* 8, no. 2, 15–20.

———. 1986a. "Will Mr. Reagan Denounce Pretoria." *New York Times*, 21 July, § A, 17.

———. 1986b. "The Sanctions Debate." *Africa Report*, September–October, 37–39.

———. 1986c. "Can Opportunity Return?" *New York Times*, 16 October, § A, 31.

———. 1986d. "Two New Straws in the Wind from the Soviet Union." *Washington Post*, 16 February, § C, 1.

———. 1987c. "The Sanctions Are Working." *Washington Post*, 16 October 1987, § A, 23.

———. 1990. "Humanitarianism and the Legacy of Mickey Leland." *TransAfrica Forum* 7, no. 1, 31–37.

Kennedy, Edward M., Mark O. Hatfield, Edward J. Markey, and Silvio O. Conte. 1983a. "The Best Way to End the Nuclear Arms Race." *New York Times*, 16 March, § A, 26.

———. 1983b. "The Experts Who Favor a Freeze." *New York Times*, 21 April, § A, 26.

"Kennedy Seeks International Indochina Conference." 1979. *New York Times*, 3 April, § A, 9.

"Kennedy, 40 Congressmen Call Chile's Vote a Fraud." 1980. *Washington Post*, 11 September, § A, 26.

Kenworthy, Tom. 1987. "Wright Calls for Effort to Curtail Trade Deficit: Legislation Top Priority, House Leader Says." *Washington Post*, 3 January, § A, 15.

Kernell, Samuel. 1991. "Facing an Opposition Congress: The President's Strategic Circumstance." *The Politics of Divided Government*, ed. Gary W. Cox and Samuel Kernell. Boulder: Westview.

———. 1997. *Going Public: New Strategies of Presidential Leadership*. 3rd edn. Washington: CQ Press.

Kettle, M. 1999. "Clinton U-Turn on Abortion Deal." *Guardian* (London), 16 November, 13.

Kinder, Donald R. 1983. "Diversity and Complexity in American Public Opinion." *Political Science: The State of the Discipline*, ed. Ada W. Finifter. Washington: American Political Science Association.

King, David C. 1994. "The Nature of Congressional Committee Jurisdictions." *American Political Science Review* 88, 48–62.

————. 1997. *Turf Wars: How Congressional Committees Claim Jurisdiction*. Chicago: University of Chicago Press.

Kingdon, John. 1989. *Congressmen's Voting Decisions*. 3rd edn. Ann Arbor: University of Michigan Press.

————. 1995. *Agendas, Alternatives, and Public Policies*. 2nd edn. New York: Harper Collins.

Kissinger, Henry. 1979. *White House Years*. Boston: Little, Brown.

Klein, Herbert G. 1980. *Making It Perfectly Clear*. Garden City: Doubleday.

Klein, Joe. 2002. *The Natural*. New York: Doubleday.

Koger, Gregory. 2003. "Position Taking and Cosponsorship in the U.S. House." *Legislative Studies Quarterly* 28, no. 2, 225–46.

Koh, Harold. 1990. *The National Security Constitution*. New Haven: Yale University Press.

Korb, Lawrence. 1973. "Congressional Impact on Defense Spending, 1962–1973: The Programmatic and Fiscal Hypotheses." *Naval War College Review* 26, 49–61.

Kramer, M. 2002. "W's U.N. Vote Pure Politics." *Daily News* (New York), 28 July, 10.

Krehbiel, Keith. 1991. *Information and Legislative Organization*. Ann Arbor: University of Michigan Press.

————. 1998. *Pivotal Politics: A Theory of U.S. Lawmaking*. Chicago: University of Chicago Press.

Krutz, Glen S. 2002. "Omnibus Legislation: An Institutional Reaction to the Rise of New Issues." *Policy Dynamics*, ed. Frank R. Baumgartner and Bryan D. Jones. Chicago: University of Chicago Press.

————. 2005. "Issues and Institutions: 'Winnowing' in the U.S. Congress." *American Journal of Political Science* 49, no. 2, 313–26.

Landay, Jonathan S. 1996. "GOP Hawks Set Sights on Missile-Defense System—Remember the 'Star Wars' Idea to Defend against Nuclear Attack? Some Republicans Vow Its Return." *Christian Science Monitor*, 5 February, 4.

Lardner, George, Jr. 1980. "Some in House Join Bid to Stop CIA." *Washington Post*, 2 September, § A, 12.

Lashmar, Paul. 1999. "War in Europe: Serbia's London Connection." *Independent* (London), 25 April, online at http://findarticles.com/p/articles/mi_qn4158/is_19990425/ai_n14219017/print.

Leach, Jim. 2001. Personal interview, Washington, 12 September.

LeLoup, Lance T., and Steven A. Shull. 1993. *Congress and the President: The Policy Connection*. Belmont, Calif.: Wadsworth.

Leogrande, William, and Philip Brenner. 1993. "The House Divided: Ideological Polarization over Aid to the Nicaragua 'Contras.'" *Legislative Studies Quarterly* 17, no. 1, 105–36.

Lindblom, Charles E. 1959. "The Science of 'Muddling Through.'" *Public Administration Review* 19, no. 2, 79–88.

Lindsay, James M. 1990. "Parochialism, Policy, and Constituency Constraints: Congressional Voting on Strategic Weapons Systems." *American Journal of Political Science* 34, no. 4, 936–60.

———. 1993. "Congress and Foreign Policy: Why the Hill Matters." *Political Science Quarterly* 107 (winter), 607–28.

———. 1994a. "Congress, Foreign Policy, and the New Institutionalism." *International Studies Quarterly* 38, 281–304.

———. 1994b. *Congress and the Politics of U.S. Foreign Policy*. Baltimore: Johns Hopkins University Press.

———. 2000. "The New Apathy: How an Uninterested Public Is Reshaping Foreign Policy." *Foreign Affairs* 79, no. 5, 2–8.

———. 2003. "Deference and Defiance: The Shifting Rhythms of Executive-Legislative Relations in Foreign Policy." *Presidential Studies Quarterly* 33, no. 3, 530–47.

Lindsay, James M., and Randall B. Ripley. 1993. "How Congress Influences Foreign and Defense Policy." *Congress Resurgent: Foreign and Defense Policy on Capitol Hill*, ed. Randall B. Ripley and James M. Lindsay. Ann Arbor: University of Michigan Press.

Lippman, Theo, Jr. 1976. *Senator Ted Kennedy*. New York: W. W. Norton.

Lippman, Thomas W. 1995a. "Helms Ends Impasse on Most Envoy Nominations." *Washington Post*, 30 September, § A, 9.

———. 1995b. "GOP Allies Sign Letter for Helms." *Washington Post*, 20 November, § A, 5.

———. 1998a. "Measure Granting Millions in Aid to Cuba Introduced." *Washington Post*, 15 May, § A, 5.

———. 1998b. "Senate Kills Two Agencies, Reorganizes Foreign Affairs Roles." *Washington Post*, 22 October, § A, 23.

———. 1999. "Helms Faces Off with White House on Missed ABM Treaty Deadline." *Washington Post*, 21 June, § A, 5.

Lippman, Thomas W., and Bradley Graham. 1996. "Helms Offers Bill to Force U.S. Out of ABM Treaty." *Washington Post*, 8 February, § A, 20.

Loomis, Burdett A. 1998. *The Contemporary Congress*, 2nd edn. New York: St. Martin's.

Loomis, Burdett A., and Wendy J. Schiller. 2004. *The Contemporary Congress*, 4th edn. Belmont, Calif.: Wadsworth.

———. 2005. *The Contemporary Congress*, 5th edn. Belmont, Calif.: Wadsworth.

Lowi, Theodore J. 1963. "Bases in Spain." *American Civil-Military Decisions: A Book of Case Studies*, ed. Harold Stein. Birmingham: Twentieth Century Fund / Inter-University Case Program / University of Alabama Press.

MacLeod, Michael C. 2002. "The Logic of Positive Feedback: Telecommunications Policy through the Creation, Maintenance, and Destruction of a Regulated Monopoly." *Policy Dynamics*, ed. Frank R. Baumgartner and Bryan D. Jones. Chicago: University of Chicago Press.

Maltzman, Forrest. 1997. *Competing Principals: Committees, Parties, and the Orga-nization of Congress*. Ann Arbor: University of Michigan Press.

———. 1998. "Maintaining Congressional Committees: Sources of Member Sup-port." *Legislative Studies Quarterly* 23, 197–218.

Mann, Judy. 1999. "How the White House Sold Out Women." *Washington Post*, 19 November, § C, 11.

———. 2000. "This Deal Was No Triumph of Diplomacy." *Washington Post*, 7 April, § C, 13.

Mann, Thomas E. 1990. "Making Foreign Policy: President and Congress." *A Ques-tion of Balance: The President, The Congress and Foreign Policy*. Washington: Brookings Institution.

Mann, Thomas E., and Norman J. Ornstein. 1993. *Renewing Congress: A Second Report*. Washington: American Enterprise Institute.

Mansbridge, Jane J. 1999. "Should Blacks Represent Blacks and Women Represent Women? A Contingent 'Yes.'" *Journal of Politics* 61, 628–57.

———. 2003. "Rethinking Representation." *American Political Science Review* 97, 515–28.

Marshall, Bryan W. 2005. "Explaining Congressional-Executive Rivalry in Inter-national Affairs." *Divided Power: The Presidency, Congress, and the Formation of American Foreign Policy*, ed. Donald R. Kelley. Fayetteville: University of Arkansas Press.

Martin, Edward McCammon. 1994. *Kennedy and Latin America*. Lanham, Md.: University Press of America.

Martin, Lisa L. 2000. *Democratic Commitments: Legislatures and International Cooperation*. Princeton: Princeton University Press,

Mason, Robert. 2004. *Richard Nixon and the Quest for a New Majority*. Chapel Hill: University of North Carolina Press.

Matthews, Christopher. 1996. *Kennedy and Nixon: The Rivalry That Shaped Post-war America*. New York: Simon and Schuster.

Mayhew, David R. 1974. *Congress: The Electoral Connection*. New Haven: Yale Uni-versity Press.

———. 1991. *Divided We Govern*. New Haven: Yale University Press.

———. 2000. *America's Congress: Actions in the Public Sphere, James Madison through Newt Gingrich*. New Haven: Yale University Press.

———. 2005. "Actions in the Public Sphere." *The Legislative Branch*, ed. Paul J. Quirk and Sarah A. Binder. New York: Annenberg Foundation Trust at Sunny-lands / Oxford University Press.

McCartney, Robert J. 1984. "Salvadoran Vote Today: Clashing Candidates, Views of U.S. Role." *Washington Post*, 25 March, § A, 14.

McClelland, David C. 1961. *The Achieving Society*. Princeton: D. Van Nostrand.

McCarran, Pat. 1952. "The Communist World Conspiracy." *Vital Speeches of the Day* 19, no. 2, 55–58.

McCormick, James M. 1985. "Congressional Voting on the Nuclear Freeze Resolutions." *American Politics Quarterly* 13, 122–36.

———. 1993. "Decision Making in the Foreign Affairs and Foreign Relations Committees." *Congress Resurgent: Foreign and Defense Policy on Capitol Hill*, ed. Randall B. Ripley and James M. Lindsay. Ann Arbor: University of Michigan Press.

McCormick, James M., and Michael Black. 1983. "Ideology and Voting on the Panama Canal Treaties." *Legislative Studies Quarterly* 8, 45–63.

McCormick, James M., and Eugene R. Wittkopf. 1990. "Bipartisanship, Partisanship, and Ideology in Congressional-Executive Foreign Policy Relations, 1947–1988." *Journal of Politics* 52, no. 4, 1077–1100.

McCormick, James M., Eugene R. Wittkopf, and David Danna. 1997. "Politics and Bipartisanship at the Water's Edge: A Note on Bush and Clinton." *Polity* 30, no. 1, 133–50.

McCubbins, Mathew D. 1991. "Government on Lay-away: Federal Spending and Deficits under Divided Government Control." *The Politics of Divided Government*, ed. Gary W. Cox and Samuel Kernell. Boulder: Westview.

McFarland, Linda. 2001. *Cold War Strategist: Stuart Symington and the Search for National Security.* Westport: Praeger.

McGrory, Mary. 1983. "Imagine If the House Hadn't Voted against the Secret War." *Washington Post*, 2 August, § A, 3.

———. 1987. "The Wright Way." *Washington Post*, 24 September, § A, 2.

McManus, John, and Lori Dorfman. 2002. "Silent Revolution: How U.S. Newspapers Portray Child Care." *Issue* 11 (January), online at http://www.gradethenews.org/pagesfolder/Issue_11.pdf.

McNamara, Robert S. 1995. *In Retrospect.* New York: Random House.

Melanson, Richard. 2005. *American Foreign Policy since the Vietnam War: The Search for Consensus from Richard Nixon to George W. Bush*, 4th edn. Armonk, N.Y.: M. E. Sharpe.

Meyer, Ken. 2001. Personal interview, Washington, 10 September.

Mintrom, Michael. 2000. *Policy Entrepreneurs and School Choice.* Washington: Georgetown University Press.

Moe, Ronald, and Steven Teel. 1970. "Congress as Policy Maker: A Necessary Reappraisal." *Political Science Quarterly* 85 (September), 443–70.

Monk, J. 1992. "One Senator's Stranglehold on Nicaragua." *Houston Chronicle*, 8 November, § A, 26.

Morgan, Dan. 1990. "'Battle of Choppers' Enmeshes Congress, Army; Concern for Voters' Jobs Complicates Decisions on Copter Projects." *Washington Post*, 28 May, § A, 1.

Munson, Lester. 2001. Personal interview, Washington, 10 September.

Myers, Steven Lee. 1997. "A Paradox for Helms on an Abortion Issue." *New York Times*, 1 August, § A, 18.

NASA. 2006. "Response to Sputnik: The Creation of NASA." Online at http://history
.nasa.gov/SP-4211/ch7-1.htm.

National Post (Canada). 1999. "Tycoon Brothers Join Cast in Diplomatic Effort."
6 May, § A, 12.

Nelson, Thomas E., and Zoe M. Oxley. 1999. "Issue Framing Effects on Belief Importance and Opinion." *Journal of Politics* 61, no. 4, 1040–67.

Nicoll, Alexander. 1999. "New Bid for Kosovo Peace: Clinton Awaits Messages from
Russian and Yugoslav Presidents in Fresh Move to Broker Settlement." *Financial Times*, 3 May, 1.

"No Applause for Sen. Helms." 1993. *Washington Post*, 11 September, § A, 20.

Nokken, Timothy P. 2000. "Dynamics of Congressional Loyalty: Party Defection
and Roll-Call Behavior, 1947–97." *Legislative Studies Quarterly* 25, 417–44.

Norton, Noelle H. 1999. "Committee Influence over Controversial Policy: The Reproductive Policy Case." *Policy Studies Journal* 27, no. 2, 203–16.

"Not an Abortion Issue." 1999. *Washington Post*, 26 July, § A, 18.

Oberdorfer, Don, and Lou Cannon. 1987. "Gorbachev Arrives, Urging Progress on
Broader Treaty." *Washington Post*, 8 December, § A, 1.

Observer. 1999. "War in the Balkans: Embassy Fiasco: Bomb Blunder Ambushes
Peace Hope: NATO's Flawed Tactics Will Help Milosevic." 9 May, online at
http://infoweb.newsbank.com.ezproxy.tcu.edu/iw-search/we/InfoWeb?p_
product=AWNB&.

O'Donnell, Kenneth P., and David Powers, with Joe McCarthy. 1970. *Johnny We
Hardly Knew Ye*. Boston: Little, Brown.

Oldfield, Duane, and Aaron Wildavsky. 1989. "Reconsidering the Two Presidencies." *Society* 26 (July–August), 54–59.

Ottaway, David B. 1987a. "Tightening Intelligence Scrutiny: Proposal for Change
Sparks Sharp Debate at House Hearing." *Washington Post*, 2 April, § A, 23.

———. 1987b. "U.S. Shuns Joint Effort on Mozambican Food Relief." *Washington
Post*, 2 June, § A, 26.

Parker, Glenn R. 1992. *Institutional Change, Discretion, and the Making of Modern Congress: An Economic Interpretation*. Ann Arbor: University of Michigan
Press.

Peterson, Paul E., ed. 1994. *The President, the Congress, and the Making of Foreign
Policy*. Norman: University of Oklahoma Press.

Pianin, Eric. 1987. "Wright, Shultz Say Feud Over: Joint Statement Is Issued on
Search for Nicaraguan Peace." *Washington Post*, 18 November, § A, 1.

———. 2000a. "A GOP 'Pit Bull' Puts Missile Defense Front and Center." *Washington Post*, 13 June, § A, 8.

———. 2000b. "An Offbeat Housing Alternative; Rep. Weldon's Congressional Village Is a Hit with Lawmakers, Kin." *Washington Post*, 3 August, § A, 15.

———. 2001. "Lawmakers Seek Russia Initiatives." *Washington Post*, 8 November,
§ A, 7.

Pichirallo, Joe. 1988. "Wright Warns Latin Parties against War Preparations: House Speaker Urges Nicaraguan Government, Contras to Get Peace Talks Back on Track." *Washington Post*, 6 May, § A, 4.

Pincus, Walter, and Dusko Doder. 1986. "Wright Says Iran Paid $12 Million for Arms: Hill Criticism of White House Intensifies." *Washington Post*, 22 November, § A, 1.

Polsby, Nelson W. 1984. *Political Innovation in America: The Politics of Policy Initiation*. New Haven: Yale University Press.

Pomper, Miles A. 1999a. "House Passes State Department Bill, Leaving Tough Issues of Abortion and U.N. Debt until Conference." *Congressional Quarterly Weekly* 57, no. 30, 1806–8.

———. 1999b. "House GOP Votes to Hold Up Foreign Operations Spending Bill If Abortion Riders Are Challenged." *Congressional Quarterly Weekly* 57, no. 31, 1881–82.

Porteous, Samuel D. 2000. "Financial Sanctions: A Better Way to Target Rogue Regimes." *Backgrounder* (C. D. Howe Institute, Toronto), 7 December.

Powell, Lee Riley. 1984. *J. William Fulbright and America's Lost Crusade: Fulbright's Opposition to the Vietnam War*. Little Rock: Rose Publishing.

Power, Samantha. 2002. *A Problem from Hell: America and the Age of Genocide*. New York: Perennial.

Price, David E. 1971. "Professionals and 'Entrepreneurs': Staff Orientations and Policy Making on Three Senate Committees." *Journal of Politics* 33, no. 2, 316–36.

Priest, Andrew. 2006. *Kennedy, Johnson and NATO: Britain, America and the Dynamics of Alliance, 1962–1968*. London: Routledge.

Priest, Dana. 1999. "Cohen Says U.S. Will Build Missile Defense Weapon to Be Pursued Despite '72 ABM Treaty." *Washington Post*, 21 January, § A, 1.

Purvis, Hoyt, and Steven J. Baker, eds. 1984. *Legislating Foreign Policy*. Boulder: Westview.

Reed, Roy. 1967. "U.S. Stands Firm on Price of Gold; Stresses Supply." *New York Times*, 25 November, 1.

Reeves, Richard. 1993. *President Kennedy: Profile of Power*. New York: Simon and Schuster.

Reston, James. 1967. "President Faces Arms Dilemma." *Dallas Morning News*, 26 July, 3.

Reuss, Henry S. 1958. "Foreign Aid: Misspent, Mislabeled, and Misunderstood." *Reporter* 18 (6 February), 24–26.

———. 1960. "A Point Four Youth Corps." *Commonweal*, 6 May, 146–48.

———. 1961. "The United States Foreign Aid Program: An Appraisal." *Annals of the American Academy of Political and Social Science* 336 (July), 23–29.

———. 1962. "Should the Non-communist Nations of the World Work toward Establishing an Economic Community? Pro." *Congressional Digest* 41 (October), 232, 234, 236.

———. 1963. "America Gets an Unexpected Break." *Harper's Magazine*, May, 33–42.

———. 1964. *The Critical Decade: An Economic Policy for America and the Free World*. New York: McGraw-Hill.

———. 1965. "Let the U.N. Handle It." *Commonweal*, 23 July, 523–26.

———. 1967. "Should Order of Induction into Military Service Be Determined by Lottery? Pro." *Congressional Digest* 46 (May), 150, 152, 154, 156.

———. 1999. *When Government Was Good: Memories of a Life in Politics*. Madison: University of Wisconsin Press.

Reuters. 1999. "Weldon Drops U.S.–Russia Belgrade Visit." *Washington Post*, 24 April, § A, 16.

———. 2007. "Republican Senator: Bush Should Begin Iraq Withdrawal." 23 August, at http://www.reuters.com/article/politicsNews/idUSN2336185420070823.

Ridgeway, James. 1999. "Peace Blitz: Hawks in the Dark over Belgrade." *Village Voice*, 5–11 May, online at http://www.villagevoice.com/generic/show_print .php?id=5341&page=ridgway&issue=99.

Rieselbach, Leroy N. 1995. *Congressional Politics: The Evolving Legislative System*. 2nd edn. Boulder: Westview.

Riker, William H. 1980. "Implications from the Disequilibrium of Majority Rule for the Study of Institutions." *American Political Science Review* 83, 193–213.

———. 1986. *The Art of Political Manipulation*. New Haven: Yale University Press.

———. 1997. *The Strategy of Rhetoric: Campaigning for the American Constitution*. New Haven: Yale University Press.

Ripley, Randall B. 1983. *Congress: Process and Policy*. 3rd edn. New York: W. W. Norton.

———. 1998. "Congress and Foreign Policy: A Neglected Stage." *Great Theatre: The American Congress in the 1990s*, ed. Herbert F. Weisberg and Samuel C. Patterson. Cambridge: Cambridge University Press.

Ripley, Randall, and James Lindsay. 1993. "Foreign and Defense Policy in Congress: An Overview and Preview." *Congress Resurgent: Foreign and Defense Policy on Capitol Hill*, ed. Randall Ripley and James Lindsay. Ann Arbor: University of Michigan Press.

Roberts, Jason M. 2007. "The Statistical Analysis of Roll-Call Data: A Cautionary Tale." *Legislative Studies Quarterly* 32, no. 3, 341–60.

Roberts, Nancy C. 1992. "Public Entrepreneurship and Innovation." *Policy Studies Review* 11, no. 1, 55–74.

Robinson, James. 1962. *Congress and Foreign Policy-Making*. Homewood, Ill.: Dorsey.

Rockman, Bert. 1994. "Presidents, Opinion, and Institutional Leadership." *The New Politics of American Foreign Policy*, ed. David Deese. New York: St. Martin's.

Rodan, Steve. 1998. "US Congressman: Iran's Israel-Range Rockets Nearly Ready." *Jerusalem Post*, 26 April, 2.

Rodman, Peter W. 1994. *More Precious Than Peace: The Cold War and the Struggle for the Third World*. New York: Charles Scribner's Sons.

Rohde, David W. 1974. "Committee Reform in the House of Representatives and the Subcommittee Bill of Rights." *Annals of the Academy of Political and Social Science* 411, no. 1, 39–47.

———. 1994. "Partisan Leadership and Congressional Assertiveness in Foreign and Defense Policy." *The New Politics of American Foreign Policy*, ed. David A. Deese. New York: St. Martin's.

———. 2005. "Committees and Policy Formulation." *The Legislative Branch*, ed. Paul J. Quirk and Sarah A. Binder. New York: Annenberg Foundation Trust at Sunnylands / Oxford University Press.

Rowan, Hobart. 1988. "Gephardt's Protectionist Campaign." *Washington Post*, 11 February, § A, 27.

Rudalevige, Andrew. 2005. "The Executive Branch and the Legislative Process." *The Executive Branch*, ed. Joel D. Aberbach and Mark A. Peterson. New York: Annenberg Foundation Trust at Sunnylands / Oxford University Press.

Rusk, Dean. 1990. *As I Saw It*. New York: W. W. Norton.

Russell, Mary. 1978. "House Votes Cut in Aid as Retaliation." *Washington Post*, 23 June, § A, 1.

Safire, William. 1999. "Holbrooke on Hold." *New York Times*, 18 March, § A, 25.

Salisbury, Robert H. 1969. "An Exchange Theory of Interest Groups." *Midwest Journal of Political Science* 13. no. 1, 1–32.

Schaffner, Brian F., Wendy J. Schiller, and Patrick J. Sellers. 2003. "Tactical and Contextual Determinants of U.S. Senators' Approval Ratings." *Legislative Studies Quarterly* 28, no. 2, 203–23.

Schickler, Eric. 2001. *Disjointed Pluralism: Institutional Innovation and the Development of the U.S. Congress*. Princeton: Princeton University Press.

Schiller, Wendy J. 1995. "Senators as Political Entrepreneurs: Using Bill Sponsorship to Shape Legislative Agendas." *American Journal of Political Science* 39, 186–203.

———. 2000. *Partners and Rivals: Representation in U.S. Senate Delegations*. Princeton: Princeton University Press.

Schlesinger, Arthur M., Jr. 1965. *A Thousand Days: John F. Kennedy in the White House*. New York: Houghton Mifflin.

Schmitt, Eric. 1998. "White House Plays Down Device's Loss in China in '96." *New York Times*, 25 June, § A, 15.

———. 2001. "Helms Urges Foreign Aid Be Handled by Charities." *New York Times*, 12 January, § A, 4.

Schneider, Greg. 2000a. "A Strategy of Silence on Missile Defense." *Washington Post*, 4 June, § H, 1.

———. 2000b. "Boeing Plans Ads to Promote Missile Defense; 'Education' Drive to Address Criticism." *Washington Post*, 16 June, § E, 3.

Schneider, Mark, and Paul Teske. 1992. "Toward a Theory of the Political Entrepreneur: Evidence from Local Government." *American Political Science Review* 86, no. 3, 737–47.

Schumpeter, Joseph A. 1939. *Business Cycles*, vol. 1. New York: McGraw-Hill.

Sciolino, E. 1995. "Awaiting Call, Helms Puts Foreign Policy on Hold." *New York Times*, 24 September, 1.

Scott, James M. 1996. *Deciding to Intervene: The Reagan Doctrine and American Foreign Policy*. Durham: Duke University Press.

———. 1997. "In the Loop: Congressional Influence in American Foreign Policy." *Journal of Political and Military Sociology* 25 (summer), 47–76.

———, ed. 1998. *After the End: Making U.S. Foreign Policy in the Post–Cold War World*. Durham: Duke University Press.

Scott, James M., and Ralph G. Carter. 2002a. "Acting on the Hill: Congressional Assertiveness in U.S. Foreign Policy." *Congress and the Presidency* 29, no. 2, 151–69.

———. 2002b. "Leading the Charge: Frank Church and Post-Vietnam Foreign Policy Entrepreneurship." Paper presented at the Annual Meeting of the International Studies Association, New Orleans, 24–27 March.

———. 2005. "The Politics of IMF Reform: Asian Flu and Abortion Politics." *Contemporary Cases in U.S. Foreign Policy: From Terrorism to Trade*, ed. Ralph G. Carter. Washington: CQ Press.

Sellers, Patrick J. 2000. "Manipulating the Message in the U.S. Congress." *Harvard International Journal of Press/Politics* 5, no. 1, 22–31.

Shepsle, Kenneth A. 1989. "The Changing Textbook Congress." *Can the Government Govern?*, ed. John E. Chubb and Paul E. Peterson. Washington: Brookings Institution.

Shepsle, Kenneth A., and Barry R. Weingast. 1987a. "The Institutional Foundations of Committee Power." *American Political Science Review* 81, 85–104.

———. 1987b. "Why Are Congressional Committees Powerful?" *American Political Science Review* 81, 937–38.

Shields, Mark. 2005. "Wisconsin's Maverick Liberal." Online at www.cnn.com/2005/POLITICS/12/19/proxmire.shields/index.html.

Shultz, George P. 1993. *Turmoil and Triumph: My Years as Secretary of State*. New York: Charles Scribner's Sons.

Silverstein, Gordon. 1994. "Judicial Enhancement of Executive Power." *The President, the Congress, and the Making of Foreign Policy*, ed. Paul E. Peterson. Norman: University of Oklahoma Press.

Silverstein, Ken, Chuck Neubauer, and Richard T. Cooper. 2004. "Lucrative Deals for a Daughter of Politics." Los Angeles Times, 20 February, online at http/www.latimes.com/news/nationworld/nation/la-na-weldon20feb,1,2050409,print.story.

Simpson, Alan, and Edward M. Kennedy. 1985. "Choosing the U.N.'s Next Refugee Commissioner." *New York Times*, 10 October, § A, 31.

Sinclair, Barbara. 1993. "Congressional Party Leaders in the Foreign and Defense

Policy Arena." *Congress Resurgent: Foreign and Defense Policy on Capitol Hill*, ed. Randall B. Ripley and James M. Lindsay. Ann Arbor: University of Michigan Press.

———. 2000. *Unorthodox Lawmaking: New Legislative Processes in the U.S. Congress*. 2nd edn. Washington: CQ Press.

———. 2005. "Parties and Leadership in the House." *The Legislative Branch*, ed. Paul J. Quirk and Sarah A. Binder. New York: Annenberg Foundation Trust at Sunnylands / Oxford University Press.

Shanker, Thom. 2002. "Administration Says Russia Is Preparing Nuclear Tests." *New York Times*, 12 May, 4.

Small, Melvin. 1999. *The Presidency of Richard Nixon*. Lawrence: University Press of Kansas.

Smith, Christopher H. 1997. ". . . But Funds Promote Abortions Abroad." *St. Louis Post Dispatch*, 12 February, § B, 7.

———. 1998. "Foreign Aid and Abortion Overseas." *Washington Post*, 16 March, § A, 21.

———. 1999. "Getting Our Money's Worth From the U.N." *Washington Post*, 3 November, § A, 34.

———. 2002. "U.N. Program Abets China Travesties." *Atlanta Journal and Constitution*, 14 May, § A, 12.

Smith, Jean. 1989. *The Constitution and American Foreign Policy*. New York: West.

Smith, R. Jeffrey, and David Hoffman. 1997. "No Support Found for Report of Lost Russian Suitcase-Sized Nuclear Weapons." *Washington Post*, 5 September, § A, 19.

Smith, Steven S. 1989. *Call to Order: Floor Politics in the House and Senate*. Washington: Brookings Institution Press.

———. 1994. "Congressional Party Leaders." *The President, the Congress, and the Making of Foreign Policy*, ed. Paul E. Peterson. Norman: University of Oklahoma Press.

———. 2005. "Parties and Leadership in the Senate." *The Legislative Branch*, ed. Paul J. Quirk and Sarah A. Binder. New York: Annenberg Foundation Trust at Sunnylands / Oxford University Press.

Smith, Steven S., and Gerald Gamm. 2001. "The Dynamics of Party Government in Congress." *Congress Reconsidered*, 7th edn, ed. Lawrence C. Dodd and Bruce I. Oppenheimer. Washington: CQ Press.

Sorensen, Theodore C. 1965. *Kennedy*. New York: Harper and Row.

Spiegel, Steven L. 1997. "Eagle in the Middle East." *Eagle Adrift: American Foreign Policy at the End of the Century*, ed. Robert J. Lieber. New York: Longman.

Stout, David. 1998. "Clinton Vetoes Measure to Pay $1 Billion in Late U.N. Dues." *New York Times*, 22 October, § A, 3.

Stratmann, Thomas. 2000. "Congressional Voting over Legislative Careers: Shifting Positions and Changing Constraints." *American Political Science Review* 94, no. 3, 665–76.

Strobel, Warren P. 1999. "The CNN Effect: Myth or Reality?" *The Domestic Sources of American Foreign Policy: Insights and Evidence*, 3rd edn, ed. Eugene R. Wittkopf and James M. McCormick. Lanham, Md.: Rowman and Littlefield.

Swoboda, Frank. 1988. "Timetable Accepted on Trade Bill: Wright Says Objective Is to Put Trade Measure to Floor Vote Next Month." *Washington Post*, 16 February, § A, 3.

Sundquist, James L. 1992. *Constitutional Reform and Effective Government*. Rev. edn. Washington: Brookings Institution.

Szulc, Tad. 1978. *The Illusion of Peace: Foreign Policy in the Nixon Years*. New York: Viking.

Tarnoff, Curt. 2004. *The Former Soviet Union and U.S. Foreign Assistance in 1992: The Role of Congress*. Congressional Research Service Report for Congress. Washington: Library of Congress.

Tate, Bill. 2001. Personal interview, Washington, 12 September.

Taylor, Paul. 1986. "White House Labeled 'Arrogant, Partisan': Sen. Byrd Decries 'Reliance on Ramboism.'" *Washington Post*, 13 December, § A, 3.

"That 'Dear Commandante' Letter." 1984. *Washington Post*, 3 May, § A, 20.

Thiessen, M., ed. 2001. *Empire for Liberty: A Sovereign America and Her Moral Mission*. Washington: Regnery.

Thurber, James A. 1991. *Divided Democracy: Cooperation and Conflict Between the President and Congress*. Washington: Congressional Quarterly Press.

Tonkin Gulf Resolution. 1964. Public Law 88-408. 88th Congress, 7 August 1964. Washington: U.S. Government Printing Office.

Torry, Saundra Saperstein, and John Mintz. 1987. "Free Jews, Thousands Demand: Demonstrations Converge on D.C. to Make Pleas." *Washington Post*, 7 December, § A, 1.

Treverton, Gregory, and Pamela Varley. 1992. *The United States and South Africa: The 1985 Sanctions Debate*. Washington: Institute for the Study of Diplomacy.

Trubowitz, Peter. 1998. *Defining the National Interest: Conflict and Change in American Foreign Policy*. Chicago: University of Chicago Press.

"UN Dues, Round 3." 1999. *Christian Science Monitor*, 23 June, 10.

University of New York-Stony Brook Javits Collection. 2003. Online at http://www.stonybrook.edu/library/javitsb.htm.

UPI. 1960. "Rep. Reuss Wants Cruise Cancelled." *Dallas Morning News*, 27 November, 7.

———. 1961. "Dillon Sees Free Trade between U.S., Europe." *Dallas Morning News*, 9 November, 4.

———. 1966. "McNamara Says Cong Building Up." *Dallas Morning News*, 16 February, § A, 2.

———. 1967. "Proposal on Attacks Defeated: Owl Group." *Dallas Morning News*, 3 March, § A, 2.

U.S. Embassy. 2002. "Ambassador Tony P. Hall." Online at http://www.usembassy.it/usunrome/files/hall.htm.

U.S. News and World Report. 1976. "Two Sides of the Question: Interview with Senator Edward M. Kennedy." 8 March, 43.

Van Doren, Peter M. 1990. "Can We Learn the Causes of Congressional Decisions from Roll-Call Data?" *Legislative Studies Quarterly* 15, 311–40.

Vogel, Ralph H. 1987. "The Making of the Fulbright Program." *Annals of the American Academy of Political and Social Science* 491 (May), 11–21.

Walker, Jack L. 1981. "The Diffusion of Knowledge, Policy Communities, and Agenda Setting: The Relationship of Knowledge and Power." *New Strategic Perspectives on Social Policy*, ed. John E. Tropman and Roger M. Lind. New York: Pergamon.

Walsh, Edward. 1987. "Wright Urges Reagan to Admit Errors: Speaker Calls Iran Sales Illegal as Democrats Challenge President." *Washington Post*, 4 March, § A, 1.

Warburg, Gerald F. 1989. *Conflict and Consensus: The Struggle between Congress and the President over Foreign Policymaking*. New York: Harper and Row.

Wawro, Gregory. 2000. *Legislative Entrepreneurship in the U.S. House of Representatives*. Ann Arbor: University of Michigan Press.

Weissert, Carol S. 1991. "Policy Entrepreneurs, Policy Opportunists, and Legislative Effectiveness." *American Politics Quarterly* 19, no. 2, 262–74.

Weissman, Stephen R. 1995. *A Culture of Deference: Congress's Failure of Leadership in Foreign Policy*. New York: Basic Books / Harper Collins.

Weldon, Curt. 1989. "A Moment of Truth in Defense?" *Washington Post*, 27 June, § A, 22.

———. 1999. "Finding a Way Out of Kosovo." *Washington Post*, 10 May, § A, 22.

———. 2002a. Personal interview, Richardson, Texas, 22 June.

———. 2002b. "Russia's Arms Stocks." *New York Times*, 14 December, § A, 28 [letter to the editor].

Weldon biography. 2007. Online at: http://www.montcogop.org/gopteam_weldon.htm.

Western, Jon. 2005. *Selling Intervention and War: The Presidency, the Media, and the American Public*. Baltimore: Johns Hopkins University Press.

Wheeler, Linda. 1993. "Israel First to Pay Fines for Parking." *Washington Post*, 2 November, § A, 1.

White, Josh. 2005. "Defense Document Bans Detainee Torture." *Washington Post*, 9 November, § A, 25.

White, Josh, and R. Jeffrey Smith. 2005. "White House Aims to Block Legislation on Detainees." *Washington Post*, 23 July, § A, 1.

Wicker, Tom. 1991. *One of Us: Richard Nixon and the American Dream*. New York: Random House.

Wildavsky, Aaron. 1966. "The Two Presidencies." *Transaction* 4, December, 7–14.

Wilson, Charlie. 2008. Personal interview, Fort Worth, Texas, 3 September.

Wilson, George C. 1981. "Opponents Find Vought Corporation's A7 Impossible to Shoot Down." *Washington Post*, 13 March, § A, 3.

Wisconsin Historical Society. 2006. "Turning Points: Sen. William Proxmire's Campaign against Genocide." Online at www.wisconsinhistory.org/turningpoints/
search.asp?id=1512.

Wittkopf, Eugene R., and James M. McCormick. 1998. "Congress, the President,
and the End of the Cold War." *Journal of Conflict Resolution* 42, no. 4, 440–67.

Wittkopf, Eugene R., Charles M. Kegley Jr., and James M. Scott. 2003. *American Foreign Policy: Pattern and Process*. 6th edn. Belmont, Calif.: Wadsworth /
Thomson Learning.

Woods, Randall Bennett. 1998. *J. William Fulbright, Vietnam, and the Search for a
Cold War Foreign Policy*. Cambridge: Cambridge University Press.

Wright, Jim. 1987. "We Can't Dictate the Terms of Peace." *Washington Post*, 29
September, § A, 19.

———. 1993. *Worth It All: My War for Peace*. Washington: Brassey's.

———. 1996. *Balance of Power: President and Congress from the Era of McCarthy
to the Age of Gingrich*. Atlanta: Turner Publishing.

———. 2001. Personal interview, 20 November.

Wright, John R. 2000. "Interest Groups, Congressional Reform, and Party Government in the United States." *Legislative Studies Quarterly* 25, 217–35.

Ybarra, Michael J. 2004. *Washington Gone Crazy: Senator Pat McCarran and the
Great American Communist Hunt*. Hanover, N.H.: Steerforth.

INDEX

James M. Scott is a professor of political science at Oklahoma State University.

Ralph G. Carter is a professor of political science at Texas Christian University.

Library of Congress Cataloging-in-Publication Data
Carter, Ralph G.
Choosing to lead : understanding Congressional foreign policy entrepreneurs /
Ralph G. Carter and James M. Scott.
p. cm.
Includes bibliographical references and index.
ISBN 978-0-8223-4490-2 (cloth : alk. paper) —
ISBN 978-0-8223-4503-9 (pbk. : alk. paper)
1. Government executives—United States. 2. Political entrepreneurship—
United States—History—20th century. 3. Political entrepreneurship—
United States—History—21st century. 4. United States—Foreign relations.
I. Scott, James M., 1964– II. Title.
JK723.E9C46 2009
327.73—dc22
2009005698